Dr. Abdul Galil Shaif

SOUTH YEMEN:
GATEWAY TO THE WORLD?

AuthorHouse™ UK
1663 Liberty Drive
Bloomington, IN 47403 USA
www.authorhouse.co.uk
UK TFN: 0800 0148641 (Toll Free inside the UK)
UK Local: 02036 956322 (+44 20 3695 6322 from outside the UK)

Because of the dynamic nature of the Internet, any web addresses or links contained in this book may have changed
since publication and may no longer be valid. The views expressed in this work are solely those of the author and do not
necessarily reflect the views of the publisher, and the publisher hereby disclaims any responsibility for them.

Any people depicted in stock imagery provided by Getty Images are models,
and such images are being used for illustrative purposes only.
Certain stock imagery © Getty Images.

This book is printed on acid-free paper.

ISBN: 978-1-6655-9314-4 (sc)
ISBN: 978-1-6655-9315-1 (e)

Print information available on the last page.

Published by AuthorHouse 02/07/2022

authorHOUSE®

This book is dedicated to my beloved mother, God rest her soul, Zara Abdulla Musaid Alshaibi. Without her encouragement, I would have never completed my PhD thesis, which forms part one of this book. It is also dedicated to the thousands of brave Yemeni men and women who lost their lives in the struggle for statehood, and to the next generation of Yemenis who will, inshallah, live in an independent, democratic South Yemen.

Contents

CONTENTS

Acknowledgements

First and foremost, I would like to thank my colleague, and friend Karen Dabrowska, who helped me to write this book and assisted in all aspects of its production. My thanks also to Jonathan Derrick for his meticulous proofreading and thought-provoking questions that encouraged me to augment the text and include a lot of information that otherwise would not be in the publication. Qais Saeed kindly supplied some excellent, exclusive photographs. Numerous colleagues provided valuable insights and material about the struggle for independence in South Yemen. Professor Chris Searle helped organise publicity and reviews. The understanding and support of my wife and children while I was busy writing and editing in the time I would have otherwise spent with them is greatly appreciated.

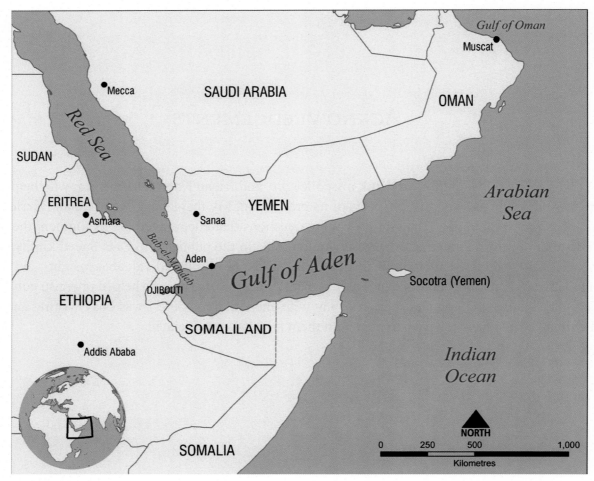

Location Map

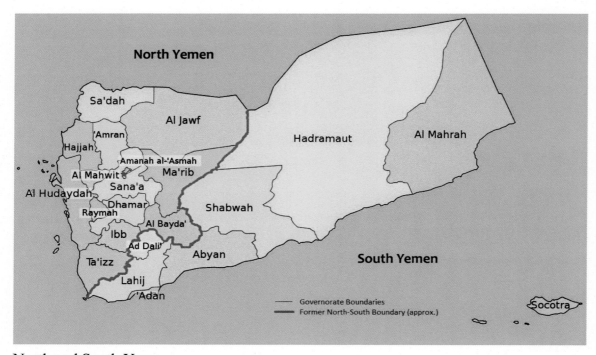

North and South Yemen

CHRONOLOGY

1839   The British occupy Aden with local resistance to occupation.

1869   Opening of Suez Canal.

1900–30 Extension of British protectorate system into the hinterland.

1937   Aden becomes a Crown Colony.

1947   Creation of the Legislative Council in Aden.

1948   Emergence of the first Yemeni nationalist movement in North Yemen.

1950–1952   Adeni nationalists call for self-rule in Aden itself.

1954   BP refinery opens in Buraika, Little Aden.

1956   Founding of the Aden Trade Union Congress.
        Suez crisis.

1959   Formation by the British of the Federation of South Arabia.

1961   Foundation of the People's Democratic Union.

1962   Overthrow of Imam in the North and proclamation of the Yemen Arab Republic. Egyptian forces arrive in support of the revolution in YAR.
        Formation of People's Socialist Party by Aden Trades Union Congress.

1963   Formation of National Liberation Front (NLF).
        Aden joins Federation of South Arabia.
        Radfan campaign: revolution begins on 14 October.

1964   Britain announces it will grant independence to the federation in 1968, retaining its base.

1965   First NLF Congress in Taiz issues the National Charter.
        Guerrilla war in Aden against the British.

1966   Second and Third NLF Congresses. NLF joins and leaves FLOSY. Internal conflict ignited.
        Britain decides to abandon its military base in South Yemen.

1967   NLF and FLOSY fight for control of Aden.
        NLF takes control of large parts of the country outside Aden.
        The June War sees military defeat of Egypt by Israel and withdrawal of Egyptian forces in YAR. Suez Canal closed.
        30 November: South Yemen becomes independent as the People's Republic of South Yemen.
        NLF becomes NF.

1968   Fourth NF Congress.
        Qahtan Al-Shabbi's victory over the left.

1969   Glorious Corrective Move to enforce socialist policies.
        South Yemen breaks relations with the United States.
        Nationalisation of all banks and insurance companies.
        Overthrow of Qahtan Al-Shabbi, the first president of South Yemen.
        New Presidential Council: Salem Rubayi as chairman, Abdul Fattah Ismail as secretary general of the NF, and Muhammad Ali Haytham as prime minister.

1970   Proclamation of the People's Democratic Republic of Yemen.
        Agrarian Reform Law.
        National Reconciliation in the YAR.

1971   Resignation of Muhammad Ali Haytham.
        Ali Nasser Muhammad becomes prime minister.
        The three-year plan starts.
        First Supreme People's Council meets.

1972   Fifth NF Congress.
        The "Seven Glorious Days".
        First Border War between the PDRY and the YAR.
        Housing law.

1973   October Ramadan (Yom Kippur) War.
        Abolition of private medical practice.

1974   Ibrahim Al-Hamdi becomes president of the YAR.
        Family law issued.
        The first five-year plan starts.
        First congress of the General Union of Yemeni women.
        Emigration is banned.

1975   Sixth NF Congress and the Unification Congress.
        Merger of the NF with the People's Democratic Union and the Popular Vanguard Party (al-Tali'a).
        Unification Congress in Aden.
        Aden University Medical School created.
1975–78 The second five-year plan starts.
1976   Establishment of diplomatic relations with Saudi Arabia.
        Formation of Peasants Union.
1977   President Al-Hamdi murdered in the North; Al-Ghashmi succeeds him.
        Relations between South and North worsen.
        Qat consumption law in the South.
        Government takeover of BP refinery by agreement.
1978   Assassination of President Al-Ghashmi in the North by Southerners.
        Killing of Salem Rubayi in Aden.
        Ali Abdullah Salih becomes president of the YAR.
        NF becomes the Yemeni Socialist Party; first conference of the YSP. Abdul Fattah Ismail becomes
        secretary general of the YSP and chairman of the presidium.
        Formation of the Northern Branch of the YSP.
1979   Second border war between YAR and PDRY.
        Kuwait agreement on unity of North and South Yemen.
        Treaties of friendship and cooperation signed between PDRY and Soviet Union, German Democratic
        Republic and Ethiopia.
1980   Fattah Ismail resigns and leaves for Moscow.
        Second "exceptional" YSP Conference.
        Ali Nasser Muhammad becomes president, secretary general of the YSP, and prime minister.
        Iraq attacks Iran, leading to war that lasts until 1988.
        Discovery of oil.
        New Literacy Law.
1981   Civil Defence law.
        Clashes on Oman border.
        Ali Antar is removed from Defence Ministry and replaced by Saleh Musleh Qassim.
1982   Establishment of the General People's Congress in the YAR.
        Disastrous floods.
1983   Supreme Yemeni Council meets in Sanaa.
        PDRY-Oman diplomatic recognition.
1984   Central Committee appointed; new members join the politburo.
        Mohsin Al-Shargabi brought back from exile in Addis Ababa to serve as minister of housing.
1985   Haydar Al-Attas becomes prime minister.
        Fattah Ismail returns from Moscow and is received by the party as a hero.
        Third YSP Congress.
1986   Failure of a coup attempt by Ali Nasser Muhammad leads to virtual civil war. Ali Nasser kills politburo
        members with devastating reaction by the opposition. Defeated militarily in subsequent fighting, he leaves
        for the YAR with thirty thousand of his followers.
        Haydar Al-Attas becomes president, Ali Salim Al-Beidh becomes secretary general, and Yassin Said
        Numan becomes prime minister.
1987   Fourth YSP Congress.
1988   Meetings between YAR and PDRY leaders to discuss unity.
1989   Fall of Berlin Wall.
        PDRY and YAR sign unity agreement.
1990   Proclamation of the Republic of Yemen with Ali Abdullah Salih as president and Ali Salim Al-Beidh as
        vice president. Haydar Al-Attas made prime minister.
        Iraq occupies Kuwait.
        Saudi Arabia expels eight hundred thousand Yemenis.
1993   First parliamentary elections.
        Ali Salim Al-Beidh leaves Sanaa permanently for Aden.
1994   Ali Abdullah Salih and Ali Salim Al-Beidh sign Document of Pledge and Accord.
        May–July: Civil war ends in decisive victory for the Northern forces, weakening the YSP, which
        proclaimed the Democratic Republic of Yemen before being defeated. Al-Beidh leaves Yemen.

1995	Eritrean and Yemeni forces clash over control of the Hanish Islands, located just north of the Bab El-Mandeb. Arbitration through the UN gives Yemen the right to Hanish Islands.
1996	Yemeni troops put down anti-government protests in Mukalla.
1997	Parliamentary elections won by Ali Abdullah Salih. Some eleven people killed in violence linked to the vote. Participation estimated at 80 per cent.
1998	The National Opposition Front (MOWJ), a group of people who fought with the socialists against the Northern regime, is set up in London, led by Abdul Rahman Aljiffiri.
	Kidnapping of foreign tourists.
1999	A Yemeni court sentences three Islamic militants to death for their role in the abduction and killing of Western tourists.
	Abu Hassan (a nom de guerre for the head of the Islamic Army of Aden and Abyan) is executed.
2000	Saudi Arabia and Yemen sign an agreement to end decades of border disputes. MOWJ closes down as part of this deal.
	US naval vessel USS *Cole* damaged in Al-Qaeda suicide attack in Aden. Seventeen US personnel killed.
2001	Violence overshadows disputed municipal polls and referendum which backs extension to presidential term and powers.
2002	Around one hundred foreign Islamic clerics expelled in a crackdown on Al-Qaeda.
	Al-Qaeda attacks and badly damages oil supertanker MV *Limburg* in Gulf of Aden. One person killed and twelve injured. Yemen loses substantial port revenues.
2004	Hundreds die as government troops battle insurgents led by Hussein Al-Houthi in the North.
2005	Resurgence of fighting between government forces and supporters of the slain cleric Hussein Al-Houthi claims more than two hundred lives.
2007	Clashes continue between security forces and Al-Houthi rebels in the North. Houthi leader Abdul-Malik al-Houthi accepts a ceasefire in the summer.
	The Southern Movement (Al-Hirak Al-Janoubi) is formed. Its protests calling for the return of the South Yemen republic are brutally suppressed.
2008	Police fire warning shots at opposition rally in Sanaa. Demonstrators demand electoral reform and fresh polls.
2009	Saudi and Yemeni Al-Qaeda branches merge. Al-Qaeda in the Arabian Peninsula (AQAP) is formed.
	The Yemeni army embarks on another offensive against Houthi rebels in the Northern Saada province. Tens of thousands of people are displaced by the fighting.
2010	Thousands flee government offensive against Southerners in Shabwa province demanding independence.
	General strike in South Yemen against repression and discrimination by the regime in the North.
2011	President Salih agrees to hand over power to his deputy, Abdroba Mansour Hadi, after months of protests in Yemen's Arab Spring. A unity government is formed.
2012	Abdroba Mansour Hadi is inaugurated as president after an election in which he is the only candidate. He is unable to counter Al-Qaeda attacks in the capital.
2013	National Dialogue Conference held in Sanaa as a key part of the agreement brokered by the UN and the Gulf Cooperation Council that saw Salih hand over power to Hadi.
2014	The Houthis take over Sanaa, saying they are unhappy at Hadi's staying in power beyond the expiry of his two-year mandate and the lack of implementation of the recommendations of the National Dialogue conference.
	The Houthis appoint a presidential council, known as the Supreme Political Council, to replace President Hadi.
2015	The battle for Aden; rebels and their allies seize control of Aden International Airport, and Hadi manages to escape Houthi imprisonment and flee to Saudi Arabia. Saudi Arabia, requested by Hadi to support the legitimate government, unilaterally launches an attack on Yemen under the name Operation Decisive Storm with the aim of restoring the government of Hadi and preventing the Iranian-backed Houthis from taking over the country. A civil war starts between the Houthis and the Saudi-led Arab Coalition militarily backed by the United States, the United Kingdom, and France. The UN Security Council imposes an arms embargo on the Houthis.
	Among incidents in the war: Houthi rebels fire mortar rounds and rockets at the Saudi city of Najran, near the border, killing at least three civilians; international pressure is put on the Saudis regarding indiscriminate bombing; Hadi returns to Aden after the Saudi-backed government forces retake it.
2016	UN-sponsored talks between the government and rebels begin.
	An air strike by the coalition hits a crowded funeral in Sanaa, killing at least 140 mourners.
2017	The Southern Transitional Council (STC), which calls for the independence of the South, is established

after Hadi dismisses governors of the Southern governorates.

The coalition imposes a complete blockade on Yemen in response to a missile fired by the Houthis at Riyadh airport. On 22 November, the coalition announces a partial lifting of the blockade.

Houthis kill former president Saleh following days of street fighting in Sanaa, after he reached out to the coalition, indicating he might switch sides.

2018	Fighting breaks out between Hadi's forces and the STC, which is supported by the UAE. The STC seizes military control of Aden.

Hadi visits the United Arab Emirates for the first time, but the relationship between the legitimate government of Yemen and the Emirates worsens.

The coalition launches an offensive on Hodeidah, Yemen's main entry point for food and humanitarian aid.

An air strike by the Saudi-led coalition hits a bus driving in a busy market in the Northern Saada province, killing at least fifty people, including children, and wounding seventy-seven.

2019   Houthi drone attacks on Saudi Arabia, hitting an oil pipeline and the airport in Abha. Drone attacks on Saudi Arabia's oil facilities halt about half of the supplies from the world's largest exporter of oil. One attack is on Saudi Arabia's Shaybah oil field, near the kingdom's border with the UAE.

Al-Qaida militants join in the war, targeting a military camp in Abyan province, killing at least twenty troops.

The STC, backed by the UAE, clashes with forces of the internationally recognised government near the presidential palace in Aden, and the STC wrests control of Aden. Emirati aircraft target Yemeni government troops as they head to retake Aden from separatists, killing at least thirty.

The internationally recognised government and the STC sign the Riyadh Agreement, a power-sharing deal, aiming to end the fighting in the South.

2020   A missile attack by the Houthis hits an army camp in the central province

of Marib, killing at least at least 111 troops and wounding at least 68. Houthis strike a Saudi oil facility in Jeddah with a new cruise missile.

The STC, unhappy with the lack of progress in implementing the Riyadh Agreement, withdraws from it and declares self-rule in Aden and the areas in the South under its control. Later, the STC announces it is "rescinding its self-rule declaration" to allow implementation of the Riyadh Agreement, acknowledging that Saudi Arabia and the UAE had exerted pressure to row back on the proclamation.

A US drone strike kills Al-Qaeda leader Qassim al-Rimi in Marib province. Air strikes by the coalition kill at least three dozen people, including twenty-six children and six women, in the mountainous northern province of Jawf. The attack comes after Houthis shoot down a coalition military aircraft.

Houthis take control of the strategic city of Hazm, the capital of Jawf province.

Yemen announces the first confirmed case of the new coronavirus pandemic; the coalition announces a two-week cease-fire in Yemen to fight the pandemic.

The STC takes control of Socotra archipelago from forces of Yemen's Internationally Recognized Government.

Yemen's warring sides complete the war's largest prisoner exchange.

Iran announces the arrival of its ambassador in the Houthi-held capital, Sanaa.

New power-sharing government formed by the IRG and STC. But then, on December 31, a large explosion strikes the airport in Aden, shortly after a plane carrying the newly formed cabinet lands there. At least 25 people are killed and 110 wounded.

2021   Outgoing US secretary of state Mike Pompeo announces he will designate the Houthis as a foreign terrorist organisation. He says the designation will take effect on 19 January, one day before Joe Biden takes office. But after Biden takes office, the designation is rescinded. The Biden administration places at least temporary holds on several big-ticket arms sales to the UAE and Saudi Arabia, and the new president says the United States is ending support for the Saudi-led coalition and calls for a cease-fire. The United States appoints Tim Lenderking as special envoy to Yemen.

In the war, there is prolonged fighting for Marib; Houthis target Saudi Arabia's Abha airport with bomb-laden drones, causing a civilian plane on the tarmac to catch fire. Oman seeks to mediate between the Houthis and the IRG. However, fighting continues between the IRG and the STC.

Demonstrations in Aden about non-payment of pensions and salaries and lack of provision of basic services.

No progress made with peace talks or implementation of the Riyadh Agreement.

The world's worst humanitarian crisis continues in Yemen.

US envoy to Yemen says he has met a dead end on the crisis.

Houthis continue attacks on Marib.

Yemen to get $655 million of IMF reserves.

Biographical Notes

Qahtan Muhammad Al-Shabbi (1923–81) was the first president of the People's Republic of South Yemen. He held the presidency until 22 June 1969, when the hard left-wing group from within the NLF seized control. He was jailed, placed under house arrest until the 1970s, and lived quietly in Aden from his release until his death in 1981. Al-Shabbi was originally an agricultural officer from Lahej region who fled to Cairo in 1958. In 1962 he was announced the head of a National Liberation Army, formed in Egypt, and in 1963 he was chosen as the founding head of the NLF. Upon independence in 1967, he was the best-known NLF leader and the only one over forty years of age with some education. The government declared that his deposition was "in the absence of true democracy". Al-Shabbi's son Najeeb Qahtan Al-Shabbi ran unsuccessfully against President Ali Abdullah Salih in the 1999 Yemeni presidential election. His followers were persecuted by the so-called left of the NLF.

Salem Rubayi (1934–78), known by his comrades as Salimin, was the head of state of the People's Democratic Republic of Yemen from 22 June 1969 until his execution on 26 June 1978. Rubai led the left wing of the National Front for the Liberation of South Yemen (NLF), which forced the British to withdraw from southern Yemen on 29 November 1967. Rubayi's radical left-wing faction gained dominance over the more moderate President Qahtan Al-Shabbi's elements, allowing Rubayi to seize power; he retained the title of chairman of the Presidential Council throughout his term, even as the NF changed the name of the country from the People's Republic of South Yemen to the People's Democratic Republic of Yemen in 1970. He opposed the idea of the Yemeni Socialist Party's (YSP) future creation. In 1978, he was assassinated by his comrades in the left wing after a short battle in Aden's Almodowar Palace, which Rubayi used as a fortification. He was the most popular leader in the history of the South.

Abdul Fattah Ismail (1939–86) was the Marxist de facto leader of People's Democratic Republic of Yemen from 1969 to 1980. He served as chairman of the Presidium of the Supreme People's Council (head of state) and was the founder, chief ideologue, and first leader of the Yemeni Socialist Party from 21 December 1978 to 21 April 1980. In March 1968, he was arrested by the right wing of the NLF and went into exile, where he drafted the programme for Accomplishing National Democratic Liberation, a leftist manifesto. He undertook a leading role in the consolidation of the left wing of NLF which subsequently regained power in the 22 June 1969 "Correction Step". He undertook a leading role in the dialogue between the NLF and other left parties in South Yemen leading to the formation of the Yemeni Socialist Party (YSP) and was elected secretary general. Ideologically, he favoured the Soviet model of socialist development. In 1980 he resigned from all his posts allegedly for health reasons and went to Moscow for medical treatment until 1985, when he returned in the face of a mounting crisis in the YSP. In October 1985, he was elected to the YSP Politburo, but armed conflict broke out in 1986 between his supporters and those of Nasser. He died in the fighting that resulted in thousands of casualties, but his body was never found. He is credited as being the mastermind behind establishing the YSP.

Ali Nasser (1939–) was a former leader of South Yemen serving as general secretary of the Yemeni Socialist Party between 1980 and 1986. In 1978 he took over power in South Yemen after the assassination of President Rubayi. On 13 January 1986, a violent struggle began in Aden between Ali Nasser's supporters and those of the Abdul Fattah Ismail. Fighting lasted for more than a month and resulted in thousands of casualties. Despite initiating the crisis, Nasser was militarily defeated in the South and fled to North Yemen. During the 1994 civil war in Yemen, he pushed his supporters to operate alongside the forces of the Sanaa government against the recently re-established Democratic Republic of Yemen, seeking revenge for his ouster. The Southern secession was repressed in July 1994 after the surrender of the Aden and Mukalla strongholds. The former president became an opposition figure in the 2011 Yemeni uprising, being named to a seventeen-member transitional council intended by some anti-government factions to govern Yemen during a prospective transition from the authoritarian regime led by President Ali Abdullah Salih to a plural democracy. Ali Nasser continues to live outside Yemen but still takes a regular interest in the politics of Yemen.

Ali Salem Al-Beidh (1939–) served as the general secretary of the Yemeni Socialist Party (YSP) in South Yemen after the ousting of Ali Naser and later became vice president of Yemen following the unification in 1990. He left the unification government in 1993, sparking the 1994 civil war in Yemen, and then went into exile in Oman. He was one of the leaders of the Southern independence movement Al Hirak. He joined the National Liberation Front in 1963. After independence, he joined the YSP. In 1971 he was selected as the general secretary of the Hadhramaut Provincial Committee and was admitted into the YSP National Central Committee. Al-Beidh took the top position in the YSP following a twelve-day 1986 civil war between forces loyal to Abdul Fattah Ismail and Ali Nasser. Following the unification of South Yemen with the Yemen Arab Republic in 1990, he took up the position of vice president in the transitional government of unified Yemen. In 1993, Al-Beidh quit the government and returned to the former Southern capital of Aden, claiming that the new government was systematically marginalising the southern people. On 21 May 1994, Al-Beidh declared the separation of South Yemen. He served as the only president of the DRY, from 21 May to 7 July 1994, and subsequently fled to Oman after the secession failed. After fifteen years of living in exile, Al-Beidh resumed his political career and called for a return of South Yemen as an independent state. Many commentators blame him for the unity project.

Salih Mosleh Qasim was born in Marais in the Dhala region of South Yemen. He became minister of interior and a strong supporter of the hard left. He was well-known for his iron fist approach to politics. He came from a poor family in the peasantry and became a hard veteran of the revolution in South Yemen. He was a strong supporter of Yemen unification and gave much support to those leaders who fled the North of Yemen and joined the NLF and later the YSP. He was killed by Ali Naser in the 13 January 1986 catastrophe. Saleh played politics in the background and didn't like much publicity, but his influence in the politics of South Yemen was significant. Those close to him followed his orders, and the killing of the northern president Al-Gashmi is attributed to him because the suicide assassin was one of his close friends.

Ali Antar (1937–86) was a veteran of the 14 October revolution. He became the minister of defence and vice president of South Yemen to Ali Nasser Muhammad. He was killed in the 13 January 1986 catastrophe, which led to the South Yemen civil war. Ali Antar was born in 1937 in Khraibeh, Dalea. He was known for his simplicity in speech. He became a vocal opponent to the policies of Ali Nasser throughout the 1980s, and the tensions between the two leaders came to a head in 1986. Ali Antar had very good connections within the army and ordinary members of the party, and his assassination led to a devastating negative reaction to Ali Nasser supporters.

Haidar Abu Bakr al-Attas (1939–) was appointed prime minister of Yemen by President Ali Abdullah Salih when the People's Democratic Republic of Yemen and Yemen Arab Republic united in 1990 to form present-day Yemen. Al-Attas served until 1994. He was a member of the Yemeni Socialist Party. Before unification, Al-Attas served as prime minister (1985–86) and chairman of the Presidium of the Supreme People's Council (1986–90) in the southern PDRY. When southern Yemen seceded seceded in May 1994, Al-Attas served as the prime minister of the secessionist Democratic Republic of Yemen until the rebellion ended less than two months later. He was recently appointed as an advisor to president Abdroba Mansur Hadi and takes a keen interest in the politics of Yemen.

Abdul Rahman Jiffri (1943–) was the vice president of the Presidency Council of the short-lived Government of the Democratic Republic of Yemen that was established on 21 May 1994. He was also the president of the National Opposition Front (MOWJ), an opposition group set up in London after the northern regime won the 1994 war. In 1964, Jiffri was granted the Culture Award for his thesis on the *Positive Neutrality and Non-Alliance Policy.* In 1956, at the age of thirteen, Jiffri joined the Rabitat Party Youth, and he was one of the pioneers in founding the Youth Organisation of the Afro-Asian Peoples Solidarity. Rabitat Abna Al-Yaman (RAY) was one of the country's oldest but smaller Yemeni opposition parties. He took part in the anti-colonial struggle against the British. In 1970 Jiffri was involved in the National Unity movement, which was then newly formed in Sanaa. The National Unity was a coalition that included the League Party, the Liberation Front, the Front for the Liberation of Occupied South Yemen (FLOSY), and the secessionists from the National Liberation Front (NLF). He was appointed as vice president of the new seceded state of South Yemen in 1994 and became a prominent figure during the war in 1994.

Major General Aidarus Qassem Al-Zubaidi (1967–) is the current president and commander of the Southern Transitional Council (STC) and the de facto leader of the Southern Movement in Yemen. He previously served as the governor of Aden Governorate from December 2015 to April 2017. Al-Zubaidi is a former military commander from Dhale province who remained loyal to President Abdroba Mansur Hadi during the Yemeni civil war. He was appointed as Governor of Aden in early December 2015 after the previous one, Major General Jaafar Mohammed Saad, was assassinated in a car bombing. In early January 2016, he survived an assassination attempt by ISIS when a bomb exploded near his convoy, and at least one bodyguard was killed. He was fired on 27 April 2017 by President Hadi. On 3 May, major rallies were held in Aden to protest the decision. One week later, the Southern Transitional Council was formed, with the membership of the governors of Dhale Governorate, Shabwah Governorate, Hadhramaut Governorate, Lahij Governorate and Socotra, and Al Mahrah Governorate. On 29 January 2018, in the Battle of Aden, Al-Zubaidi announced the state of emergency in Aden and said that "the STC has begun the process of overthrowing Hadi's rule over the South". He was a key member of the team negotiating the Riyadh agreement.

South Yemen: Gateway to the World?

South Yemen could be the Hong Kong of the Middle East. Centred on the strategic port of Aden located on the southern tip of Arabia, there is tremendous potential for the development of a free trade zone or a special economic zone, a container terminal with huge capacity for transit containers, a transport hub, and an important tourist destination with unique mud-brick architecture and the island of Socotra—an ecotourist's dream come true. This opportunity since independence from the British colonisation has not been realised, and South Yemen as a gateway to the world has become a living hell for its people.

Sadly, the country's leaders, both in the days of the People's Democratic Republic of Yemen (PDYR) and today, have not taken advantage of God-given natural resources which were never utilised or developed for the advantage of the people of the South. Internal politics and feuds rather than the exploitation of economic opportunities dominated the agenda of the National Liberation Front (NLF) and the Yemeni Socialist Party, which ruled the South from 1967 to 1990. When the South united with the North, its resources were exploited for the benefit of the Northern elite rather than the benefit of the people of Yemen. Today, opportunities to attract investment have not been taken advantage of, the economy is in ruins, and the Southerners are unable to free themselves from a power-sharing government that is taking them closer and closer to the abyss. Investment in the people of the South and investment from Yemeni business people residing in the Gulf and from Gulf States themselves could turn South Yemen into a thriving economy and an economic gateway to the world.

This book tells the story of South Yemen and asks whether it can become a gateway to the world and what really happened to destroy that opportunity. The struggle for power, internal fighting, and regional and international tensions are some of the issues this book analyses in detail.

From 1839, the south of Yemen, or South Arabia, was a British protectorate. Control of Aden was central to Britain's imperial strategy.

An Adeni university student I interviewed for my PhD thesis *Revolutionary: Politics in South Yemen 1967 – 1986,* Adel Mohammed, brilliantly summed up British rule: "British colonial history is characterised by the divide and rule policy. In occupation the British would sometimes side with the sheikhs and sultans against the people and sometimes with the people against the sheikhs and sultans. If they wanted something from the sheikhs they would side with the people and vice versa. The British wanted to leave South Yemen without incurring further loss of life to their soldiers. I do not think that they had forgiven the National Liberation Front when they left, otherwise they would have given economic support."

The British, in order to maintain their authority in colonial South Yemen and prevent a rebellion in the hinterland, initiated the idea of the Federation of South Arabia in the 1950s. The emergence of the NLF and the Front for the Liberation of Occupied South Yemen (FLOSY) as the dominant opposition movements was inspired by Egypt's nationalism under Gamal Abdul Nasser. The two leading organisations absorbed many splinter groups and individuals but were unable to come together under common objectives and fought against each other. The NLF prevailed as the new power to take over the governance of the South from the British in 1967.

The British had drawn up documents to hand over the Federation of South Arabia to a successor state, but the NLF, with a clear revolutionary objective and ambition to unite Yemen, decided to call the new state the People's Republic of South Yemen. This issue was not the source of tension between the new leadership because although unity was an objective, many in the NLF saw unification as a long-term objective they would achieve by building a socialist state in the South that would inspire the people in the North to revolt against what they saw as a backward reactionary regime. Unification of Yemen through various propaganda sources was highlighted as a priority for Southerners, with children and army cadets taught to bring about this objective into reality.

In my interviews with central committee members in both visits, they stressed that efforts must be continued towards unification by taking practical steps. This should be done by broadening common ties and interests which constitute a practical basis for unity. The Central Committee of the YSP, in its fifteenth session in 1989, stressed the importance of continuing the struggle to achieve our people's great objective, namely the establishment of a single Yemeni entity, without further delay. The reality of this rhetoric was used by the party hierarchy to better strengthen its own position by playing on the emotions of Southerners. In the North of Yemen, the Zeidi Northern leaders have generally been less enthusiastic about unity than the Shafei South. It is interesting to note that for most South Yemenis, since independence it has been an article of nationalist faith and one of the revolutionary major objectives that the two Yemeni states should unite. The slogan in Arabic used to motivate a whole generation of South Yemenis was "We swear to realise Yemeni unity", and I remember in my visit in 1990 and many interviews, Yemen united as one country with optimism about the future. Those hopes were to be cruelly disappointed thanks to the destructive, self-serving record and rivalry of Yemen's political elites.

This book explains in detail that the real divisions between the comrades in the South were based on the internal policy programme, foreign policy particularly towards the Gulf States and the Soviet Union, and the continued internal power struggle with big clashes in personalities in a struggle for power and control.

These continued power feuds and subsequent events led to new tensions between the different wings of the Yemeni Socialist Party, which subsequently culminated in the massacre between the rival factions within the YSP in the catastrophe of 1986. This crisis was the worst experienced by South Yemen. It robbed the party of its brightest cadets and had a huge negative impact on its structures of governance and destroyed its credibility internationally.

During the time of the People's Democratic Republic of Yemen (PDRY), some resistance leaders, including prominent political theorist Abdul Fattah Ismail, saw the Soviet model of nationalisation and central planning as the best model for postcolonial South Yemen. This was perceived by the Gulf States and the West as opposition to their own interests in the region, and hence the new state in the South was treated by many external powers as an enemy state.

This relationship between the new independent state, regional powers, and the West was problematic and compounded by internal fighting about the strategy for the development of the new state. South Yemen was later declared a "socialist republic", the Yemeni Socialist Party was established, and the People's Democratic Republic of Yemen became the only Arab country to openly align itself with the Soviet Union and declare itself a socialist state.

The revolution in South Yemen has many achievements to be proud of, and progress was made to support the poor and disadvantaged. But left-wing leaders by Arab standards became their own worst enemies, mainly because political power has its own logic. Individual power became a source of envy and conflict between the comrades, and very little time was given to build institutions. Individual political elitism and internal conflicts dominated the political arena. Sadly, these conflicts ended by one or other group overthrowing the other with huge negative consequences for the development of the country.

During my numerous visits to Yemen and the many interviews I conducted with officials and members of the YSP, it was clear to me that they really believed South Yemen had become a socialist society. The positive aspects of South Yemen society were the continuing emancipation of women and girls from the age-old tribal bondage, with women playing a much bigger role in society; equal rights for minorities that were previously ignored, including the country's most oppressed groups; and increasing access for ordinary people to education, medical care, decent housing, and sanitation. During two visits in 1980–81, I saw the beginnings of progress: women worked together in handicraft co-ops, where for the first time they could be paid decently for their work and control the money they earned. I saw illiterate adults, both women and men, learning to read. Women working as professionals were holding leading government positions, including central committee members of the YSP. Unfortunately, I also saw totalitarianism with no room for dissent or opposition, with people getting assassinated for having a different viewpoint than South Yemen's authority. There was a combination of positives and negatives with no room in the system for flexibility or change of leaders through the ballot box.

The post-1978 developments following the creation of the YSP also included Soviet aid to economic and social projects, with a new South Yemen–Soviet Friendship Treaty and a variety of new projects, including infrastructure, resource prospecting and exploration of oil and water resources, health services, education, and agricultural demonstration projects. It is fair to say that during my visit to Aden in late 1985, I witnessed the politically charged negative atmosphere between the comrades with a real possibility that that things could explode, and it seemed to me all these positive gains would be lost because of the internal power struggles. Somewhere beneath the ruins of all the internal struggles and today's torn and impoverished South, some of these positive seeds still remain, but only in the memories and minds of most socialists who lived through that period; even now, in the darkest of times, within the hearts of the Southern people, they know there is still a better future for this country.

In my interviews with several surviving leaders of the YSP, they failed to acknowledge the reasons that their socialist experiments failed to materialise for their people. Sadly, they also failed to draw the right lessons from their failure. Their analysis was usually an attack on their comrades, and recent interviews with ex-leaders like Ali Nasser and Haider Al-Attas demonstrate the inability to draw lessons from the past or even have the humility to apologise for so much damage and killings. In their analysis, they refused to accept that their policies were based on a vague vision of an all-encompassing utopian idea of worker and peasant control. South Yemeni society in reality was unprepared for these ideas or their implementation. Neither were the leaders themselves willing to give up their own power base to achieve real democratisation in the YSP. These same problems underpinned the failed socialist systems in the Soviet Union and other communist countries. When South Yemeni socialist leaders talked about a non-autocratic, non-authoritarian, participatory, and humanitarian version of socialism, they were not being as original as they would like to believe. One can argue that immediately following independence from their colonial masters, the leaders of South Yemen did not start out with totalitarian aspirations, but political and military power corrupted their minds and hence the general direction of their politics. Despite holding some noble ideas, South Yemeni leaders ended up oppressive and authoritarian in their actual practices to preserve their own power base. Their own lack of flexibility in implementing any form of real democracy in the country and recognising their own totalitarianism created the seeds of their downfall.

Whilst socialism was a unique experiment in South Yemen, and many of the socialist leaders made sweeping utopian promises in their party propaganda about the nature of the future South Yemeni society—all people are equal; from each according to his ability, to each according to his need; the end of the bourgeoisie, the rise of the proletariat; the end of poverty—in reality, the nature of the South Yemeni state that emerged was very different from this utopian vision. It was a socialism in which the comrades themselves competed for power at the expense of each other and at the expense of the economy. Implementing a leftist ideology in a traditional Islamic society with hostile neighbours, and pursuing aggressive and revolutionary domestic and foreign policies without realistically considering their chances of success, led to a withering away of the socialist state and a vacuum in political society.

I agree socialism did fail to materialise and turn South Yemen into a success story, but I don't believe that the failure lies with the ideology itself; it lies rather with those leaders who engaged in power struggles and endless infighting. There are plenty of examples of the success of the socialist experiment in South Yemen, and this book will look at these progressive measures. When the leaders allowed it to work, socialism did bring about some positive progress, but when the leaders were corrupted by power, they were unable to implement their noble ideology.

The problem in South Yemen lies in the fact that so many times leaders corrupted the socialist ideals and deviated from their principles. The leaders in the South from 1967 to 1990 became very selfish, self-centred, and preoccupied with their own destinies. When in positions of power, they quickly abused that power. This is why socialism did not thrive in South Yemen: one leader always wanted more power and authority at the expense of his comrades. The result was a system run by a dictator or a totalitarian party with a very limited democratic outlook. The interests of the people were mainly disregarded, and the interest of the leaders became paramount.

Some may argue that this is human nature running its course because politicians are more interested in their own power, but I would argue it is something more fundamental than this. By 1990, the leadership in South Yemen speedily gave up on the socialist project and appeared to agree to embark on a new experiment that brought with it new difficulties and even more difficult challenges. The book will reveal that socialist leaders were themselves the victims of their own corrupt politics and selfish needs.

It gives me no pleasure to point out that the first socialist experiment in the Arab world failed not because of the genuine progress it made to help the poor and marginalised but rather because of the struggle for power at the top by the children of the revolution themselves. None of the people in the South wanted to see those who made the revolution possible end up eaten by the very revolution they led. If the violence-promoting leaders had a bit more respect for the fire they played with, the history of South Yemen would have been different and less blood-soaked. They needed to study history more carefully, learn from past mistakes, and understand why it is so dangerous to ride the tiger of unlimited power.

Fearing the spread of Soviet influence in the region, Saudi Arabia and the United States began to massively increase financial and military aid to the North Yemen government, to counterbalance the South. The collapse of South Yemen's close ally the Soviet Union, which had supported the YSP financially and militarily, pointed to further economic difficulties. This spurred Al-Beidh, the head of the state and party, to an escape plan towards unification without any thorough analysis of the pros and cons of unification. He took a leap into obscurity that weakened the YSP even further.

The people in the South were emotionally charged towards unification through party propaganda, and therefore there was very little resistance if any from the public. There were a number of leading YSP members who cautioned against the move, but Al-Beidh explained his decision as the YSP achievement of a long-desired unified Yemen, in which the YSP would play a critical role in the new partnership.

The war in 1994 proved Al-Beidh wrong, and the Northern political class took over the state machinery, making the YSP redundant in the process and the Southern people without a partnership voice in the new unity republic. This war was a setback to the unification process, which allowed the Northern political class to govern the North and the South on its own terms.

The division between North and South thus continued until 1990, and two independent states pursued their own domestic and foreign policies. However, following the collapse of the Soviet bloc and significant internal power struggles, particularly in the South, the governments of South and North Yemen entered into a voluntary treaty of unification on 22 May 1990.

The US government, emerging out of the Cold War as the world's only superpower, aimed to increase its influence over regions of the world that had previously been satellites of the Soviet Union, and the United States made its mark on Yemen, more often than not in a negative way.

The United States worked closely with the Gulf States on Yemen without any real positive engagement to support the new unified state. The constitution of the new unified republic of Yemen guaranteed democratic rights for both regions with much focus on civil liberties. However, it became clear in the first few years of unification that the constitution was brilliant in theory but very weak in practice. Throughout the years of unity, land concessions in the South were given to Northern tribal leaders, and oil, a scarce resource explored in the South, was transferred mostly to meet the needs of the national budget, with much emphasis on developing the North rather than the South. The Southerners were unhappy with their new positions in the unified state, and internal fighting became a feature in the new Yemen.

These continued antagonisms led to an uprising in the South in 1994, but this rebellion was viciously put down by the army of the North supported by Southerners within the Northern regime. Following the 1994 conflict, the regime in the North began a five-year programme in 1995 that removed all controls on the exchange rate, cut the interest rate, and initiated trade policy reform, privatisation, and the elimination of price controls. In return, the World Bank and the International Monetary Fund (IMF) provided aid. The Southerners, with very little power and no advocate in the unity partnership, had very little say in the management of the economy or in their own destiny within the unified state of Yemen. The unity entered into voluntarily in 1990 had by 1994 become a unity forced by military means.

It is in this context that the current, growing independence movement in the South should be viewed. The war for secession in 1994 became a campaign to end the influence of the Southern partner in the unity experiment. The democratic constitution promised at unification has not been adhered to. Parliamentary elections since 1990 have been marked by corruption and violence, and the elections scheduled for April 2009 were postponed for two years. The movement that developed in South Yemen, started by retired Southern military officers, was a reaction to perceived infringements of the democratic rights of South Yemenis and the implementation of unpopular economic reforms which left them marginalised and with no power base.

The Southern movement was initiated by MOWJ (the Southern opposition movement established in London by Abdul Rahman Jiffri) and later Hatem (the Southern Liberation Movement that believed in military action). A group of former army officers who had been forcibly retired after unity in 1990 was rapidly gaining support. The Society of Retired Military Officers began a series of small protests in 2007. The size, scope, and organisation of the movement have continued to grow over many years. This movement became Al-Harakat Al-Janubiyya, a broad coalition including many different Yemeni political parties and factions.

The dominant force is clearly members or ex-members of the YSP. However, the coalition also includes Nasserists, Ba'athists, and a number of different religious groups and young people gaining force. On January 10, 2010 a general strike swept through many regions in the South. The Hirak movement was gaining much political support in the South but lacked unity or a command structure, with too many leaders eyeing for positions rather than building a wide coalition. The emergence of the Arab Spring brought with it a new revolutionary fever demanding the overthrow of the ruling regime in Yemen, which obscured the role of the Hirak movement. The international community was less concerned with what they perceived as a separatist movement and gave their support to the Arab Spring movement in Yemen. I spoke to a number of foreign ambassadors regarding the Hirak movement, and they did not see it as a potent force, citing the divisions within the group and their own view favouring unification of the country.

In contrast, the Houthis have emerged as powerful force in Yemeni politics. Through the Northern Yemen Imamate, they dominated the North of Yemen for centuries, with many incursions into the South that were met with Southern resistance to the Northern regime's domination. The Houthis have shown little interest in Southern separation and are more concerned with their assumed God-given right to govern the whole of Yemen.

When the Ottoman Empire collapsed after the First World War, the Northern Yemen region was for decades ruled by a Shia royal family from a Zaidi Shia sect. Supported by Saudi Arabia, they remained in power until the September revolution of 1962 when, with Egyptian support, the regime was overthrown.

After unification of the two Yemens in 1990, the Houthis became increasingly marginalised in the new republic. Demanding more autonomy and a bigger share within the power structures of the new state, they rebelled against the ruling regime, and some of their leading lights were killed, including the older brother of Abdul Malik Al Houthi.

The Arab Spring came to Yemen in 2011 following Tunisia, Egypt, and Libya, and it played its part in undermining the presidency of Ali Abdullah Salih, who had been in power since 1978. Those close to him in the regime were of the opinion that Salih no longer had the confidence of the international community, and his resignation was seen in the best interest of Yemen. The Houthi movement in the beginning was one part of the nationwide uprising against Salih but was primarily concerned with advancing its own narrow political and economic interests. Many in the South were initially sympathetic to Houthi demands and grievances, but later, as the Houthis advanced militarily into the South, they became bitter enemies.

A National Dialogue Conference (NDC) with regional and international assistance was instituted to address the future of Yemen after Salih agreed to step down. It proposed a federal solution with six provinces with some autonomy. The Zaydi-dominated North got two landlocked entities, which the Houthis argued was gerrymandering against them. The Houthis and many in the Southern Hirak movement were unhappy with the six-region federal states proposed by the NDC. The conference was hailed as a success but in reality achieved nothing for the people of Yemen.

In 2014 the Houthis began colluding with Salih against the new president, Abdroba Mansur Hadi. This was a dramatic change of loyalties as Salih and Houthis were long-standing enemies. Much of the army no longer remained loyal to Salih, but he failed to understand the new realities and stayed in the country. Hadi took over as the new president of Yemen, but the Houthis moved quickly into his power base and put him under house arrest. He later escaped to the South and then to Saudi Arabia. Ex-president Salih was later viciously assassinated by the Houthis when they no longer had any use for him. The Houthis were upset when he criticised them and withdrew from the alliance.

The Yemeni government launched a major offensive against the Houthi rebels, who retreated into the border region between Yemen and Saudi Arabia. The Houthis aligned themselves to Shia Iran, and their relationship with Iran was seen by Saudi Arabia as a threat to their kingdom. President Salih had weakened the Houthis through the six wars but was unable to subdue them. They were able to reorganise and mobilise much quicker than many thought possible. In 2014 the Houthis, supported by the state of Iran, overthrew the government in Sanaa, and they are now in control of more than 80 per cent of the North. When they tried to take over the South in 2015, an Arab coalition led by Saudi Arabia, with the assistance of Southern fighters, expelled them. The intervention of the coalition marked the start of a seven-year civil war which is continuing at the time of writing. It is destroying the country and has been described by the United Nations as the world's worst humanitarian disaster. Numerous peace negotiations have failed, and there is no end in sight to the war. There is widespread recognition that the international community and the United Nations have failed the Yemeni people.

Adding to and underpinning the political crisis in Yemen is an acute and deepening economic crisis. Yemen is now one of the world's twenty-five poorest countries. Out of twenty-four million people, 45.2 per cent live below the poverty line. There has been a steep decline in oil income, which makes up an estimated 70 per cent of total state revenues. Oil production in Yemen has been in decline for years: crude oil production was down from five hundred thousand barrels per day in 2000 to three hundred thousand barrels per day in 2009. There is no available data to show the level of production as I write this book, or to show where the oil revenues are channelled to.

An estimated 34 per cent of Yemen's 6.5 million strong workforce is currently unemployed. A contributing factor to this was Yemen's stance during the 1990–91 Gulf War, when the Yemeni government refused to condemn the Iraqi invasion of Kuwait. As a result, 800,000 Yemeni workers were expelled from Saudi Arabia and a further 50,000 were expelled from the Gulf States. Not only did the Yemeni state have to deal with a population increase of 850,000 newly unemployed workers, but the money they sent back to Yemen had accounted for almost 40 per cent of Yemen's gross domestic product. This was accompanied by drastic cutbacks in US aid.

The Yemeni government's response to these economic problems has been appalling, with no economic policy or programme. The only individuals who have benefited from the current government have been the warlords and individual politicians; this is disastrous for the majority of the population. Proof of this can be seen in the weakening local currency, which has become worthless for the ordinary person in the street. The average public employee in 2009 earning eighty thousand riyals could buy four hundred dollars, whereas in 2021 the same salary buys only sixty dollars. The economic situation is becoming unbearable for many, and only a very few are benefiting.

For most of its history, North Yemen has had a rural economy based on private ownership of land. The communist government nationalised all private-sector companies, including the port and the oil refinery. After the 1994 civil war, this was reversed. Privatisation has led to serious economic problems. For example, farmers have shifted to growing cash crops such as bananas that, though profitable for individual landowners, cannot be grown in sufficient quantities to provide much-needed food for Yemen's population.

All the problems Yemen is now experiencing have a common cause: imperialism, whether it is the legacy of British imperialism in the South or the current interventionist policy of regional and international powers. The Houthis' rebellion is the result of their marginalisation by the Yemeni state. The growing movement in the South is largely the result of the imposition of unity by force and the worsening economic conditions.

As with the rest of the Middle East, so long as the Yemeni people are given no control over their own country, their economy, and particularly their oil, the situation can only go from bad to worse. The

South is eager to separate itself from the fundamentalist religious Houthi regime in the North and be independent once again. This dream is opposed by the Northern regime and has received little support from the international community, which, like a one-trick pony, clings to the idea of a united Yemeni state without any real consideration for the politics on the ground.

As a young man in my twenties, I completed my master's degree in economics in Sheffield University and then decided to write a PhD thesis on South Yemen, "Revolutionary Politics in South Yemen, 1967–1986". The thesis was submitted in 1990, and my external examiner, the late Professor Fred Halliday, was an expert on South Yemen. It was always my ambition to publish a book based on this work and my own experience of leading a Yemeni government authority from 2008 to 2014. But life got in the way, and I spent six brilliant years in Yemen as chairman of the Aden Free Zone, which gave me an in-depth understanding of the country and its people. The book project was delayed until 2020, when I set up Friends of South Yemen with Karen Dabrowska, a journalist specialising in Islamic and Middle Eastern affairs. Karen has worked tirelessly with me on its publication.

This book charts the history of the struggle for Southern statehood (1967–2021). The lessons of history described in part one were disregarded, and the same struggles continue to be repeated in current post-revolutionary conflicts. The new revolutionaries are repeating the same mistakes without realising they will be the first to be eliminated if they are not prepared to heed the lessons of previous conflicts. The history of the South was less about economic and social development and more about conflict and the lack of conflict resolution.

An independent Southern state or a Yemen made up of a self-governing Northern region and a self-governing Southern region is, in my opinion, the only viable options out of the current crisis, which is destroying Yemen and propelling it towards the abyss. The civil war, which is now seven years long and is continuing between the Houthis and the internationally recognised government (IRG) and the Southern Movement, has led to the world's worst humanitarian crisis and widespread famine. But regional powers and the international community have not acted in the best interests of the people of Yemen and still cling to the idea that one state, which does not exist in reality because the Houthis are governing 80 per cent of the North, is the best possible option. For the South, unity with the fundamentalist, repressive Houthi regime in the North is not possible. History has shown that the Southerners will continue their struggle for independence. This book is a historical analysis of South Yemen's politics with its ups and downs, it failures and successes. The future is unknown and insecure.

London, January 2022

PART ONE

The People's Democratic Republic of Yemen (PDRY)

Chapter 1

The Struggle for Independence

Britain forced its colonial entry into the Arab world from India and the East in the early part of the nineteenth century. The first British outpost was established on the Red Sea in Aden. British intervention in the Arab world never went unchallenged throughout the period of colonisation, and resistance to the British invasion of South Yemen can be traced as far back as 1837.

South Yemen under British Rule

The military occupation of Aden took place on 16 January 1839. A military force of over five hundred men and three warships was sent to Aden to ensure its capture. Resistance to the British resulted in bloodshed, but the military strength of the British Royal Navy proved to be superior. Aden therefore became one of the first acquisitions of Britain's Victorian Empire. The objectives behind the occupation were twofold: Aden had a superb natural harbour seen as vital to serve and safeguard trade routes to India and the Middle East, and it was seen as an important future military base for British military power and political influence in the Middle East.

By the Government of India Act of 2 August 1935 (effective 1 April 1937), Aden was disannexed from British India and split into two parts, the Colony of Aden and the Aden Protectorate. In order for the British to administer it more effectively, the protectorate was split into a Western Aden Protectorate, with headquarters in Lahej, and an Eastern Aden Protectorate, with headquarters in Mukalla. Western Aden included sixteen states and several subdivisions near the colony, and Eastern Aden included the Hadhramaut, Socotra, and several smaller divisions west of Muscat and Oman. Government was by individual rulers, with cooperation of the British resident, subject to the governor of Aden. The residents were represented locally by British advisers under the advisory treaties signed in 1937. Rulers of the four most prominent states—Lahj, Qu`aiti, Mahra, and Fadli—were entitled to a hereditary salute of nine guns. All states were abolished in 1967 when South Yemen became independent.

The population of Aden grew rapidly because of its international importance as a trade route; it was well-known to travellers on steamers between Suez and India. By 1935 it had reached 80,000 people, and by 1950 it had increased to 275,000. The sudden rise in the total population was mostly due to the need for a labour force, particularly to work in the harbour. More than one-third of those who migrated to Aden were from North Yemen, a separate state ruled by a conservative monarch, Imam Yahya. In 1954 Britain established an oil refinery in Aden, and by 1960 it became the headquarters of British military forces in the Middle East.

In the mid-1950s, Aden's economy was thriving, and the profits made by British and foreign businesses were substantial. The existence of this socioeconomic structure gave rise to workers and nationalist opposition. Aden was transformed into a large consumer market, and its wealth was open to exploitation. As a result of lack of investment in the economy, workers began to demand an increase in wages and solutions to their accommodation problems. Opposition by the workers led to strikes, demonstrations, and frequent upheavals or violence.

Aden was a small city, and the colonial state was aware that such a large concentration of workers might inspire revolutionary violence. It thus pursued a policy of involving the police and intelligence services to infiltrate workers' organisations. This was usually done through arrests and terrorisation. The British state was adamant that Aden would not become a centre for violence, militancy, and revolutionary movement.

Aden Port. Source Author.

The mid-1950s also witnessed frequent rebellions in the hinterland of South Yemen, a vast area of mountainous land which the British, throughout their occupation, had completely ignored economically. The hinterland was dominated by a peasant farming economy and was ruled by sultans supported by the British. There were two dozen sultanates and other forms of local states over which the British gradually extended the protectorate system. Frequent upsurges of violence against the ruling sultanic regime and the British colonial system resulted from the oppressive conditions under which people lived. The British and the sultans squashed the opposition, and these rebellions failed owing to non-existent organisation and lack of any genuine leadership.

The Emergence of the Revolutionary Movement

The revolutionary movement in South Yemen was a response to what was perceived as oppressive British rule. It appeared during an era of high Arab nationalist sentiments when other Arab countries had successful revolutions. At this time, Syria became independent and experienced a series of military coups, King Farouk of Egypt was ousted by a group of army officers in 1952, and the monarchy in Iraq was overthrown in a bloody revolution in 1958.

The inspiration behind Arab nationalism came from Gamal Abdul Nasser, the Egyptian leader. He appealed to all the Arabs to struggle against European colonialism and to fight against their traditional oppressive feudal rulers. The Arab Nationalist Movement (ANM) embraced a variety of ideologies and inspired the nationalist movements in Yemen. It generally adopted Nasser's Arab socialism, called Nasserism, the objective of which was to regain Palestine, unify the Arab world in a single state, and support Arab liberation movements determined to eliminate colonialism from all Arab states. This movement had a substantial influence on the formation and development of the nationalist movement in South and North Yemen.

Conflict within the ANM between those who associated themselves with Nasserism and those who held socialist left-wing views caused the movement to split into several factions. Those who associated themselves with Nasserism accepted that the correct path towards socialism was to attain Arab unity and struggle for an alliance of all classes. The left-wing faction of the ANM rejected this theory and said such an alliance with other classes necessarily included and legitimised the Arab bourgeoisie, which was inevitably a natural ally of colonialism and neocolonialism. This faction held the view that socialism in the Arab world could not be built by peaceful cooperation among the social classes; it required the militant leadership of the working class.

The South Yemeni branch of the ANM suspended relations with the umbrella organisation and chose to act independently. This was a complex period in South Yemen's political development. By suspending relations with the ANM, former members of this organisation began to act independently, struggling on the basis of ideological conviction rather than by tying themselves to mainstream Arab politics. A period of political uncertainty now emerged in Yemen along with conflicting nationalist and socialist ideologies.

The Nationalist Movement in South Yemen was characterised by a multiplicity of groups and splinter groups. Each grouping represented and reflected a different social base and leadership and approached the struggle for independence with different tactics, ideology, and internal and external support. It was during this period that the seeds of political conflict, which were to play such a prominent role in shaping South Yemen's politics, were first sown.

The South Arabian League

The first nationalist organisation in South Yemen was the South Arabian League (SAL), founded in 1950 by the al-Jifri family. Its aims were to try to unite the divided British-dominated principalities, and its origins owed much to the influence of Arab nationalism during the 1940s. Because of the character of its conservative leadership, the SAL tended to adopt traditional nationalist ideas and orientate its policies and strategies towards the traditional pattern of South Yemeni politics, uniting different Yemeni notables and sultans to further its own political ambitions.

Although the SAL was a nationalist movement based in South Yemen, it lacked two essential characteristics needed for appealing to the wider population. First, the SAL rejected the notion of anti-colonial armed struggle and was willing to compromise with the British colonial authority. Second, the militants and other militant factions began by the late 1950s to suspect that the SAL was being supported by the conservative regime in Saudi Arabia.

Saudi Arabia tended to see the SAL as a counterweight organisation to other nationalist organisations that were sponsored by Egypt. Between 1956 and 1958, the SAL readily lost its influence and appeal in South Yemeni politics and was soon marginalised. Many SAL members split from the organisation because they disagreed with its ties to traditional rulers. Southern Yemen in this period was called South Arabia, established by the British.

The Federation of the Emirates of the South was an organisation of states within the British Aden Protectorate in what would become South Yemen. The federation of six states was inaugurated in the British Colony of Aden on 11 February 1959, and the federation and Britain signed a treaty of friendship and protection that detailed plans for British financial and military assistance. It subsequently added nine states and on 4 April 1962 became known as the Federation of South Arabia. This federation was joined by the Aden Colony on 18 January 1963.

There is currently a debate within Southern intellectual circles about whether Southerners should call the new state they seek to establish a South Yemeni state or the state of South Arabia. Some would argue that the NLF leaders were determined that the postcolonial state be called South Yemen because one of the fundamental aims of their revolution was to unify Yemen. Others, including the SAL, believed that this was a big mistake because the state that developed during British colonial rule was called the federal state of South Arabia (*Alhuraibi Alarabi*) and hence was not linked to Yemen but rather to the Arab states in the region. Furthermore, they argued that linking the Southerners to Yemen has taken away the opportunity to be part of the rich Gulf states. This topic continues to be discussed with passion in current times.

United National Front

Some SAL members split from the organisation because they disagreed with its ties to traditional rulers. Those who left set up another organisation, the United National Front (UNF). During the period of its formation, it was very influential, especially among the working class and peasantry. Its aims and objectives were briefly summarised by the then governor of Aden, Sir Reginald Stuart Champion:

"The UNF's stated policy is union with the protectorate, the Yemen and the Sultanate of Muscat and Oman and the setting up of a South Arabian independent state. This policy is an amalgamation of the nationalists who insist on independence and will be content with nothing less, the left-wing of the South Arabian league and a few free Yemenis who work for a more liberal form of government in their own country, the Yemen."

Because of a gradual increase in workers' awareness of their exploitation, trade unions in Aden started forming in the 1930s. As a result of trade union formation, the United National Front was short-lived and ceased to function as a separate organisation. It became very ineffective and split into different factions, with its members joining the new trade unions, instead of remaining with the UNF. Trade unions were seen by the working class and members of the intelligentsia as radical organisations which were capable of improving their standards of living and working conditions.

The Aden Trade Union Congress

During the 1950s, there were a series of strikes in Aden. These strikes disrupted the colony and had great effects on the socioeconomic structure. As a result of these strikes, and as the 1950s progressed, the second major trend in South Yemen's politics was that which manifested itself in the Aden Trade Union Congress (ATUC).

On 20 March 1956, twenty-five separate trade unions joined to form the umbrella organisation which became known as the Aden Trade Union Congress. Many members of the working class in Aden came from the hinterland. These workers were politicised through the experience of exploitation and through learning about the developments in other Arab nationalist movements. As a result, there was a growing political consciousness of themselves as exploited, oppressed, and colonised. The central role of the ATUC can be summed up what is described as its pledge to march forward towards the Arab socialist society and its unity and to free it of all means of exploitation and colonialization."

In 1962, the ATUC established its own political party, the People's Socialist Party (PSP), which was the political extension of the ATUC. It was led by the late Abdullah Alasnaj. Born in 1934 in Sanaa, he spent most of his life in Aden. He expressed his gratitude for his father's poetry and his mother's inclination to Arab literature, history, and religion, which exposed him to Arab nationalism very early in his life. He was also influenced by central inter-Arab issues. He studied in a teacher's college but did not finish his course and became a clerk in the local branch of British Overseas Airways Corporation. He also became general secretary of the ATUC and then its president, and he emerged as a nationalist, shrewd, seemingly flexible, but stubborn leader.

The ATUC conducted most of the opposition towards British colonial rule during the 1950s. However, its Arab nationalist orientation and reformist political ideas did not appeal to the masses. It had close links with Egypt's Nasserism and with the British Labour Party. It was also weak outside Aden, particularly in the hinterland. Its aims were similar to those of the SAL: it called for British withdrawal and the unification of Yemen.

Although the PSP was committed to an anti-colonial strategy, this did not include a strategy of armed struggle as a way of achieving its political objectives. The PSP relied upon achieving political and diplomatic solutions to the problems in South Yemen. Nevertheless, in the early 1960s, the PSP and the ATUC began to be actively political, dominating all political opposition to the British colonial authority in Aden.

The British government in the early 1960s was certain that the PSP-ATUC were the representatives of the nationalist movement in South Yemen. Yet the government ignored the fact that the PSP was only active in Aden, and therefore its influence was limited to Aden itself and did not extend to the hinterland. By failing to realise this, the British also ignored the fact that during this period of history, there was emerging a revolutionary movement from the hinterland. The British government and the PSP were perhaps overconfident of their capacity to bring about a political solution to the existing challenges. Indeed, it was generally felt internationally that the PSP's moderate views would eventually prevail and lead to independence.

But when the PSP's political strategy of negotiations with the British began to fail to deliver any of its promises, its members became dissatisfied with its leadership, whom they perceived as opportunists. As a result of these policy failures, by 1965 the PSP itself had lost the initiative in Aden and had ceased to be the major political force in South Yemen. After the August 1960 law banning strikes was introduced, the ATUC claimed that the British were trying to destroy Aden's Arab character and to turn it into a city of foreigners.

Because of the decline of its political influence, it initiated a series of meetings in the summer of 1966 with other nationalist groups, especially those representing the bourgeois and the petit-bourgeois class. These meeting resulted in the formation of the Organisation for the Liberation of Occupied South (OLOS), a coalition embracing both the PSP and the SAL.

Internal conflicts within the leadership as to which strategy to adopt ensured this organisation's downfall even before it began. The conflict centred around two major issues: tactics and strategies to gain independence and the leadership of the future government.

The National Liberation Front

The third and major nationalist grouping within South Yemen's politics in the 1960s was the National Liberation Front (NLF), formally announced in June 1963 in Taiz (North Yemen). It consisted of several different Yemeni nationalist groups, some of which represented tribal groups like the League of Tribes, the Mahra Youth Organisation, and the Yafai Reform Front. Others represented Arab political tendencies which were influential at that time: the Nasserite Front, the Secret Organisation of Free Officers and Soldiers, the Revolutionary Organisation of Free Men, the Patriotic Front, the Aden Revolutionary Vanguard, and the Revolutionary Organisation of Youth in Occupied South Yemen. These groups were organised in opposition to British rule and were determined to carry out armed struggle to achieve their purpose.

The creation of the NLF marked the beginning of a serious decline in support for the established political organisations based in Aden. It attracted many of the educated youth and those from traditional lower classes like the peasants. Its main support came from the hinterland because the majority of people living in the hinterland wanted to free themselves from oppressive and exploitative relations that they endured throughout the colonial period.

Following the failure of OLOS to produce political results, the NLF believed it was necessary to use military force to oust the British. Encouraged by the North Yemeni Revolution of September 1962 which ousted the Imamic regime, the NLF used North Yemen as its base for organisation. The NLF was supported by Arab and Third World revolutionary movements to carry out armed struggle. It launched the armed struggle campaign on 14 October 1963. The British saw this violence as merely tribal and expected it would eventually be crushed. They were at the time unaware of the fact that the NLF was a potential revolutionary movement determined to force them out of South Yemen.

The British never imagined that four years later, the NLF would take political power in the occupied South. Unlike previous nationalist organisations, it drew massive support from a broad base in South Yemen, appealing to the masses as a strong and viable organisation to take charge of the struggle.

Abdullah Alasnaj's close relationship with Nasserism meant that it was in the interest of Egypt to force a merger between OLOS and the NLF. Egypt wanted to install a leadership in South Yemen that it could work with, a leadership which had Nasserite ideological conviction. OLOS was much closer to Egypt's political ideology and organisation, and it had been created at a time when sections of the NLF were critical of Egypt as a petty bourgeois state, one that was prevented by its class character from giving full support to revolutionary movements which challenged the capitalist system. Egyptian intelligence officers concentrated all their energies on bringing about the merger, their view being that once a merger was formed, Egypt could control and direct the movement. By January 1966, the Egyptians thought they had succeeded when the leadership of the NLF agreed to a merger, and the Front for the Liberation of South Yemen (FLOSY) was formed.

Nasserites with the NLF supported the merger, but the majority of the rank and file members did not. This Egyptian-imposed unity in fact exposed deep divisions within the NLF ranks. Such unity was opposed by the rank and file activists of the NLF, who denounced members of the leadership who had agreed to a merger without consultation with the grass roots of the organisation.

To avert divisions within the NLF, Qahtan Al-Shabbi, a leading figure in the NLF, immediately issued a statement condemning FLOSY. He was detained by the Egyptians in Cairo for a year and half. In November 1966, the NLF formally broke away and described FLOSY as nothing more than the armed wing of the PSP, a pro-Nasserite faction which even included a sultan.

There was strong political opposition within the NLF to the structure and programme of FLOSY, particularly as they opposed the participation of sultans and the national bourgeoisie in this movement.

As a result of the NLF's resistance to integration with FLOSY, Egypt publicly began to support FLOSY and immediately responded with political, financial, and military pressures. Its goal was to force the unification of these organisations in order to keep them under its own direction. It exerted substantial pressure to amalgamate FLOSY and the NLF but failed. Their failure was partly due to their own intelligence information about the nature of the revolutionary situation and partly due to the NLF's belief that cooperation with Nasserism would defeat the revolution in South Yemen and open the door to neo-colonialism. The result of the failure of these negotiations to reach any kind of compromise was an open struggle between the NLF and FLOSY.

FLOSY was totally crushed by the NLF, which went on to declare the South as an independent socialist state. South Yemen, previously a colonial-Islamic state, by 1970 had a socialist government that undermined Islamic religion in favour of communism. This blending of Marxism, which believed that Marxist Leninism was the answer to South Yemen's problems, became a big concern for pro-Western Arab governments and US interests in the region. This fear was based on the notion that the South of Yemen could export its Marxist revolution to other pro-Western Arab states. The real threat to US interest was also the Soviet military base at this important location of the world. The YSP, through political communist education, did undermine Islam in the South, and Islam played a minor role in its political development for at least two decades.

In June 1965, the NLF held its first congress, which was largely devoted to discussing a long-term programme, eventually published as the National Charter. It did not bind itself to any particular ideology but was influenced both by what it perceived as capitalism, in the sense that it still saw an important role to be played by the petty bourgeoisie, and by socialism, in the sense that it saw the economy as being guided by an overall development plan. There was emphasis on the fundamental importance of the alliance between the workers and peasants as the guarantor of social progress. The second NLF congress held in June 1966 focused on rejection of a merger with FLOSY. This was upheld by the third congress in November 1966. The NLF by this stage was adamant that it could act independently in waging the war against colonialism.

Intensification of the Armed Struggle

By 1966, the NLF was involved in three different wars and struggles. The first was a bloody civil war with FLOSY in which the intensity of the battle to gain recognition among the population grew. Politically, the NLF wanted to be seen as capable of taking over power from the British; to achieve this successfully, FLOSY had to be eliminated from Yemeni politics. The NLF drew its members from all over South Yemen and from broad sections of the social strata. During this struggle, it clearly believed that it was a credible and authentic nationalist movement in South Yemen. The difficulties faced by FLOSY in this conflict were mainly because it was active only in Aden and tainted by political intrigues; as a result, it lost much-needed support. By September 1967, FLOSY had been politically and militarily defeated by the NLF, and most of its leadership went into exile in Saudi Arabia and Egypt.

The second struggle was waged against the British army. This began in the mountainous Radfan region on 14 October 1963. The objective was that NLF revolutionary fighters would, through armed struggle, ensure Britain's military and political withdrawal. In its military operations, the NLF unquestionably showed good internal discipline. As one British soldier explained, "The NLF proved to be a sophisticated and well-organised force, with excellent security, based on the traditional insurgent system of 'cells', whereby the members are divided into a number of small groups or 'cells' each of which is isolated from the other, except for trusted 'link men.'"

British intelligence finally began to realise the strength of the NLF, both in terms of political support within the South Yemeni population and with respect to the strength of the NLF's military strategy and tactics. On those grounds, Britain therefore decided that it was time it withdrew its forces from South Yemen.

It would have preferred to hand over power to the federal rulers. These rulers formed the Federation of the Arab Emirates of the South, a British initiative of forming a state consisting of the ruling class, under British protection and advice. The idea behind the federation was that the ruling class became the governing council, and their union was formed less for shared constructive aims and more to pool their strength against national and external enemies.

The failure of the federation to form a government and the failure of FLOSY to gain broad support meant that the British could not, as they would have wished, hand over power to any of these forces. Yet because of the NLF's political and military strength, it was clear that it was the only organisation capable of taking political power, a situation grasped by the British government, despite immense political pressure by Saudi Arabia to persuade Britain to remain in Aden until it found a government which could ensure peace and stability. Saudi Arabia had no faith in the NLF from the very beginning.

In his memoirs, former British prime minister Harold Wilson described the situation: "King Faisal of Saudi Arabia was still in London, expressing his concern about our proposed evacuation of Aden and South Arabia. On Friday 19th May, we had long talks in which he gravely urged us not only to leave militarily units in the area but to accept a binding military commitment to use them to defend the new South Arabian state against attack or infiltration from the new independent state of South Yemen inspired by Arab nationalism. Unless we hold firm in Southern Arabia, the Gulf would be subverted within months."

The third and final struggle which the NLF simultaneously carried out was against the traditional tribal rulers. The NLF had a clear policy regarding the transformation of Yemeni society. The organisation was clear in its understanding that Yemeni society was a class society and that it was therefore absolutely essential to wage this particular armed struggle against the Yemeni ruling class.

The NLF held a view of South Arabia in which it considered the conflict between the reformist Irshadi and the conservative Alawi as the first clear manifestation of a class-based conflict in South Arabia. The Irshadi Society was formed in 1915 representing the poor sections of Yemeni society, and it contested the privileged position of the Alawis. The movement was successful in reducing the influence of the ruling class.

The left within the NLF identified with the Irshadi as its spiritual ancestors. As a result of the military campaign waged against the ruling class, the sultans and sheikhs began to fall one after another in the period 1967–68. Sections of the population in the hinterland took up arms in response and joined the NLF, ensuring its victory and rise to power.

By 1967 much of the NLF's finance was coming from ordinary people, who were willing to give whatever they owned to rid themselves of what they saw as the exploitative ruling class. Many members of the ruling class had fled into exile in neighbouring Gulf countries by the end of 1967 and joined the other defeated elements of the SAL and FLOSY in an attempt to regroup and become an effective political force opposing the NLF. This to a large extent did not materialise.

The Achievement of Independence and Its Implications
The various political organisations in South Yemeni politics before independence, though mainly nationalist in character, were in conflict and bitterly opposed to each other. The NLF was able through political and

military struggle to defeat the opposition forces. As a result of its considerable efforts and those of other nationalists, British rule ended in South Yemen on 30 November 1967, and power was taken by the NLF.

In Britain's colonial history, the NLF victory over British colonialism in South Yemen inflicted a defeat which was unique. In other countries colonised by Britain in which nationalist revolutionary struggle had broken out, it had generally been the case that a British withdrawal was preceded by lengthy diplomatic negotiations, and that the subsequent regime had soon harmonised its relations with the British state.

This had certainly been the case in neighbouring Gulf countries such as Kuwait, Abu Dhabi, Bahrain, Oman, and others which had not been fully colonised. Unlike these countries, South Yemen's nationalist movement abandoned any kind of political or economic relations with Britain and continued what it called its anti-colonial struggle. The revolutionary struggle of the NLF has great similarities to that of Cuba, where the revolutionary movement was also started by nationalists who were non-communist to begin with but at a later stage in the revolution declared an adherence to communism.

An Adeni university student, Adel Mohammed, who I inter viewed for my PhD thesis *Revolutionary Politics in South Yemen 1967 -1986* brilliantly summed up British rule: "British colonial history is characterised by the divide and rule policy. In occupation the British would sometimes side with the sheikhs and sultans against the people and sometimes with the people against the sheikhs and sultans. If they wanted something from the sheikhs they would side with the people and vice versa. The British wanted to leave South Yemen without incurring further loss of life to their soldiers. I do not think that they had forgiven the NLF when they left, otherwise they would have given economic support."

The NLF not only forced the British to withdraw completely from South Yemen but also succeeded politically and militarily in undermining Britain's colonial strategy for transferring power to a pro-Western state that would be accommodating to British and Western interests in South Arabia and the Indian Ocean.

Ahmed Ali Musaid and Saif Aldhali take their seats in the United Nations as the Representatives of the new South Yemen state. Source Author.

Although Britain had spent four years fighting the NLF and British soldiers had lost their lives fighting an outdated colonial war, the British high commissioner, Sir Humphrey Trevelyan, recognised the ability of the NLF to govern South Yemen when he summed up the British position. Fred Halliday quotes Trevelyan in his book *Arabia Without Sultans:*

> So we left without glory but without disaster. Nor was it humiliation. For our withdrawal was the result not of military or political pressure but our decision, right or wrong, to leave, and if we failed to hand over our colony in the manner which we should have wished, it was principally because the South Arabians were unable to produce in time a responsible political party having the support of the majority of the people and prepared to negotiate a more civilised approach to independence. All we could say at the time was that it might have been much worse. And, in the end, another little independent Arab country came into being, desperately poor and probably destined to go through periods of violence and revolt. The mark of the British on it was light and will soon have disappeared save for the great barracks, the airport and disused churches and a few half-obliterated signs to the NAAFI or the sergeants' mess. Our period of occupation did the country little permanent good, for all the selfless work of many devoted Englishmen and so many good intentions. Whatever the rights or wrongs of the way we left, whatever was to come after us, the time for us to be there was over. And if we were to go, it was better not to linger on.

However, this did not mean that all were ready to begin the transformation of Yemeni society. The revolution encountered internal and external opposition from the outset. This was because the revolutionary struggle itself had taken place amidst violence and bloodshed. Members and leaders of tribes and business families had fled to neighbouring countries because their interests and status were tied up with the former colonial socioeconomic structure. These people presented a threat to the new regime by fomenting hostility towards it in their places of refuge, notably Saudi Arabia.

In contrast, the objective economic conditions facing the NLF were unfavourable. There were three main sources of income during colonial rule: the Aden port free zone, which made up 60 per cent of the state budget; the commercial sector, including the banks and insurance companies tied into the international capitalist market; and the service sector. The NLF faced huge economic difficulties immediately after taking power from the British without an economic plan to deal with these difficulties.

When the NLF took over, these sources of income were discontinued, partly as a result of the British withdrawal and partly as a result of the closure of the Suez Canal during the Arab–Israeli war in 1967. The NLF faced many political and economic problems as well as having to overcome the divisions of the hinterland into twenty-four separate states or sultanates.[1]

The NLF organisation was a broad coalition of nationalist forces who believed that the only way to drive the British out of South Yemen was to engage in a revolutionary struggle. However, this did not mean that all the different nationalist groups were in agreement about other strategies and policies which concerned the NLF in general.

Since the NLF's formation in 1963, there had always been political and ideological disputes within the organisation. During the period of armed struggle, such factionalism, although apparent during the NLF conference in Taiz, took second place to actually concentrating on the battle against the British and the traditional ruling class. However, those political disputes and differences began to become apparent and real as soon as the NLF took power.

---

[1] States of the Western Aden Protectorate: Alwai, Aqrabi (Akrabi), Awdhali (Audhali), Bayhan (Beihan), Dali (Dhala), Dathina, Dubi, Fadli (Fadhli), Hadrami, Hawshabi (Haushebi), Lahj (Lahej), Lower Awlaqi (Aulaqi), Lower Yafa, Maflahi (Muflahi), Mawsata, Shaib, Upper Awlaqi Sheikhdom, Upper Awlaqi Sultanate, Upper Yafa.
States of the Eastern Aden Protectorate: al-Hawra, al-Irqa, Mahra, Sayun (Kathiri of Seiyun), Tarim, Shihr and Mukalla (Qu'aiti), Wahidi, Wahidi Sultanate of Ba'l Haf, Wahidi Sultanate of `Azzan, Wahidi Sultanate of Ba´l Haf and `Azzan (from 1962, Wahidi Sultanate), Wahidi Sultanate of Bi´r `Ali `Amaqin, Wahidi Sultanate of Habban.

Strategies and ideologies on how best to respond to the many pressing economic, social, and political issues which faced the NLF and South Yemen as a whole provided the immediate battleground. The struggle between what they perceived as the left wing and the right wing within the NLF emerged as the dominant problem of the new regime, and early political and policy decisions reflected the thoughts and ideas of one or the other faction. As a result of political conflict between these groups, there was a gradual increase in left-wing political thinking within South Yemen. It was a very simplistic approach that missed the many opportunities to reconcile differences between comrades and resolve conflict through political compromise.

Political conflict within the NLF, and later the Yemeni Socialist Party, went on throughout South Yemeni politics until the final dramatic explosion on 13 January 1986 when a military civil war within the YSP began; it continued for two weeks, causing substantial bloodshed and loss of lives and considerable damage both to the economic system and to South Yemen's political reputation locally and internationally. And as expected, the postcolonial period for the NLF meant that the internal conflicts and power struggles during the independence period did not simply disappear with independence. Hence the postcolonial NLF often had to grapple with the problem of what it meant to be independent. Was it enough to be formally independent, or was the new state to be different from the old one? And did they simply need to rid themselves of those who were perceived as reactionaries who simply could not mould into their type of socialist politics? One thing was for sure: the NLF were keen to replace the colonial system and structures with a new system based on their supposedly authentic political identity. The internal power struggles had not been expected to cause so much damage that the youthful spirit to gain independence turned sour for the very people who struggled to make it happen.

This period reflected two conflicting tendencies. On the one hand, there was the radical left which wanted to restore the revolutionary fervour and transform a feudal system into a socialist one. On the other hand, there was the right wing of the NLF, which wanted slow and gradual reforms based on the idea of Arab nationalism. The right wing was influenced by Nasserism and showed a tendency to support capitalism as a system, whereas the left wing was influenced by the Soviet Union. The development of a system based on socialist principles was unique in the Arab world. It was a new experiment that was likely to be resisted by South Yemen's rich, powerful neighbours.

Mohammed Lashoon Colonel in South Yemen National Security Office (left) and Saleh Muslih Qasim Minister of Defense and Interior. Source Author.

Mohammed Lahsoon described the NLF politicians as a bunch of nationalist leaders with conflicting views born out of the armed struggle against British colonialism, trying to do this by mobilising mass support by expressing popular demands. They intended to use their central power and mass support to unite all the people of the country into a single nation in which there would be economic justice. They didn't realise that the conflict between fellow nationalists during the colonial resistance would continue to haunt the new comrades in the postcolonial period.

Internal political struggles within the NLF and within the YSP didn't just destroy the revolutionaries themselves but often led to external conflicts with neighbouring states within the international system. The Gulf states were adamant that the political system in the South was a danger to the survival of their own states built on a completely different system of authority. Revolutions are characterised by the ideology and methods employed by revolutionaries, which not only have domestic problems but also have huge international implications. Domestically, internal revolutionary conflict causes massive upheavals of the political structures within the South Yemeni state, which negatively impacted on its relations with neighbouring states. The Saudis in particular were concerned that a successful socialist state on its own border might actively export its ideology to their people by means of propaganda, or by supporting revolutionary movements, or by directly deploying military forces to confront neighbouring states. They saw the South Yemeni socialist state with Soviet support as a threat to the prevailing regional order and perceived their left-wing leaning as a threat to their state's sovereignty, which prompted these states to intervene at some stage or another directly or indirectly to ensure that this experiment of socialism did not succeed.

CHAPTER 2

Development of the Post-independence Socialist State (1967–74)

The NLF took power in South Yemen in 1967 following the defeat of its rivals. The National Charter manifested certain ambiguities in its internal politics, and this was reflected in the differences and political debates. Although the major issue of independence and the adoption of armed struggle was a policy issue everyone could agree on, there still existed major divisions on other issues, such as economic planning and foreign affairs, which featured prominently in the evolution of both the NLF and the post-independence government of South Yemen. The post-independence state-building project fell short of achieving its goals mainly because of internal conflict between the different factions in the NLF that were unable to develop unity amongst themselves or realise the weaknesses of the structures required to build consensus, the weak economic position the British left South Yemen in, and the hostile regional and international powers. Between 1963 and 1967, the NLF focused on ousting the colonialists. Once this was done, internal struggles came to the fore.

Divisions within the NLF: The Right and the Left Wings

Two political wings emerged as a result of these divisions. The right wing's leadership consisted of those who spent some of their time during the struggle for independence outside South Yemen. They were influenced by the politics of Nasserism and upheld social democratic Arab nationalist values. The left wing of the NLF consisted predominantly of radical revolutionary fighters whose ideological views had been radicalised both by the experience of armed struggle and by the exploitative and oppressive conditions under which they lived in South Yemen.

The left wing of the NLF was pressing for a commitment in the National Charter towards a radical, socioeconomic transformation at independence, but the right wing resisted this, insisting on the adoption of a more moderate line, which generally prevailed despite the success of the left in obtaining reference to some radical ideas, such as the discussion on the character and composition of the new state and the introduction of a planned, centralist economic system. The debate on which political path to adopt was very intense, and many within the NLF found the charter too right-wing and were keen to challenge its politics. During the years of the independence struggle (1965–67), the issue of FLOSY had to be resolved, and this delayed political debates, which resumed once independence was achieved. The NLF succeeded in mobilising the peasants in the hinterland and the working class in Aden. The majority of the population were influenced by the NLF mainly because they wanted freedom from both colonialism and their local ruling class.

When South Yemen became independent, the General Command of the NLF was composed of twenty-one members who appointed Qahtan Al-Shabbi as president for two years. "Apart from the President who was 47, they were all young men in their thirties and hardly known in South Arabia, let alone outside it. This was partly due to their working underground in the NLF for almost four years. They were men of some education and most of them with training in government service under the British. Some were not educated but did have military fighting experience. When they emerged in power it became clear that they had made a very thorough study of both the military and political aspects of the revolution all the way from Marx and Lenin to Castro and Mao. They were for the most part Arab socialists of the Nasser type rather than communists except perhaps for the minister of national guidance, Abdul Fattah Ismail, who was reputed to be a Marxist. They had prepared very carefully for the moment when they would take power. They were well documented in all the issues and greatly surprised the British who expected them to be revolutionary fighters rather than politicians by their grasp of the issues at stake."[2]

The questions of how best to respond to the many pressing economic, political, and social issues confronting the new Republic of South Yemen provided the context of an immediate battleground for the ideological disputes between the two wings of the NLF. The right wing and their traditional leadership consisting of moderates and conservatives led by Qahtan stressed the importance of restoring the ailing economy to pre-independence levels through gradual reforms. This group opposed radical measures and supported only very limited reforms. They were keen to find foreign aid from any source, including the British, and to have good relations with other Arab states, including Saudi Arabia. Because of this attitude, the leadership was also unwilling to give any support to the Popular Front for the Liberation of Oman.

The left wing of the party subordinated all issues to the cause of social and political revolution in South Yemen. They called for a complete transformation of Yemeni society based on socialist construction. The service-oriented economy had to become independent and geared towards agricultural and industrial production. In foreign affairs, they called for close association with the socialist camp and were adamant in their fullest support for national liberation movements in the Arab world.

On only a few practical and theoretical issues could the left and right wings of the NLF agree: the need to repress the South Arabian League and FLOSY, the importance of the public sector, the desirability of Yemeni unity, support for the Palestinian cause, and solidarity with the Arab revolution. However, on major issues of internal affairs such as the economy and some foreign affairs issues, conflict and political struggle were imminent.

The Problems Facing the New State

The difficulties faced by the new Republic of South Yemen were immense. In the first year of independence, the economy was bankrupt because it had lost three sources of income. First, international trade to South Yemen was affected by the closure of the Suez Canal; as a result of this, Aden port lost its revenue from shipping. Second, the British government refused to keep its promise of sending aid to Aden. Third, the lack of finance in the economy and the lack of finance from international aid resulted in an immediate economic decline and hardship for the people. It also became clear within the first few months that neighbouring Gulf countries like Saudi Arabia were hostile towards the NLF and were assisting FLOSY and the South Arabian League to regroup and attack the NLF as a counter-revolutionary force.

---

[2] *Le Monde Diplomatique*, April 1972, 6.

The First NLF Government Headed by Qahtan Al-Shabbi

The first NLF government was headed by Qahtan Al-Shabbi, who took the post of president, prime minister, and the supreme commander of the armed forces. His government was under tremendous pressure from progressive Arab states to integrate South Yemen into the Arab world and adopt Arab socialist politics based on nationalist Nasserite ideological thinking. But the strength of the left did not allow Qahtan to follow a policy of rapprochement with Gulf countries, which included Saudi Arabia.

The balance of power in the first NLF government was in the hands of the right wing, and hence they managed to delay the fourth congress. The differences between the left and right wings were fundamental differences on issues of policy. The right was moderate and reformist, whereas the left was concerned that the revolution had to continue with a radical transformation of Yemeni society which focused on the dismantling of the existing colonial administration and its replacement by a new revolutionary state. At independence, the influence of the British colonial state remained in the new state, and the colonial state structure remained intact to some extent. The left was determined to dismantle these structures at any cost.

An example of this was in Aden: The administration was still managed by members of the Adeni colonial bureaucracy. The left was against using the pre-existing administrative structure, whereas President Qahtan and his allies were in favour of building on the remains rather than starting to build new systems.

The right and left wings started working against each other. Qahtan and his supporters began the process of building close ties with state institutions, especially the army and the colonial established bureaucracy. The left began to set up new embryonic state structures, popular committees, and a popular guard and administrative group separate from the ex-colonial administration. These new structures were followed by explicit calls from the left that there should be the creation of a new Yemeni state, abolishing the old army and civil service, and building a militia of 150,000 armed men and women who would defend the revolution internally and against external enemy forces. The basis of political control should be popular committees in each village, which in turn would elect members to the highest legislature, the Supreme People's Council. The left also stressed the need for a radical economic policy incorporating the nationalisation of foreign capital and a low limit on land ownership.

By 1968, however, Qahtan had built strong ties with the army which had served the British and subsequently merged with NLF fighters, and the NLF left had to contend with this. It was preoccupied with establishing new forms of state institutions in the hinterland against the wishes of the right-wing leadership.

The Programme of National Democratic Liberation and the Fourth NLF Congress

The Programme of National Democratic Liberation presented to the Fourth NLF Congress by Abdul Fattah Ismail represented left-wing thoughts and argued for a national democratic revolution. In this programme, political power would be vested in the hands of the workers, peasants, and revolutionary intellectuals. It also called for the establishment of a Supreme People's Council and a series of economic measures to enable the national democratic revolution to continue, with the nationalisation of foreign banks and foreign trade and an end to Aden's free port status except for tourism and goods in transit. Only in this way, the left believed, could South Yemen avoid the fate of other Third World countries which had passed from colonialism to neocolonialism.

When the Fourth NLF Congress took place on 2–8 March 1968, the left criticised Qahtan for his inability to call for a purge in the army and bring about land reform. There was a feeling amongst many in the left that the revolution and policies which were essential to bringing about some form of change had not been pursued.

Qahtan wanted to maintain and extend his position and influence in South Yemen in the face of the growing strength and influence of the left, and he cleverly took measures which he hoped would swing the congress his way. The Agrarian Reform was issued on 5 March 1968. This involved the distribution of land to the peasants and the turning of many farms which belonged to colonial-era rulers into state farms. Just before the congress was due to convene, its postponement until March was announced, enabling members of the army who supported the right to be included as delegates. Had the Congress been held earlier, these delegates would not have qualified because they would not have fulfilled their probationary period as members of the NLF.

The right put forward its opposition to the programme in a statement entitled "A viewpoint concerning the issue on the agenda of the congress". This document explicitly attacked the unclear views and vagueness of the left's espousal of a non-capitalist path of development and advocated a transitional stage of state capitalism. Senior army officers demanded the liquidation of the NLF's irregular forces, the Liberation Army, and the People's Guards.

Debate at the congress was protracted and tense, and the Zanjibar resolutions issued at the end clearly reflected left-wing policies:

1. Developing the NLF into a political party based on the ideology of scientific socialism.
2. Opening the NLF to other national democratic forces.
3. Reorganising the NLF.
4. Liberating the economy of South Yemen from the control and hegemony of foreign capital.
5. Purging the state structure and the army of all undesirable and reactionary elements.
6. Electing a new forty-one-member general command to be the supreme authority in South Yemen and act as a legislative authority until a Supreme People's Council could be established.
7. Implementing land reforms whereby the land belonging to the sultans and ex-ministers under the British would be confiscated without compensation.

No appeal was made to attract national capital, and the right was unable to get any of its resolutions passed owing to its lack of appeal amongst NLF activists. The left was adamant about severing all links with the petty bourgeoisie, as expressed in the speech by the leading ideologist of the left Abdul Fattah Ismail, who said, "The compromising petty bourgeois leadership in the epoch of imperialism is even more dangerous for the national democratic revolution than the explicit counter revolutionary policies of the semi feudal-semi bourgeois alliance." This differed from the experience of the Russian and Chinese revolutions in which the petty bourgeoisie was considered by communists to be a revolutionary force. Neighbouring Gulf countries criticised this line. Qahtan refused to implement the resolutions and to appoint Abdul Fattah Ismail as prime minister.

On 19 March 1968, after the local leadership in Aden called for a rally to support Ismail and the resolutions of congress, Qahtan arrested and jailed the principal opposition figures, including Ismail and Ali Salem Al-Beidh, without trial. This led to widespread protests through the country coupled with calls for Qathan's resignation.

The Post-congress Crisis
Almost all politicians felt that the army's arrest of left-wing politicians was definite interference in what was an entirely political conflict. The imprisoned politicians were released, and both Ismail and Beidh resigned their ministerial positions because they felt they could not compromise with what they saw as

a reactionary leadership. A full-scale uprising was launched on 14 May 1968 by the left in Abyan, but it was limited due to lack of coordination and quickly suppressed by the military.

In late 1968 and early 1969, the left began to reorganise itself both within the state machinery and within the NLF. The left in the NLF believed that Qahtan was pursuing an individualistic and authoritarian political style. He resigned as prime minister in April 1969 under pressure from both the left and even some on the right. On 22 June 1969, the left launched an active political and military attack, supported by the politicians on the left, the liberation army, the militia, and lower army ranks. President Qahtan, known as Abu Al-Shujan, the father of the people, was forced to resign and was eventually imprisoned. Many top army officers were purged or fled to neighbouring countries. Those who had fought together against British colonialism had by now become bitter enemies in a struggle for political control of the new state. The continuation of internal power struggles demonstrated structural failures in the newly independent state, which in turn resulted in weak state institutions, inadequate political cohesion, and a clear absence of any political consensus on fundamental issues of social, economic, and political organisation. Many of these internal bloody struggles could have been avoided through conciliation and political understanding.

Salem Rubayi, a leading NLF guerrilla fighter in the nationalist movement and a key member of the left, became chairman of the Presidential Council and assistant secretary general of the National Front. Abdul Fattah Ismail was appointed secretary general of the Central Committee of the National Front and chairman of the Supreme People's Council. Muhammad Ali Haytham became the prime minister, Ali Salem Al-Beidh occupied the post of minister of defence, and Ali Antar became commander of the army.

On 22 June 1969, the new General Command, the top organ of the NLF, issued a press statement announcing the resignation of Qahtan. It blamed "individualistic actions which caused the revolution to deviate from its proper course to a different course. Thus action by the general command in carrying out a natural corrective operation within its ranks was in response to an urgent necessity felt by every citizen and especially all members of the organisation."

The new leadership referred to this period starting on 22 June 1969 as "the corrective movement", emphasising that the National Charter of the NLF (see Appendix 1) was the leading guide for the 14 October revolution. The new leadership adopted a more radical line in foreign policy and stressed its support for the Palestinians and the People's Front for the Liberation of Oman, fighting in Oman. It was committed to strengthening relations and building ties with Arab countries and to improving relations with socialist countries, in particular with the Soviet Union. This became a guiding principle of the new government's foreign policy.

The corrective movement marked the beginning of revolutionary socialist debate within the NLF. The right of the NLF and the military were purged, and in January 1970 some twenty leading members were expelled from political office. The left was clearly by now in a position of undisputed power in the new state. The new General Command stressed the importance of building new democratic institutions to replace those which had been built by the colonial state.

Internal economic problems were even worse than they had been in 1967. By the beginning of 1970 the left was in a position of political power in South Yemen but the economy was in deep trouble. However, because the revolution was only just born, the economy was not a major issue: the population was simply informed by the NLF to expect the worst and struggle to survive in order to defend independence.

Policy Implementation: Nationalisation, Women, Defence, and Security
On 27 November, foreign banks and insurance companies were nationalised, but the time to nationalise was badly chosen because private investors, in anticipation of this move, were able to transfer their

assets abroad, and the NLF acquired only a large number of overdrafts. The execution and timing of nationalisation initiatives were not a thought-through process to help build the new economy but rather a desperate political move of popular radicalism that actually drove investors out of Aden into neighbouring states. The successful port economy managed by the colonial power hugely suffered the consequences of nationalisation.

The Housing Law of 1972 was another radical measure taken by the new left-wing government. The law nationalised all absentee property, in particular that belonging to the rich. Many of those who were homeless were able to find housing, and the poor benefited from this measure. However, it again caused economic problems because the nationalisation of housing led to a sudden drop in expatriate remittances. Mistakes were made in this programme which later became an obstacle for subsequent governments to deal with.

Another area of priority was agrarian reform. The sultans and sheikhs who dominated the ownership of land were ousted during the revolutionary struggle between 1963 and 1967 because they were seen by the left as stooges and traitors. In the post-independence period, the struggle over land was carried out in what the left saw as class struggle. This was to take it away from the few rich peasants and redistribute it amongst the majority of the peasants.

In December 1969, left-wing activists, with government backing, began encouraging insurrections. Hundreds of armed peasants started a revolutionary process of arresting big landlords and redistributing land through popular committees which were set up to administer this. The strategy behind these uprisings was to create the political circumstances to bring about a socialist-oriented economy in agriculture.

An NLF activist described how the peasantry was encouraged to rise: "We persuaded the peasants that the exploiters of land and capital would never change and that they had to act. They took their hatchets and sickles and immediately arrested all the sheikhs, sada (descendants of Prophet Mohammed) and other feudalists—82 in all. The population was stupefied. They thought these people were untouchable and that whoever lifted a hand against them would die on the spot. When they saw that the lords remained in prison and that the town was not struck by any cataclysm, all tongues were loosened and all the other peasants joined those who had taken part in the risings and came to the peasant leagues. It was important that the peasants themselves took the people to prison. Some were armed but we did not distribute arms because we were afraid of a massacre."[3]

Public support for these changes was immense, and there was a type of revolutionary fervour which at the early stages of the uprising looked uncontrollable. The social implications were certainly tremendous. The rural economy was restructured, and this led to a marked improvement in the living and material standards of a large majority of peasants. Medical care and other social services which were previously unavailable were now provided. By 1975 the feudalist economic and social structure was almost dismantled, and the new revolutionaries saw a new socialist state emerging on the horizon.

Women played an important role in the revolutionary struggle to gain independence, and this was taken to mean that their struggle must continue and their participation in all walks of life was necessary. For over a century, colonialism had ensured that a a backward, oppressive, traditional way of life was imposed on Yemeni women, limiting their participation to the management of their own homes and nothing else.

There were a number of demonstrations in the 1970s chanting *Tahrir Almera Wageb* (Liberating woman is an obligation). Woman burned their face coverings, and many South Yemeni women wore modern clothes, including jeans, for the first time and joined the armed forces.

---

[3] Lackner, *People's Democratic Republic of Yemen: Outpost of Socialist Development in Arabia* (London: Political Studies of the Middle East, 1985), 69.

One of the ideas most vigorously pursued by the General Union of Yemeni Women, established in 1974, was the integration of women into the economic life of South Yemen. To put this idea into practice, energy and resources were used to give women better training and education. The long-term political benefit was an increased participation of women at all political and economic levels.

There was an influx of women studying in the non-educational field, particularly in the vocational and technical areas. This was encouraged, especially in the rural areas where many women from the peasantry, in comparison to other groups, had entered the field of work and education. Because of the backward nature of British political rule, women were amongst the 90 per cent of the population who were illiterate. Yet in 1975–77 alone, 59,065 women attended literacy courses. This was a very high attendance considering that the population of the country was approximately two million.

Members of the right wing who still occupied important state positions were reluctant to assist this development, hoping it could be contained and traditional and religious values would restore the status quo. FLOSY and other right-wing organisations who had fled the country used the radio to exploit the fears of those Yemenis who felt their tradition and customs were in danger. The attacks, as this radio broadcast shows, were vehement: "What do they mean by giving women equal rights? Islam defined women's relationships with men. But now Marxism has destroyed this basis It has rendered women's equality with men a basis of sin and whoredom." Generally the South Yemeni public saw these broadcasts as enemy propaganda which was not unsettling, partly because of the support for the new state as the state which had defeated colonialism, and partly because of the strength of policies influencing sociopolitical change which were being pursued. The left had succeeded in this particular radical initiative, turning women's oppression into some form of liberation.

A radical transformation also occurred in the army by 1974. It had been decided that the army had to be fully involved in the social and economic transformation of South Yemen. An example of this involvement was the army's drive towards agricultural collectivisation by establishing and operating a number of state farms. Because of the lack of manpower, particularly for labouring jobs, the army made a significant contribution to fulfilling this gap and was most successful in the Lahej and Abyan regions.

Like other Marxist regimes, South Yemen's regime also built a system of popular defence committees for the defence of the revolution, which involved the population in a variety or revolutionary programmes like education, housing, and security tasks in general. The first popular defence committee was established in May 1973 in Aden's Sheikh Uthman district. People were recruited to the popular defence committees from all backgrounds, the purpose being to break down tribal and other subnational loyalties and provide some formal basic political education and training in order to instil support for the revolution amongst important groups of people. In 1982, the popular defence committees had a membership of 160,000. Suspicion about the regular army, which was recruited from the sons of sheikhs, emirs, and big landowners and formed on tribal lines, continued throughout the post-revolutionary period; a military intelligence department was established in 1983. There was a need for a security system, but questions had to be raised about the issues of suppression by the security services, which proved effective in preventing sabotage on some occasions but were ruthless on others.

The early 1970s were a time of great optimism and euphoria in South Yemen. The people were so enthusiastic about the revolution and changes it made to Yemeni society that in 1971, the workers came out in the street demanding lower wages and chanting, "A reduction in our salaries is a revolutionary duty" (*kafed alrawtib wagib*). This was unique not just in the Arab world but also internationally. The South Yemeni working class were demanding a reduction of their wages, and these protests were designed to help the new state manage the economy but also to show solidarity with the popular President Rubayi. The population was successfully psyched up to support the radicalisms of the new state, and the country was captivated by revolutionary fervour.

The Fifth Congress and the Unification Congress

The Fifth Congress was held in March 1972. This period was characterised by a degree of high political activism and militancy. A period of post-revolutionary activity had passed and the socialist programmes had been implemented to some extent, some with limitations. Many members of the right had been expelled from the party, and the new congress was dominated by the radical wing of the NLF. Discussion took place in a comradely atmosphere and with little conflict.

Women in the workplace. Source: Qais Saeed.

A *Le Monde* journalist commented, "Aden had been filled for days with demonstrating workers and peasant crowds of militants shouting 'long live Marxism-Leninism' greeted the delegates. The average age of the delegates was between twenty and thirty, most of them from poor backgrounds—and many were hardly able to read or write but despite the difficulties the sessions were long, serious and highly politicised."[4]

Many issues concerning the way forward in terms of political and economic policies relevant to the socialist construction of Yemeni society were discussed. Although the leadership wanted to see such programmes and policies in place, it tended to take a more cautious and realistic stand towards policy decisions. The experience of governance had brought home the difficulty of the actual economic and political situation faced on the ground by the new state.

Delegates in congress wanted to pursue the political policies of the Fourth Congress, but the leadership did not want to attack the petty bourgeoisie because they realised it could bring in much-needed capital into the economy. No indication was given on the role this group could play within the economy. The congress devoted most of its time to discussing party development, indicating above all its determination to move towards the formal structure of a socialist political party. The NLF itself was renamed the National Front Political Organisation, and the previous General Command was replaced by an elected central committee of thirty-one members and fourteen candidate members, which in turn elected the political bureau. This new system was aimed at transforming the NLF from a loosely structured organisation into a more orthodox, centralised socialist party similar to those of the Eastern bloc. There was a call for the development of relations between Yemen and socialist states.

On 30 April 1974, the minister of foreign affairs and some of the best diplomatic brains in South Yemen were killed in a plane crash.

---

[4] *Le Monde,* 27 May 1972.

Some of the government members who died in the plane crash of 30 April 1974:

13a. Mohamed Saleh Al-Awlak, minister of foreign affairs

13b. Ahmed Saleh Al-Shaer, minister of agriculture

13c. Seif Ahmed Al-Dhalei, minister of foreign affairs

13d. Abdullah BinSalman, Presidential Office director

13e. Fadhal Ahmed Al Sallami, Presidential Office director

13f. Nour Alderm Kassim, governor of Aden

13g. Mohamed Nasser Mohamed, ambassador to Beirut

13h. Saeed Shahbel, ordinances director, Ministry of Foreign Affairs

13i. Mohamed Naji Mohamed, consul general to Jakarta

No official inquiry was ever made into the causes of the crash. Most commentators agree that the plane crash wasn't an accident and believe that a bomb was planted on the plane to explode in the air. Most of those killed were supportive of the Qahtan wing of the NLF, and their deaths definitely weakened his authority in South Yemen. The crash was a major blow to the government's capacity to operate externally, and the cover-up later on was almost an indication of the guilt of those in opposition to Qahtan. The crash caused major mistrust between the two factions in the NLF and significantly increased tensions. The NLF and the YSP lost its cadres due to internal disputes, and this weakened their administrative capacity.

The Unification Congress was held in October 1975 to bring two small parties operating within South Yemen, the People's Democratic Union and the People's Vanguard Party, into the NLF. The union was opposed by President Salem Rubayi, who began to launch his anti-bureaucratic campaign of urban uprisings, a form of mass mobilisation influenced to some extent by the Cultural Revolution in China, primarily designed to break the hold of bureaucrats within the state machinery. A new organisation, the United Political Organisation National Front (UPONF), was created.

The majority of left-wing activists firmly believed that the UPONF in 1975 would lead to the establishment of a new socialist party of South Yemen. They saw the organisation as marking the transitional stage, and as a tool of the national democratic revolution within the general framework of a broad class alliance between all social democratic forces who had a real interest in the national democratic revolution: the workers, peasants, soldiers, revolutionary intellectuals, and petty bourgeoisie.

The whole idea of a vanguard party was unique in the Arab world. A major ideological change which was clearly visible at the unification congress was a change in the attitude towards the petty bourgeoisie. This social class was violently attacked in 1968 and ignored in 1972; in 1975 it was clearly stated that the unified organisation's economic philosophy was based on public ownership. But public ownership did not prevent any form of private ownership. This statement recognised the role of the private sector, which was reinforced in the programme that stated the opportunity must be given to national capitalists to participate actively in creating a productive agricultural and industrial national economy under the leadership of the public sector. The programme also indicated that the revolution would defend all industrial projects set up in the private and mixed sectors within the development plan. This change indicated the extent to which the lack of capital in the economy held up the implementation of the first development plan. South Yemen's economic bureau claimed that only 50 per cent of its targets for the first plan had been met. This concerned many economists who had anticipated a more favourable result.

Already in 1975, a very intense political struggle was clearly emerging between the militant wing of the party led by Abdul Fattah Ismail and what was perceived as the Maoist wing led by President Salem Rubayi. The differences which emerged at this point of state development between the two factions mainly concerned internal economic policies and foreign policy. These differences were later to prove fatal in the relationship between the comrades who fought together to build a new socialist state. The inability of these left-wing members to establish a mechanism to resolve internal conflict through peaceful means proved to be fatal in the successful construction of the new socialist state. The idea that those politicians in power do things either this way or the other way without any room for compromise and negotiations appeared to haunt the revolution in state building.

Counter-revolutionary Forces

The main counter-revolutionary force was an exile group, the National Grouping of Patriotic Forces (NGPF), formed in 1980. It was made up of the United National Front (led by former Adeni Chief Minister and FLOSY leader Abdul Qawi al-Makawi), the Yemen Unity Front (led by former prime minister Muhammed

Ali Haytham), the remnants of the South Arabian League, and the June 26 Group (supporters of President Salem Rubayi Ali, who was deposed in 1978). The NGPF published a monthly information journal from Cairo and engaged in a number of sabotage plots against the new state, which were foiled by the South Yemeni security system. Counter-revolutionary forces had little influence inside South Yemen as the people took the line of their government, conscious of the need to maintain their political and economic independence. The left-wing propaganda machinery opposing what they saw as counter-revolutionaries was very effective.

Internal political resistance was similarly ineffective and focused on the issue of women and land. The resistance was sporadic and politically disorganised. It was sometimes linked to tribalism or generated by opportunistic party members mobilising fellow tribesmen in support of their political position. The main reason for the ineffectiveness of the resistance was the strength and organisation of the party and its determination to carry out radical popular policies. The removal of Qahtan and killing of some of his supporters was a clear indication of the weak capacity of the postcolonial state plagued so early on in its development with a high level of political violence. The governability of the new Yemeni state was dependent upon the political infrastructure of the state to deal with internal factionalism, in the absence of which the state increasingly relied upon the use of violence by one group against the other. This was to become a major defining feature of the development of the South Yemeni state.

CHAPTER 3

Factional Politics: The Conflict between Salem Rubayi and the Militant Left (1975–78)

The revolutionary enthusiasm apparent in the early 1970s calmed down in the middle of the decade. In the rural areas, major structural changes in land tenure and relations of production had not brought about instant prosperity or wealth, as many poor peasants had expected. Despite salary cuts and heavy food subsidies, the cost of living was rising. Peasants were becoming apathetic because of the low return on production and the inefficient working of the new agricultural institutions.

Economic Problems

In 1968–69, all workers' salaries in the public and private sectors were reduced by one-third to two-thirds; public sector salaries were cut again in 1972. In 1969 all banks and insurance companies were nationalised. In 1970 an agricultural law limited irrigated holdings to twenty acres and unirrigated holdings to forty acres. In 1972 a housing law ended all private renting and allowed individuals to own only the house in which they lived.

Cooperative farms in the PDRY. Source: Qais Saeed.

All previous economic colonial structures were dismantled, and the key to the new economic system was the gradual imposition of a state centralised planning system. The first five-year plan introduced in April 1974 projected a substantial increase in industrial output. Production rose around 260 per cent between independence and the end of 1975. Of the thirty-five factories in the country at the end of 1977, fourteen belonged to the public sector, eight belonged to the mixed sector (with the state having a 51 per cent share), and thirteen belonged to the private sector, with the state-owned units accounting for a disproportionate share of workers' output.

Despite succeeding in creating an entirely new economy, something which the British did not manage to achieve in over a century, South Yemen still faced severe economic problems and was in desperate need of economic assistance. These severe and continuing economic problems were undoubtedly a main motive for Rubayi's faction to seek economic aid from the Gulf countries. At the beginning of 1977, the PDRY joined the Arab Common Market.

This move was significant for Rubayi's faction. They felt it would create a conducive atmosphere for friendly relations with the strong economies of the Gulf countries and would also bring much-needed generation of capital necessary for the economic institutions they had set up to succeed. His more radical opponents paid little attention to this move, knowing full well that once they had established a socialist party, the decision to collaborate could easily be reversed. Rubayi's policy of rapprochement with the Gulf countries did, however, bring in economic aid which was desperately needed during that particular period.

According to the World Bank, South Yemen's GNP at market prices was $200 million in 1974. In 1977 the PDRY received $50 million in foreign loans. This improved the economic situation slightly, thus permitting an increase of international reserves to $100 million. In 1976–77, the government increased its efforts to implement Development Budget Investment, amounting to 17.2 million Yemeni dinars, of which 27 per cent was allocated to the public sector.

Salem Rubayi meeting people. Source Author.

The lack of finance in the public sector was due to the diversion of economic aid into other areas, such as defence and security. This was something that neither faction could do anything about, because they both intended to build a strong and secure state. As a result, the public sector was not developing fast enough to meet the economic demands of the population, and much of the blame for this was directed by the radical left towards Rubayi. To some extent, this began to shift the balance of power and popular support towards the militant left.

In a country which was not endowed with natural resources, state policy became a major determinant of economic performance. By taking a political stance against the rich neighbouring Arab countries, South Yemen has not been able to receive the necessary aid that was very much required. As a result of defending its political ideological principles, it had to endure additional economic difficulties which in most cases led to internal conflict.

Conflict between Salem Rubayi and the Militant Left
Whilst the masses were more concerned with the problems in the economy, the political leadership was divorced from this and engaged itself in factional politics. There was a lack of capital investment in the infrastructure, and hence the economic initiative did not achieve its intended targets. Yet there was no apparent direct opposition from the masses, and as a result little debate took place about these problems. Issues of conflict following the unification congress were political rather than economic. Rubayi was still seen as the undisputed popular leader.

President Salem Rubayi had become a political personality by the mid-1970s. He enjoyed the support of those who were devoted to him in both the state and the army. He did not give whole-hearted support to the idea of building a vanguard party. He was seen by the militant left as having vaguely Maoist leanings and objected to the process of centralisation implied by such a party. He had more confidence in people's revolutionary initiatives at the local level. By 1976 Rubayi had a network of sympathisers throughout the state hierarchy, and as president, he had a substantial budget which was beyond party control. He won support and avoided trouble by a clever allocation of funds, and he used this budget to support development projects supervised by politicians and civil servants loyal to him. However, the persons whom he chose to support him in office were loyalist, inept, and incompetent, and as a result those projects often ended in failure. Although he actually did believe in his policies and was viewed as a leader by the majority of the population, one of his mistakes was his reliance on loyalist colleagues who, to some extent, damaged his reputation.

Despite his miscalculations, Rubayi was loved by the people, as the popular slogan "Your army is your gun and your people are the ammunition" shows. He lived a simple life in a modest house like all the ordinary citizens of South Yemen. He had a good connection with the peasants and led by example. He was the pioneer of agricultural development similar to the Chinese model. The South Yemeni people generally saw him as one of them and until this day regret his removal from power and the way he was mistreated and killed. People came out demanding a reduction of wages because of their love for him personally.

The militant left, led politically by Abdul Fattah Ismail, became more hostile towards the president because they felt he was seeking to centralise political and economic power in his hands, thereby ignoring the fundamental party principle of collective leadership. As a result of Rubayi's individualistic approach towards the decision-making process, the difference between the two factions of the left-wing became more intense. There is no doubt that leading members of the militant left were also envious of Rubayi's popularity with the masses, amongst other issues.

The militants were keen to see structural centralist institutions in place before a socialist party was established. Whilst they were engaged with party cadres in ensuring this took place, Rubayi was busy campaigning for his political leadership, particularly in the rural areas. In all his speeches, the main theme was his desire to strengthen the popular masses—the workers and the peasants. He felt that this was best done if they themselves set up their own organisations rather than someone else doing it for them. He wanted them to have political control in their own communities. He gave no indication as to how this should be done, and many detected gaps in his theories, although they did not generally doubt his sincerity towards the poor and the working class.

The centralisation of the political and economic power structures was now in motion and succeeding quite quickly. As a result, the administrative structure was set up throughout the country. The "spontaneous" institutions such as the Agricultural Committees, which Rubayi had encouraged and directed himself to counter the rising centralisation process, were quickly losing control.

In foreign affairs and the international sphere, the president increasingly emphasised better relations with conservative neighbours and diversification of foreign aid sources. In particular, he wanted less dependence on the Soviet Union.

In contrast to Rubayi's policies and strategies, the militant left advocated an increasingly militant approach and stressed the importance of an alliance with the socialist camp, in particular the Soviet Union. The militants rejected any moderation of the revolution's aggressive foreign policy approach towards South Yemen's conservative neighbours, in particular Saudi Arabia, whom they saw as hostile and reactionary. Ismail was also the primary architect of the new party structure.

Both leaders and sets of positions had different supporters in the cabinet and the National Front. The loyalists and power-oriented elements tended to side with Rubayi, who also received some support from his Dathina co-tribesmen, his home region, and former members of the Liberation Army, many of whom were now serving in senior positions in the regular army. The more ideologically oriented elements tended to support Ismail, who, if less populist, was more imposing as a party figure and seen as a socialist theorist. He also enjoyed good relations with the Soviet Union.

The Political Explosion of 26 June 1978

Matters intensified in 1977–78. The crisis which brought the conflict between the president and his opponents to a head began on 24 June 1978 when the North Yemeni president Al-Ghashmi was killed by a bomb sent to him disguised as a present from the South Yemeni government. The NLF central committee accused Rubayi of organising this in the hope of provoking a crisis in the North in which he could intervene and so oust his rivals in the South. This later turned out to be untrue, and political commentators state that military strongman Saleh Musleh Qasim and close colleagues were behind this assassination. The suicide bomber dispatched to carry out the bomb explosion was one of Saleh's close associates from the region of Dhala.

The militant left's major aim was to reduce the influence of Rubayi, get rid of him and his faction, and build a new style vanguard socialist party as advocated by Ismail. The new party's basic political document was approved in December 1977, but it was decided to postpone the formal announcement of the new party until sometime in October 1978 because it was felt that major technical details had to be worked out before an open announcement could be made.

Three major goals were outlined in the document.

1. Re-evaluation of all the class organisational activities within the party, such as the practice of centralised democracy, collective leadership, criticism, and self-criticism;
2. A purge of all ailments and imperfections in the movement and of all the bad blood that had been found inside it. The imperfections were attributed to the bourgeois class—remnants of the old authority that had been transmitted from the age of colonialism and had not been able to develop or stay in step with the revolution. Another alleged cause of imperfection was the personal, Bedouin, and tribal relations which impeded social mobilisation.

3. The building of the productive forces into a foundation for the new class structure. These forces were the workers in the agricultural and fishery cooperatives which were established in 1970–71, the soldiers who defended the revolution, and the enlightened revolutionaries.

Yemeni men and women who had been educated in Eastern European countries were supposed to be equipped with socialist agendas by this stage. They were seen to be the creators of appropriate party structures and the people who would eventually serve the bureaucratic machinery. They were increasing in numbers, and most were involved in setting up administrative organisations which paved the way for establishing a political socialist party. But most of them had little experience of the economic and political situation and thus opened themselves to much criticism, particularly from Rubayi's faction.

Having succeeded in taking the political initiative, Ismail and his comrades ordered the arrest of 150 officers loyal to Rubayi in May 1978, because they were allegedly opposed to the creation of the new party. Rubayi responded by attempting to strengthen his political position within the armed forces through continual visits to army units.

By 21 June 1978, Ismail and his comrades believed that Rubayi was trying to turn the internal security forces into his own power base. Different leaders in the NLF had their links with the security services. Rubayi's officers in the security unit, similar to any spy agency, were suspected of attempting to create a network for secret contacts with Saudi Arabia. These officers were arrested, and when Rubayi, as chairman of the Armed Forces Organisational Committee, refused to hand over a report on the network's activities to the political bureau of the UPONF, he was replaced as chairman by Hussain Qamata, the commander of the popular militia and a central committee member.

On 24 June, Rubayi was put under house arrest and stripped of his political authority, but he still remained chairman of the Presidential Council. He refused to attend an extraordinary meeting of the central committee to discuss the political developments in North Yemen. The meeting approved two resolutions by 121 votes to 4. The first suspended President Rubayi for his alleged involvement in the assassination of the North Yemeni president, and the second called for an investigatory committee to look into his actions. Rubayi decided to hold on to his position and resist Ismail's faction until the end. Shortly after the meeting, his opponents reported that he deployed military units loyal to him near the presidential palace and other government buildings. The militants interpreted this as an attempted coup d'état, reconvened the central committee meeting, and decided to take immediate, firm action.

On 26 June, fighting started in Aden between armed units loyal to Rubayi and popular militia units loyal to Ismail in both the Tawahi quarter and the Aden airport area. Communications with the outside world were cut, and the airport was closed. Units loyal to Rubayi, including those from the nearby Salah al-Din military camp, began to shell the central committee building, the prime minister's office, and the Defence and State Security Ministry. At the same time, other units from Bab Al-Mandab, all loyal to Rubayi, began to move towards Aden.

Units loyal to Ismail had the upper hand, and by 9 a.m., the popular militias had gained control of at least half of Aden. They blocked and controlled the main roads and imposed a curfew. Towards noon, when Rubayi and his followers continued to resist, the air force bombed the Presidential Council Palace. At 2.55 p.m., the central committee issued a statement accusing Rubayi of staging a coup d'état "in violation of all the principles and objectives our revolution and political organisation". It also thanked the armed forces, the popular militia, and the police "for their vigilant stands protecting the organisational legitimacy represented in the collective command and its commitment and firm implementation of the decisions of the central committee and political bureau".

Following the fighting, Rubayi and his followers surrendered. They were tried by a special court established by his opponents, sentenced to death by firing squad, and executed immediately. Those who supported Rubayi in the central committee were expelled. Other associates and supporters mostly took refuge in North Yemen and Saudi Arabia. The central committee, following its meeting of 28 June, issued the following statement on Rubayi's political and economic stance.

> Sometimes he would wear the veil of extreme leftism in front of the democratic vanguards: on other occasions he would wear in an exaggerated manner the veil of bogus realism. He opposed the unity of the groups on national democratic action, which we regard as a first basic step towards the establishment of the brand new party. At the economic level he attempted to create confusion among all the groups at the present stage of the national democratic revolution of mobilizing their potential for the construction of the national economy to form the material foundation for subsequent construction. In foreign policy he adopted a reactionary attitude towards the Arab world and revolutionary movements. On the Yemen arena he attempted to drag our Yemeni people into civil war again.[5]

But even though the opponents alleged that Rubayi had deviated from collective leadership and had become an individualist in every sense and a dominant political personality, he still had wide support amongst the population because of his prominent revolutionary stand against colonialism. In *Yemen's Unfinished Revolution*, Fred Halliday noted, "He was a believer in an ethical approach to politics. His strength lay in his popularity in the countryside and his revolutionary vision. No-one has ever suspected him personally of corruption or leading an easy life. Even after his downfall he was still given praise for some of the developments which had taken place while he was still alive."[6]

His execution was a disagreeable surprise because of his popularity in the South. There are many conflicting stories about this assassination and the final hours in Rubayi's life which I don't intend to cover in this book. After Rubayi's execution, Ismail became the most prominent politician in the country, leading the militant left into a new era of Yemeni politics. Although Ali Nasser Mohammed had cooperated in bringing down his fellow tribesman Rubayi, he was still overshadowed by Ismail, who became the new head of state following the June events. Ali Nasser and Ali Antar retained their positions as prime minister and defence minister, respectively. This was the beginning of a new period and new leadership at a critical stage in the formation of the state. Rubayi's killing continued to haunt South Yemen's revolution, with so many people from all sides of the political spectrum regretting his death and the ruthless way in which he was removed from power. Almost all his opponents and supporters recognised his huge contribution to the revolution and the fact that he was an incorrupt leader. There are some commentators who emphasise that the removal of Rubayi in this way created the seeds for future confrontation between the comrades.

The cooperation between Ismail and Ali Nasser was treated with suspicion by the militants because it was well-known that Ali Nasser had never made his policies clear and had always showed concern for occupying positions of power rather than retaining political principles. Ismail enjoyed his greatest popularity amongst ideological party members and relied for his support from this source, whereas Nasser looked to a distinct base of support from his tribal homeland in Abyan.

Rubayi's execution meant the departure of the most influential figure of the first decade of independence, and this created a political power vacuum which remained to be filled. Although Ismail stepped in to take the leadership for the moment, a number of powerful personalities had become more powerful than previously, following the June events. Factional politics had not ended but entered a new phase that would continue to hinder the development of the South Yemeni state.

---

[5] Official statements on Radio Aden, June 28, 1978.

[6] Fred Halliday, *Yemen's Unfinished Revolution; Socialism in the South* (London: MERIP Reports, 1979), 18.

The removal of Qahtan and now Rubayi—not by the people of South Yemen but by their opponents—and the way in which they were removed and humiliated clearly demonstrate how political factional violence in South Yemen played a key role in the struggle of one comrade against the other or one faction against the other. Inter-party violence instead of a democratic mechanism was used by party loyalists to show their commitment to one side or the other, whereas intra-party conflict within the NLF could secure a particular faction's position in the state machinery. Such conflict always tended to prevail with even more intensity and a significant increase in violence. These factional dynamics became particularly visible in a country that had so much potential to develop politically and economically.

CHAPTER 4

New Era of Factional Politics: The Downfall of Militancy and the Rise and Decline of Ali Nasser (1978–86)

Ali Nasser Mohammed, who was confirmed as prime minister following the downfall of Rubayi, was a more pragmatic politician with a career ambition to lead South Yemen. He wanted to concentrate all political power in his hands. By 1980 he was the leader of three major institutions: the party, the state, and the executive—the first time in South Yemen's young history that this had happened.

The first Yemeni Government. Source Author.

Formation of the Yemeni Socialist Party (YSP) and Foreign Policy Orientations
Rubayi's downfall meant that Ismail and those around him had to come up with solutions to bring some economic prosperity to a people in need. Economically, this was the most difficult period for South Yemen, and the new leadership was under tremendous pressure. Priority was given to transforming the UPONF into the new Yemeni Socialist Party (YSP), which was set up on 11 October 1978. Ismail theoretically believed in party members having a big role to play in the party. The Yemeni Socialist Party objective was, according to all its documentation, to radically transform Yemeni society. As the first congress put it, "The Yemeni Socialist Party, which includes in its ranks all the vanguard struggling forces is considered to be the main implementer for building Yemeni socialist society."[7]

---

[7] Political Report of the Yemeni Socialist Party 1st Congress, Section 7 in Proceedings of the 1st Congress of the YSP, Moscow, 1978, 133.

Ismail was a strong advocate of the Soviet model of development. In 1978 and 1979, South Yemen signed several friendship and cooperation treaties with a number of communist countries, including the Soviet Union, East Germany, and Ethiopia. His determination to bring South Yemen into the socialist camp was clearly expressed: "Our revolution believes that the unity of the socialist camp and the unity of the world revolution will cut the road to world imperialism, which has tried to benefit from every dispute among the socialists to extend its influence throughout the world. Democratic Yemen considers the socialist camp to be a revolutionary ally and wants to create the strongest brotherly relations with it."[8] In June 1979, the PDRY acquired observer status with Comecon, and in September 1979, the Soviet Premier Kosygin visited Aden.

In March 1976, Ali Nasser pursued diplomatic relations between Saudi Arabia and South Yemen, thus revealing two different, contradictory policy orientations. The militant revolutionaries in the leadership adopted a policy of hatred towards Saudi Arabia because they believed it had sought from the very beginning to undermine South Yemen's revolution and its social system. The moderates under the leadership of Ali Nasser felt it was important to build relations with both the Arab Gulf countries and the Eastern bloc. A contradictory policy was pursued simultaneously at the time of the cold war between the Eastern bloc and the Western bloc.

The two main factors which contributed to bad relations between South Yemen and Saudi Arabia were South Yemen's continuous support for the People's Front of the Liberation of Oman and the establishment of the YSP, accompanied by the growing Marxist orientation of the PDRY.

Both factions of the YSP understood the vulnerability of the South Yemeni system, in particular its weak economic base, and both wanted economic aid, which was a very important element in South Yemen's development strategy. The limitation of economic aid from both the Arab Gulf countries and the Eastern bloc severely constrained the economic resources available to the state to achieve economic stability and systematically prevented the formulation of a coherent foreign policy strategy.

Relations with North Yemen; the War of 1979

Ismail's camp envisaged a united Yemen based on democratic values and equality, but their Marxist-Leninist ideology on which they would not compromise clearly showed this was not a realistic expectation. North Yemen was an Islamic capitalist state governed by the traditional tribal structure with an open market economy supported by the Saudis and the international community. The two states had completely different systems with no compromise for one system to replace the other.

By June 1978, relations between the two Yemeni states were quite hostile. The National Democratic Front (NDF), formed in 1976, was a group of North Yemen politicians including Omar Garallah, who fled to the South in opposition to the regime in the North. It regrouped various nationalist and leftist groups and had the full support of the YSP. Following Rubayi's downfall, relations between the two parts of Yemen became worse, with the advent of a violent propaganda war and constant border clashes. The NDF was very active in North Yemen and had military strongholds in isolated mountain regions south and east of Sanaa and Taiz. The Northern regime believed that the South was harbouring those in opposition to the regime. The senior NDF members in Aden had close connections with Ismail and also strong military backing from two senior state officials from the Dhala region, Saleh Musleh Qassim and Ali Antar. The NDF supported and joined the YSP in an attempt to consolidate some power and influence for themselves within the South, with a clear objective of influencing politics in the North of Yemen

---

[8] The programme of the Unified Political Organisation—the National Front—for the national democratic phase of the revolution, Russell Press for the PDRY Embassy, London, 1977, 14.

In October 1978, up to 2,500 Northerners came into Aden from the North expressing their support for the YSP and the NDF. The YSP leadership argued that the NDF was pursuing a continuation of the revolutionary struggle that the militant left of the NLF had fought in the South throughout 1967–69. This influx of opposition forces from the North into the South was seen by the Northern regime as an act of war against the Northern state.

On 24 February 1979, war broke out between the two parts of Yemen with the involvement of the regular armies on both sides. Militarily this was a partial victory for South Yemen, which took over border towns belonging to the North and handed them over to the NDF to administer. A ceasefire was agreed in March 1979 facilitated by Arab mediation. At the end of March, Ismail met North Yemen's President Ali Abdullah Saleh in Kuwait to sign a peace agreement and patch up their relations. A joint statement issued by the two leaders promised unity within a single agreed constitution which the people in the North and South would approve through a referendum, a unified elected parliament, and a provisional government to oversee the referendum.

Although the agreement lessened the tension between the two countries and there was a withdrawal of forces, the problems were not completely resolved because the NDF had achieved considerable military success in the North with the support of the YSP. Ismail and Saleh Musleh Qassim, the defence minister, were very supportive of the NDF, seeing it as a progressive force essential to the political development of North Yemen. But the Northerners were very aware of the YSP's support for the NDF, and the agreement did not take effect.

Throughout 1979 and the early 1980s, both sides became politically hostile to each other, restraining themselves from entering into a military conflict and confining themselves to a propaganda war. The regime in the North asserted that the NDF was nothing more than a Marxist wing controlled by the YSP's central committee.

Ali Nasser (right) and Saleh Musleh Qasim in 1985. Source Author.

The Rise of Ali Nasser

The continuing divisions within the YSP came into the open by early 1979 with two factions emerging: the militant wing of Ismail and his followers, who perceived themselves as the radical left of a vanguard party, and Nasser's wing, whose members held influential political posts since independence but whose principles were very different from those of the other wing.

In August 1979, there was a cabinet reshuffle which highlighted the disagreement between Ismail and Nasser. Mohamed Said Abdullah, the head of the Ministry for State Security, who Nasser believed had extended his responsibilities over military security, was removed. Nasser managed to manipulate Defence Minister Ali Antar to take his side on this matter. Ismail's close allies did not take Nasser seriously as a political figure and collaborated with him only to some extent, not realising the political consequences.

By late 1979, following further internal conflicts on domestic and foreign issues, Nasser was winning the battle for political control, and many of his close allies in the YSP were promoted to key positions. He also had a tribal base of support from his home town of Dathina.

At the beginning of 1980, Ismail began to warn his comrades to stand firm against those who were trying to weaken the YSP; by this he meant Ali Nasser. Nasser's faction began a smear campaign against Ismail in an attempt to undermine his political rival. Ismail was criticised for his close ties with the Soviet Union, his hostility to Saudi Arabia and other Gulf states, and his mismanagement of the economy. His faction always stressed the value of ideological purity and the importance of adopting positions on issues confronting the system. Nasser and his faction felt that political positions on issues should be flexible and moderate. A situation was created where comrades in leading political positions were fighting against each other on issues on which they had previously fought together. Nasser saw this as a way of pushing himself forward to lead the YSP, but this could be achieved only if he removed Ismail from the position of secretary-general.

In April 1980, Nasser's allies called on Ismail to resign. They attributed the economic difficulties and the worsened domestic political situation to his political and economic incompetence. Those who were not of this opinion, in particular those in the central committee, were persecuted. On 12 April, Ismail left for Libya to attend a conference on resistance and revolution. During his absence, the YSP politburo, influenced by Nasser and his followers, convened a series of meetings in which his followers were removed from office. When Ismail returned from Libya, he refused to endorse any of the decisions taken while he was away and explicitly warned that actions against loyal and faithful comrades would sharpen the conflict in both party and state and result in irreparable damage to the revolution.

On 20 April, the YSP central committee held an emergency meeting to discuss the letter of resignation from Ismail, which raised questions about his health. It was clear that Nasser had finally secured enough support in the central committee to force Ismail's resignation as both president and party secretary. In recognition of his duties to the revolution, he was appointed to the newly created post of chairman of the YSP, a titular figure without any political duties. This time the military leaders took a pragmatic view and did not support Ismail.

In his resignation statement, Ismail explained that health reasons prevented him from continuing in political office. Before going into self-imposed exile in Moscow, he emphasised how essential it was that his comrades should take care of the revolutionary experience and should not damage this experience with trivial bickering and internal disputes. He wanted to avoid bloodshed at all costs and was determined to set an example as a leader who was not authoritarian or hungry for power. He said he genuinely felt that the most important issue was the development of the YSP and the interests of the Yemeni people. The fact that Ismail was not executed was indicative of the broad support he still enjoyed within the YSP, the militia, and grassroots party organs. The Saudis were overjoyed at his political demise because they were eager to eliminate revolutionary socialism from the south of the Arabian Peninsula. It is quite possible that had he not left for exile, he would have faced a similar fate to Rubayi.

The central committee meeting on 20 April took place in an atmosphere of fear. Members were threatened if they voted not to accept Ismail's resignation. Some felt it was inappropriate to vote while Ismail was not at the meeting, but the vote went ahead nevertheless and the central committee accepted his resignation on the grounds of illness.

The vote-taking contravened internal party rules as the numbers required for a valid vote were not there. Ali Nasser became the head of the party, the state and the executive. This was not accepted by all the grassroots of the party, and some on the radical left felt he was not capable of holding such supreme high office. Nasser's position was strengthened by the execution of the foreign minister, Mohammed Saleh Muti, accused of spying for the Saudis. Foreign Minister Muti, from the Yafa region, was an intelligent politician commanding respect particularly within South Yemen's foreign service and international political circles. Undoubtedly he could have been a contender for the leadership. The only remaining rivals were Ali Antar and Saleh Musleh Qassim, who had enormous popularity amongst the ranks of the armed forces but were more military men rather than government technocrats. Nasser intelligently befriended these two senior politicians for the time being. He knew that having them in his side or neutralising them would strengthen his power base.

Ali Nasser succeeded Abdul Fattah Ismail in leadership positions of party and state. At the time of his appointment, he was considered by those politicians with greater influence than him as weak and therefore the least threatening of all the candidates. As prime minister and secretary general of the Yemeni Socialist Party (YSP), Nasser was on good terms with Ali Antar, Saleh Mosleh Qasim Ali Shai Hadi, and many others in South Yemen's political class, having earned himself the nickname of 'Ali Marhaba ('Ali at-your-service) within political circles, a title he was known to resent because it undermined his political position. As head of state, he was able to balance off the various political power players and tribal groups against one another.

But opposition to his "personal leadership" quickly emerged as he began the process of flexing his authority, and the differences between himself and Ali Antar emerged publicly. Nasser connected with his tribal base and built around him many supporters to counterbalance the influence of his opponents. He was known as a pragmatist and continued to "service" his supporters as a way of guaranteeing their loyalty. His political adversaries did likewise, although they were not as well placed to distribute the perquisites of office. The result was a competition in generosity, with Mercedes and Volvos proliferating in the streets of Aden to key members. Meanwhile, Nasser removed a number of former National Liberation Front (NLF) militants and veterans of the independence struggle from important ministry positions and replaced them with cadres who were less prestigious but more faithful to him personally. His connections with Abyan and Shabwa were a counterbalance to the support his opponents were getting from Al Dhala and Yafa, and hence this power struggle led to the January catastrophe with devastating consequences for the party and the state from which they never recovered.

Despite the political turmoil, conflicts, and executions, considerable resilience was shown by the party and the state which, were able to overcome grave internal and external tensions. They were able to bring about internal security and normality in all walks of life after each conflict. Individual leaders in the Yemeni revolution may have been able to monopolise political power, but individuals alone were unable to change any of the basic characteristics of either party, state or society.

Ali Antar. Source Author.

Following Ismail's departure, new tensions emerged focusing on political power and how it should be managed emerged. The rival camps now consisted of Nasser's camp and Ali Antar's camp; these two men were now in a struggle for power. Antar was unhappy with the way that Nasser had occupied the power vacuum within state and party.

The Authoritarian Trend

Between 1980 and 1982, Nasser focused on eliminating all opposition either by ruthless means or by ingratiating himself with those he felt were a threat. The YSP became an authoritarian organisation where disagreement with the leadership was not tolerated. After the militants' efforts to gain the upper hand when Ismail was a prominent personality, they were once again sidelined and purged from the YSP state organs. Ali Salem Al-Beidh was dismissed from the central committee and from his post as minister of local government largely because of his opposition to improved relations with Saudi Arabia. Nasser's close colleagues were promoted to key political and administrative positions.

In mid-October 1980, Nasser convened an extraordinary general congress of the YSP with a view to consolidating his position and introducing new members, who favoured his politics, to the central committee. Following Ismail's departure, it was essential to deal with the unstable political situation and ensure that no faction had authority over another, but Nasser was seen by his opponents as indulging in intensified factionalism. The security services suppressed dissent and opponents were imprisoned. It is fair to say that many opponents of the regime were crushed with impunity, and all the political leaders were engaged in a war against anyone who opposed them.

Nasser's only remaining rivals with great political influence or importance were veterans of the anti-colonialism struggle: Saleh Musleh Qassim and Ali Antar, who were perceived as strongmen with huge influence amongst the military and were to some extent popular amongst the ranks of the security services and armed forces. Nasser, in a move that was described as manipulative by his opponents, removed his new arch-rival Ali Antar from the Defence Ministry, replacing him with Saleh Musleh Qassim, so those two men were balanced against each other and his own authority remained unchallenged. Antar was appointed head of the newly created Ministry of Local Government and first deputy prime minister, in an attempt to create the impression that the party was united. When Antar was away, Nasser dismissed fifty-five army officers who supported the militant left, but the military did not challenge this action because Qasim was in the politburo.

Liberalization of the economy, moderation in foreign policy

The liberalisation of the economy was Nasser's most controversial move. Private traders were given greater leeway, rich peasants were allowed to sell about a dozen different products at prices of up to 150 per cent above those in state cooperatives, and a mixed economy came into existence. The private sector was competing with the state sector and social and political tensions arose as those in the private sector began to have higher incomes and better living standards than those working for the state economy. There were two conflicting views about the economy. Nasser and his supporters believed that South Yemen could not be a socialist society unless it passed through the stage of capitalist development. The militant left, by contrast, believed that the transformation to socialism was possible through assistance from other socialist countries and the strengthening of a centrally planned economy. Unity between the various factions that emerged after the downfall of Rubayi rapidly disappeared with each side trying to build its major base of power in the YSP and the military. A period in history that tried to wipe out dissent and systematically purged any members or others who might oppose the regime ensued.

Modernisation of Aden. Source: Qais Saeed.

The biggest mistake made by the PDRY was to try to imitate the economic development of advanced industrialised societies. In the early and mid-1980s under Nasser's leadership, millions of pounds were spent on questionable improvements and extravaganzas such as fun fairs, bowling allies, fountains, roundabouts, and luxury hotels. This sort of political and economic behaviour was seen by those in the left of the party as unacceptable when they argued for radical socialist development, in particular when there were still inadequate water, electricity, medical, and sanitation facilities in the countryside and Aden itself.

One of the major issues which generated fundamental differences between Nasser and the militant left was the way in which Naser prioritised the areas of economic need. He was seen to distribute economic resources to those areas populated by his supporters, particularly in his tribal town of Al Ibyan. This unfair allocation of economic resources led to economic division and political disharmony in many parts of South Yemen, in particular the poorer areas of the country.

The decentralisation of the economy by Nasser went hand in hand with the rapprochement towards what left-wingers saw as reactionary states in the Gulf, especially Saudi Arabia. He hoped to obtain financial assistance from these states and strengthen his reputation in the Arab world. Financial aid from the Gulf countries did not materialise on the scale envisaged by Nasser, and the economy of the PDRY failed to improve. Economic aid would have proved vital in justifying Nasser's friendly approach to the Saudis, but it was not forthcoming. These states were still mistrustful of what they saw as a communist regime in an Islamic society.

In the meantime, the left was reorganising its power base as party cells all over the country and were criticising what they saw as the petit-bourgeois approach to economic development and the attempts to draw the South closer to the conservative Gulf states.

The Re-emergence of the Left and the Return of Abdul Fatah Ismail

By 1984 Ali Antar was gaining much political influence within the military and the party. He was advised that grassroots party cells were calling for the return of Ismail from Moscow because he was seen, with Saleh Musleh Qasim, as the only senior politicians who could galvanise opposition to Nasser into action. By this time, it became clear that Antar and Nasser were at loggerheads, and the split within the party was clear to members of the rank and file.

The struggle between the two wings of the YSP intensified once again, to such an extent that the YSP Central Committee Conference was postponed from its scheduled date of November 1983 to May 1984. It emerged from the voting that the militants had succeeded in occupying influential positions, which gave them more leverage over policymaking. Amongst the five new members elected to the politburo was Saleh Musleh Qassim. This proved significant in strengthening Antar's faction and the militant left. Qassim was a strong, charismatic figure and was feared for his iron-fist approach to the development of the revolution. He emphasised that the PDRY was not satisfied with the Gulf states' reliance on the United States for their security, arguing that they were capable of defending themselves by depending on their own people's strength. In July 1984, Mohamed Ushaysh, another revolutionary militant, was made chairman of the PDRY's delegation to unity talks between North and South Yemen.

Nothing was resolved at the party conference with regards to major differences, especially on how to run the economy and what foreign policy was to be pursued by the leadership. The militants were also concerned that there was a concentration of US naval units and espionage planes in the region, including its base in Diego Garcia and its fleets in the waters of the Indian Ocean and Arabian Gulf, and they were convinced that the PDRY's prevailing foreign policy had to change to meet the American challenge.

The membership of the YSP changed significantly towards the left. Members of the NLF who later became members of the YSP did so because of their belief in developing the revolution and transforming Yemeni society. But the situation changed once the fruition of revolutionary struggle became apparent and the YSP was in command. During the early and mid-1980s, members of the well-off peasantry and bureaucrats became representatives of the Nasser's pragmatic vision because of their relationships with local and foreign capital. They joined the party for pragmatic rather than ideological reasons. In 1984 there was little respect for political discipline: ordinary party cadres were acting under the instructions of political personalities rather than the party regulations and internal programmes, and party discipline was at an all-time low.

There was a clear, irreconcilable division between the two wings of the party. On the one hand, there were those who wanted to pursue a more bureaucratic, pragmatic, and authoritarian style of politics similar to that of Nasser. On the other hand were those who were keen to reorganise the militant left and struggle towards political collectivism and economic state control of the kind espoused by Ismail.

After having gained political ground and a grip on influential ideological and economic institutions in the PDRY, the grassroots of the party began to voice the need for Ismail to return. After being forcefully but tactfully removed from office, Ismail returned to Aden in March 1985 to a hero's welcome. He was returned to the central committee, appointed secretary of public relations, and worked directly with the committee, which was preparing for the third YSP Congress. He described the conflict within the YSP as a class struggle, insinuating that the enemy was to be found within the party.

Party activists criticised Nasser for his monopolisation of political power, and he resigned unwillingly from his post as prime minister, which was given to the moderate politician Haider Abu Bakr Al-Attas. The appointment played no significant part in solving the differences between the two factions, and they started openly appealing to tribes in the rural areas to give them political support to win the struggle. The political leaders were to blame for reviving tribalism to some extent after the revolution had succeeded in suppressing it.

After the congress held in October 1985, Ali Nasser's supporters still dominated the central committee, whereas the militant leadership was in control of the politburo without whose approval no important political, economic, or ideological decisions could be taken. Ismail was now in a position to formulate policy of a socialist character similar to that which he had attempted to pursue in 1979. The PDRY state media was jubilant at a peaceful outcome at the congress. Many party officials were predicting bloodshed and the failure of the congress. The Soviet ambassador in Aden, Vladislav Zhukov, played his part in negotiating a compromise solution between the two factions.

Nasser was obviously discontented with the re-emergence of the radical left to power. He wanted to regain his power base and pursue his own pragmatism. He was seen by his opponents as abusing his own powers in both party and state. In late November 1985, he set off on a propaganda tour of the whole country, attacking the policies of the militant left and promoting his own policies of pragmatism.

The left, as it appeared at the time, had no intention of taking military action to oust Nasser and his supporters because they were confident of the support of the rank and file and believed that they could achieve their aim of challenging Nasser without having to spill a single drop of blood. They felt it necessary to succumb to the power of the party as the guiding tool for Yemeni society. Ismail, according to his followers, had shown his reluctance in 1980 to enter again into military conflict which would result in bloodshed, and he understood that a military conflict would be catastrophic for him and the party he established.

By the end of 1985, political factionalism had not been solved or managed, and this resulted in an unstable situation where major issues of personnel appointments and the policy on the liberalisation of the economy and relations with the Gulf states and the Soviet Union remained unresolved. There was an unwillingness to discuss the issues at stake using the political means within the YSP structures available to both sides. Although the situation remained volatile, everyone, including the Soviet Union, which was supposedly monitoring the situation, ruled out the possibility of military conflict. In early January, advisers close to Minister of Defence Saleh Musleh Qassim warned him of a planned attack on the militants by Nasser's faction, but he refused to take heed of such advice. He was under the impression that reconciliation would prevail and a peaceful solution would be found. Sadly, he was mistaken.

It is fair to say that the Soviet Union had by now established strong relations with the socialist state of South Yemen and, to some extent, was supportive of Ismail and the left wing of the party and their policies. The Soviet Union, however, had very little influence on the political personalities or understanding of the internal dynamics of South Yemeni politics and made little headway towards influencing the leaders of the different factions to settle their differences peacefully or convincing either side to share power in a broadly representative national government.

CHAPTER 5

The Massacre of 13 January 1986 in the South and the Path to Union with the North of Yemen (1986–90)

Following lengthy periods of political factionalism at party and state levels through the 1980s, it seemed as though by October 1986, an explosion had been avoided and a compromise had been reached by the leadership through the party conference in 1985 and Soviet mediation. But any compromises proved to be futile, and a military explosion was waiting to happen within the YSP.

South Yemen's experiment with socialism came to a bloody end. Three leading members of Yemen's NLF (from left to right): Salem Rubayi Ali, Abdul Fattah Ismail, and Ali Nasser Muhammad in 1977. Source; Wikipedia.

False Optimism and Propaganda

The success of the YSP Third Congress was interpreted by some of the world media as indicating a relaxation in the tensions in the PDRY. An agreement was reached by both parties to solve outstanding problems and issues of conflict through peaceful discussions and negotiations rather than by military force. It was clear that no one actually explained what means and mechanism were used to come up with a compromise, but it seemed as though the lessons from conflict such as those which occurred during Qahtan's and Rubayi's leadership were not heeded.

In reality, however, the outcome of the Third Congress actually set the scene for political conflict between Ali Nasser and his opponents. Although the press, radio, and television reported on the success and unity of congress, the political reality contrasted greatly. Political instability was inevitably forthcoming, focusing on major political, economic, ideological, personal, and international issues.

Many were surprised by the actual turn of events; others expected a crisis to occur. No one really expected total harmony as the press indicated. There was a huge propaganda cover-up of the reality of the political situation. Behind the shadows of the PDRY's politics, there still existed deep political differences and personal animosities. No one in South Yemen really believed that the problems had been overcome, and some felt that the worst of the conflict was yet to come. Nasser, following the congress, was still firmly in control of the channels of communication, particularly South Yemen's media, and through these institutions, he was able to create a smokescreen which reflected his personal popularity and the popularity of his pragmatic policies. Aden's media failed to provide constructive and balanced criticism which could have brought important issues to the surface and stimulated discussion within the party ranks and externally.

13 January 1986: Massacre with Tea

A meeting of the political bureau of the YSP was agreed to by the members, starting early on the morning of 13 January 1986. Ali Nasser initiated the meeting to continue previous discussions which had taken place on 12 January, focused on the redistribution of political responsibilities and duties among the two factions in the leadership of the party. These discussions, according to a number of commentators, made Nasser uncomfortable, and the majority in the meeting apparently opposed Nasser's plans for the allocation of responsibility. He wanted to place a number of loyalists into key positions of power, but the other faction led by Antar and Ismail had a different set of loyalists they wanted to push forward. It was reported that the majority of the politburo were more supportive of the plans of the opposing faction.

On Monday, 13 January 1986, members of the politburo arrived at the meeting held at the office of the central committee of the party at approximately 9.45 a.m. While the opposing faction was waiting for Nasser and his supporters to arrive for the meeting to go through the agenda previously compromised on, they had not suspected what was about to happen and began a discussion amongst themselves in preparation for the meeting. Those present (Abdul Fattah Ismail, Saleh Musleh Qassim, Ali Antar, Salem Salah, Ali Sahi Hadi, Ali Salem Al-Beidh, Ali Assad Muthena, and Ali Saleh Munassir) supported the left wing of the party. It is reported that they thought a compromise had been reached and that Nasser and his supporters would attend the meeting to finish the business. No indication was given by the security service or Soviet intelligence to those in the meeting that Nasser had planned a major military explosion.

It was interesting that Nasser's official Mercedes was parked in the yard of the same building, and it is further reported that those in the meeting assumed he was in the office of Abdul Ghani Abdul Qadir, a politburo member, because he often spent time with him before meetings. Nasser's personal security guard came into the meeting room carrying the president's briefcase, followed by another guard carrying a tea thermos flask. The members in the meeting still did not suspect anything unusual. It was at this stage, immediately after 10.15 a.m., that the two guards who entered the meeting suddenly started shooting at the members seated on their chairs. Using submachine guns, they opened fire with impunity, hysterically shooting everyone in their sights. All those present apart from Al-Beidh, Salem Saleh, and Ismail were killed. The two strongmen within the party, Antar and Qasim, were targeted and instantly killed.

Noel Brehony described how the three survivors were able to crawl into the next room and get weapons from their guards, who were outside the building. They used these to escape to the house of Said Salih Salim. There was firing on the secretariat and other adjoining buildings. The three men remained in Salih's house until tanks came to their rescue later that day. As the tanks were ferrying them through Aden, they came under rocket fire from naval vessels. The tank carrying Ismail was blown up, incinerating him. Al-Beidh suffered a minor injury when his was attacked, but he, Salim Salih, and Said Salih reached safety.[9] It appeared by this stage that Nasser had prepared a much wider plan to get rid of his opponents militarily, as well as their supporters within the YSP. Such a plan was not contemplated by his opponents or expected by anyone else.

"It was unthinkable that a colleague could carry out such a cruel act!" Salim Salih said in an interview with the *New York Times*. "Why, only last June there was a resolution adopted by the politburo that anyone who resorted to violence in settling internal political disputes is considered a criminal and a betrayer of the homeland." Even two weeks after the killings, reporters who saw the politburo headquarters described an unsettling sight. The bodies had been left on the floor throughout the fighting that engulfed Aden, and the stench was nauseating. Pools of blood were congealed on the wall-to-wall carpeting. The walls were riddled with bullet holes. Two chairs on either side of the facing conference tables had been left tipped over where they fell, next to huge patches of blood that had been sprinkled with disinfectant. The president's black armoured Mercedes-Benz, parked outside in a privileged spot next to the front door of the building, was apparently part of the ruse to make the meeting appear normal. In odd corners of the parking lot, among the debris were grimy, crushed red berets that had apparently been worn by the party security forces who fired on each other.[10] The building where the massacre took place is now part of Aden University, but the room has been left as it was with the bloodstains on the walls and the upturned chairs, keeping history alive and warning of the consequences of violence, a warning which is still not being heeded.

Nasser's opponents in the central committee were also killed or arrested by his supporters, and militia units loyal to him started taking over parts of Aden. Nasser had planned with his key supporters, including Mohammed Ali Ahmed, to physically remove all those close to Antar, Ismail, and Qasim in a move that would destroy the opponents and give him total control of the party and the state so he could pursue his pragmatic policies and attain complete power in the South. However, in his ruthless plan, Nasser missed an important element critical to the success of the plan: he was unaware that the other faction led by Antar and Qasim had huge influence in the military and in their own tribal bases of Dhala, Yafa, and Radfan, and that their supporters were in key command positions and would immediately engage in an internal war against him that could prove very costly indeed. These key officers may have planned a counteroffensive to carry out if this situation would arise; led by Haitham Qasim and Ali Qasim Talib, they quickly managed to rally their supporters in the armed forces and in the hinterland from their tribal base and from within the ranks of the YSP. They managed with speed to move into Aden from their military bases and recapture the key sites occupied by Nasser's men, including the Ministry of Defence.

---

[9] Noel Brehony, *Yemen Divided: the Story of a Failed State in South Arabia* (London: I. B. Tauris, 2013), 152.
[10] *New York Times*, 9 February 1986.

After two weeks of an intense military conflict, there was huge damage to public buildings, infrastructure, and housing. The fighting spread to all six governorates and lasted two weeks, in which at least ten thousand people were killed, mostly party cadres and military officers belonging to one side or the other, with the majority belonging to the same YSP. Nasser's supporters were defeated, but the YSP as a ruling party was hugely weakened with the loss of many of its cadres and leading officers. The 13 January catastrophe was unique in its intensity and ruthless in its calculation and implementation. This was a catastrophe that the party may not recover from for a long time to come, if ever.

The central committee and the politburo reconstituted themselves, albeit much weaker politically and economically, with many stunned by the events of the January crisis. A new collective leadership, according to party propaganda, emerged out of the crisis and was led by Ali Salim Al-Beidh. Nasser and his close supporters managed to escape the killing fields of Aden and fled to North Yemen, where they were regrouped by the Northern regime and could be used as a bargaining chip in any future issues that might arise with the South. Some of Ali Nasser's supporters went into other neighbouring countries, as Nasser also did later. Most of South Yemen's ambassadors who were appointed for their loyalty to Nasser went into exile. Nasser attempted to secure foreign support after his failed attempt to destroy the opposition, but that did not materialise.

Nasser assumed that the army would support him because commanders loyal to him had the top posts, but middle-ranking positions and control of key units were not in their hands, and the air force was split down the middle in its attitude towards him. Nasser's opponents also controlled the armoured brigade near Aden, commanded by Haithem Qasim. Sadly for a society espousing socialism rather than tradition, another twist was introduced to this conflict: some saw the fighting between those from Abyan, Dhala, and Yafa as an indication that the tribal structure in the South was still alive and kicking. The result of the crisis was seen by some commentators, particularly in the North, as a victory for the tribes of the north-western mountains, the Yafi and Dhali, over Dathina from Abyan, to which Nasser belonged. It is fair to say that Nasser's appeal to get the backing of his tribe did not materialise in the way he envisaged, and some key members of his tribe did not stand by him and later condemned his plan as treacherous. The tribal element in these circumstances did not cause the crisis but did play some part in its intensification.

One high-ranking minister in the Gulf said the whole crisis was "cooked up in Moscow". But any objective analysis clearly demonstrates that the Soviet Union had very little intelligence on the military explosion and no genuine influence over the actors in this situation. The Soviets themselves admitted their surprise at the intensity of the fighting and repeatedly requested an end to it. Soviet intelligence and the South Yemen intelligence service had failed miserably to predict Nasser's plan or the counteroffensive or the outcome of the conflict—they were caught sleeping. Had the Soviet Union known that the crisis would occur, it might have intervened to save face and rescue its socialism project in South Yemen, particularly in view of the fact that their number one man, Ismail, a thoroughbred socialist, was back in the forefront. The January crisis did give neighbouring countries a big opportunity to undermine the socialist experiment in South Yemen, and at the same, for opportunist reasons the West was implicating the Soviet Union as a basic explanation for the latest political disaster.

Obviously, indirect Soviet influence was apparent, particularly on the PDRY's model of socialist development, but the Soviet Union had little direct influence on the political development of the revolution and certainly no influence at all on the January 1986 catastrophe. The one thousand Soviet advisers joined other foreigners in fleeing to Russian, French, and British ships in the harbour when the fighting broke out. The Russians were very surprised at the conflict and even more so when the Soviet embassy came under fire. It is worth noting that the Southern leaders, no matter which faction they belonged to, had managed to maintain their political independence throughout the revolution with very little influence from outside forces, despite the huge economic difficulties and challenges they faced. All these individual leaders from Qahtan onwards refused to be bought by foreign actors because they all believed they fought the British in order to pride themselves on their own sovereign state. Despite one faction blaming the other for selling out to Gulf states and other external forces, no evidence to date has been provided to demonstrate this.

When the dust settled, the people of South Yemen began to count the cost of the bloody political civil war. Thousands of party members, members of the armed forces, militia, and ordinary citizens were killed. The official figure was 7,229 but other observers put the figure considerably higher. Most of those killed were party cadres educated and trained in the Eastern bloc. Their loss to the state bureaucracy and party structure was huge and left a big vacuum and a much weaker system. Damage was caused to buildings, economic installations, and land. The cost was officially estimated at the time to be extremely high and unlikely to be met from the current budget of the state.

The crisis gave little confidence to the emigrant communities abroad and precipitated a sharp fall in remittances, which were already reduced because of falling revenue in the oil-producing states. Soviet, East German, and Cuban advisers returned to South Yemen in February 1986, and the PDRY leaders visited Moscow to curry favour with the Russians, who were starting to re-evaluate the relationship and still kept some contact with Nasser. Even though Soviet aid was resumed, Gorbachev urged PDRY leaders to inject a greater dose of realism into their policies and economic endeavours. The Communist Party of the Soviet Union paid for new YSP buildings in Yemen to replace those destroyed in the massacre. It also agreed to develop the power station at a cost of over $1.1 million. Arms supplies also resumed. In reality the Soviets no longer trusted the YSP with governing South Yemen, and on a practical note they began to make plans to leave the South of Yemen and concentrate on their own internal reforms.

Pravda, the Soviet party newspaper, blamed "external reactionary imperialist forces" for the strife but conceded there had been "disagreements" in the Southern Yemen party and government.

On 26 January, the *New York Times* pointed out that the YSP emerged weaker and without leadership following the bloody conflict of January 1986. After weeks of heavy fighting and loss of life, Aden lay in ruins and with it the international credibility of a significantly decimated YSP—a fact that soon took a heavy toll on the erstwhile close relations with the Soviet Union Communist Party; the German Democratic Republic (GDR) and its governing party, the Marxist-Leninist Socialist Unity Party; and the socialist state of Cuba.

The New York Times went on to say that the YSP was no longer the party of collective action by the comrades but a party that had a big vacuum staring it in the face with its international reputation in ruins and its ability to get support from socialist states ruined as well. Later, the YSP failed to realise that by entering into unification with the North in 1990, it did so as the weaker of the two partners both politically and militarily. The Soviet Union was caught by surprise by the intensity and ruthlessness of the fighting, with many internal issues to resolve about its relationship with South Yemen.

Neither the Americans nor the Soviets had an understanding of the situation in South Yemen in 1986, and they did not anticipate unity in 1990. They both pursued the wrong policies and were unable to navigate the complex quagmire of Yemeni politics. This raises a question about the quality of the information the policymakers were getting from their intelligence services.

The New Collective Leadership
Following the catastrophe of 13 January, the remaining members of the politburo and the central committee held a meeting in which they expelled members implicated as loyal to Ali Nasser. A new leadership was

established and led by the radical left. Ali Salem Al-Beidh was appointed as the YSP general secretary, and six new members were appointed to the sixteen-person YSP politburo. The winning side of the January 1986 crisis led by Al-Beidh was called the *Tuma*, and the losing side led by Ali Naser was called the *Zumra*. These two descriptions continue to characterise the two groups to this day.

When the war finished, the population knew that the crisis was over and Nasser's dictatorship had collapsed. Officially, Ali Nasser Mohammed was described in the front page of the *14 October* newspaper as "a mere stooge of imperialism, a man who never was and never will be a scientific socialist, and who is of that ilk of politicians who mix revolutionary cards with rightist reactionary cards in the foreign and domestic arena".

Unfortunately the YSP propaganda machine was in full gear with a negative projection of the realities on the ground. Nasser did plan ruthlessly to wipe out the opposition, but he wasn't a stooge of imperialism. The party did not engage in a thorough analysis of where things went wrong and what lessons needed to be learned; instead, it engaged in the same rhetoric that was actually responsible for previous internal struggles in the Southern state.

Of the fifteen politburo members elected in October 1985, those associated with Nasser went into exile, mainly in North Yemen, such as the current president of Yemen, Abdroba Mansoor Hadi. Some went to Egypt, Syria, and Libya. Ali Nasser spent most of his time exiled in Syria. The immediate priority for the new YSP leadership was to form a new government and legitimise itself locally and internationally. Although fighting had stopped on 25 January, the following weeks witnessed a level of political activity in Aden that was unprecedented in the revolution's history. The administrative and government structures had been seriously damaged, particularly in terms of absent and defecting personnel. There was a sense of urgency to tackle the problems and re-establish the system.

On 24 January, the central committee held two sessions in which a moderate politician from Hadhramaut, Haydar Al Attas, was named as the interim head of state. The next meeting of the committee was held on 6 February and dealt with the reconstruction of the YSP leadership. Ali Salem Al-Beidh, also from the Hadhramaut region, became the new general secretary, and Salim Saleh, from the Yafa region in the South, became his deputy. Others appointed to the politburo were Fadel Mohsin Abdulla and Mohammed Said Abdullah Mohsin, joining the secretariat of the central committee. Yasin Said Numan, former deputy prime minister, was appointed as prime minister. Said Saleh, former secretary general of the Peasants' Union, took up the post of minister of state security. Although the new leaders were determined to ensure there would be no more crises like the one of 13 January, they proved only a little less fractured than their predecessors, with disagreements between the civilians and military officers and, once again, reformers and hard-line radical communists.

On 8 February the Supreme People's Council convened its first meeting after the crisis and a new government was formed under the new prime minister, Yasin Said Numan. It included a number of people who had not previously held ministerial positions. But on the whole, both party and state were constituted by those who supported the radical left. Haithem Qassim, a military commander and a prominent figure during the January crisis, was appointed as candidate member of the politburo, which was not surprising considering his popularity amongst the armed forces. He led the officer corps which fought to retain Aden during the crisis. There were also other new faces who managed to climb the political ladder, one of them being political communist theorist Saif Saal, a candidate member of the politburo.

The January crisis in the PDRY was seen by the winning factions within the YSP as a triumph for the radical left YSP, as a victory of organisational party and state structure over opportunism. They felt that their victory over Ali Nasser suggested a certain degree of a strong left-wing leaning in the PDRY's political system, political violence notwithstanding. More important, it seemed as though a new party and state leadership had emerged out of the bloody crisis. This new leadership was younger and more energetic, and it had the ability to absorb the lessons of past conflict and learn from them.

Nasser tried to introduce a mixed economy to South Yemen. During the promotion of this policy, businessmen were viewed by the radical left as a source of corruption. They saw civil servants becoming a guiding tool subverting the state apparatus and resorting to bribes to bypass the rules; these included expensive gifts and financial rewards.

The economy thus became a major source of conflict. Nasser encouraged the growth of private capital. He favoured the mixed economy rather than the centralised planning system which the radical left wanted to pursue in accordance with the planning documents. By 1983, the public sector of the economy had paid twenty million dinars in taxes, whereas in the same year the private sector gained 50 per cent of all profits but paid only seven hundred thousand dinars in taxes. This actually encouraged the expansion of the private sector at the expense of the public sector and created the context for economic competition in a centrally planned economic system. In Nasser's era, the economy was serving a new class of traders while the vast majority sat watching in poverty.

A critical-analytical document of Nasser's policies was presented to the Central Committee Conference in September 1987. It was self-critical of the left and was supposed to be a guide for future political action. It was admitted that the YSP did not manage to establish a stable state. The needs of the people were neglected as the leadership quarrelled. Omar Garallah prepared this analytical document to self-criticise the party for military bloodshed and unnecessary conflict between the different wings of the party; he wrote that South Yemen needed to move to some sort of multi-party system and that there was a need for self-criticism within the party. This report was seen to some extent to challenge YSP power in the South, and though it was greeted by some within the party, it was rejected by the rank and file because it was seen as an attack on the socialist experiment. The paper had no influence on any political change in the South, and business continued as usual.

The prospects for rebuilding the economy were challenging as South Yemen lost more than half of its aid from the Soviet Union between 1986 and 1989. In the midst of the economic downturn, as Soviet support declined with the Soviet Union pursuing a policy of *perestroika* under its new leadership, the government of the PDRY opted for political reform and roll-back of the more invasive branches of the security apparatus. The government showed some interest in the possible exploration of oil reserves on the border with Saudi Arabia. Efforts towards unification proceeded from 1988, but even though the governments of the PDRY and the YAR had declared that they approved a future union in 1972, little progress was made towards unification, and relations were often strained.

South Yemen's *perestroika* consisted of the release of political prisoners, the formation of political parties, and the institution of a system of justice which was billed as more equitable than that in the North. In May 1988, the YAR and PDRY governments came to an understanding that considerably reduced tensions, including agreement to renew discussions concerning unification, to establish a joint oil exploration area along their undefined border, to demilitarise the border, and to allow Yemenis unrestricted border passage on the basis of only a national identification card.

But the fallout from the conflicts of 1986 continued to haunt the new regime running party and government. The unnecessary and divisive propaganda trial of Nasser and 141 of his colleagues on charges of treason dragged on until December 1987. The verdict—sentencing the former president and thirty-four followers to death and countless others to lengthy prison sentences *in absentia*—sparked a regional outcry and demonstrated that despite the veneer of political liberalisation, the Southern regime remained wedded to a vision of political integration through coercion. Nasser's men were in what Sanaa described as refugee camps, but the PDRY called them bases. Nasser believed he was still the legal head of state and secretary general of the party, and he issued documents in the name of the Central Committee of the YSP (Legitimate Leadership). By mid-1987, there was some willingness to heal the wounds of the past rather than seek revenge, and a general amnesty was given to those who returned to the PDRY that year. The people were shocked by the execution of five high-ranking supports of Nasser, and over the next two years, most of those in prison were released.

Writing about policies from 1986 to 1987, Noel Brehony said, "The overriding aim of the new leaders was to heal the PDYR's wounds and establish their own legitimacy, challenged by the menace of Ali Nasser in Yemen and undermined by the YSP's failure to improve the lives of ordinary people. Their priorities clearly lay in consolidating the regime, choking off support to Nasser, rebuilding the economy and reassuring the PDYR's communist friends that the country was stable. They also needed to persuade regional powers and international organisations to contribute to the costs of reconstruction and development. Unity with the North started to gather momentum after 1988."[11]

The YSP's policies were debated at an Exceptional Party Conference held in June 1987. Much of the self-criticism blamed Nasser for the country's problems, and progress was measured against the situation in 1967, as very little was achieved when Nasser was in power. The presidium and politburo were re-elected without change, but a radical group calling itself Fattahiyin (followers of Abdul Fattah Ismail and his interpretation of Marxism) emerged under the leadership of Sayf Sayl Khalid from Lahij. An interest in Islam was also evident, and Al-Beidh met a number of Islamic personalities. This was probably a pragmatic move to make sure they didn't oppose the regime and to curry favour with Saudi Arabia for economic support.

The need for democratic centralism was emphasised by the radical left, and the PDRY clearly allied itself with the socialist camp in the continuing struggle against capitalism, aiming to work to improve its relationship with the Soviet Union while also seeking assistance from regional states. A recurring theme was the need for the people to work harder to develop the country and its economy.

A significant feature of self-criticism was an admission for the first time that the country suffered from serious economic problems: inadequate management by the government, lack of investment, a lack of foreign exchange, and international debt totalling $5 billion. Saudi Arabia, Oman, and Kuwait provided some assistance. Links with left-wing regimes in Syria and Algeria and the Palestinians were maintained.

The Economic Crisis and the Inevitability of Unity

There was a vain hope that oil would be a universal panacea for the economic problems of the PDRY. Oil was discovered by the Soviet Technoexport Company in Shabwa in 1986, and the following year, production was up to ten thousand barrels a day. But the development of the oil industry was slow compared to that of North Yemen, where American companies were developing oil fields in Marib.

The economy in the South was getting worse, and the state was virtually bankrupt and unable to finance projects. Farmers got miserable prices for their food crops and stopped delivering. Only bread, onions, and potatoes were available in Aden's markets. Everyone suffered, and the people began to criticise the system for its inability to create economic stability.

Divisions emerged once again in the leadership, this time between the new prime minister Yassin Said Numan and the Fattahiyin, who had an emerging charismatic leader and a strong base within the left of the party. Al-Beidh, the last of the historical leaders of the NLF, was not a charismatic leader within the left and was not strong enough to exert his authority over the politburo whose divisions he found difficult to deal with.

---

[11] Brehony, 161.

He was perceived by those close to him as an emotional man who would take decisions in haste and sometimes without thinking. His wife, Mulki, was extremely influential in his life and was seen to interfere in political decisions from time to time. The Soviet Union, no longer able to support its communist allies in Eastern Europe or elsewhere, suggested the PDRY implement its own *perestroika*, but in fact it learned very little from the mistakes of the past, which included mechanically copying the Soviets. The leaders of the PDRY decided on a policy of partial reform in conjunction with possible unity with the North.

A working party set up by the YSP in 1988 produced a document on reform, with democracy the benchmark of the whole process. The sessions of the Supreme People's Council were televised in June 1989 and showed debates about closer relations with the West and the adoption of Western economic policies. Other political parties were allowed as long as they were set up by people who fought against colonialism and remained loyal to the principles of the revolution. Greater press freedom was allowed. The role of Islam in the lives of the people was also recognised: mosques were assisted financially, a magazine on Islamic issues was published, and religious broadcasts were given more time on state media.

The first concrete steps towards unity were taken during two meetings between President Ali Abdullah Saleh and Al-Beidh in Taiz between 16–18 April and 4 May in Sanaa. Supposedly using the unity accords of the past, the two sides agreed as follows:

- A revival of the Supreme Yemeni Council, which had not met since the downfall of Ali Nasser, and the resumption of the work of its sub-committees
- The setting up of a joint committee to work on creating a unified political organisation
- A timetable on discussions on the constitution for a united Yemen, which would be placed before the two legislatures for endorsement
- The establishment of a demilitarised zone between Shabwa and Marib and the setting up of a team to demarcate the precise border
- The establishment of a joint corporation to explore for oil and minerals in the region
- New joint investment projects, including the connection of two electricity grids
- The setting up of joint border posts as a step towards permitting citizens of one state to cross into the other using only identity cards

Both countries acted quickly to implement the agreement, and relations between the two Yemens were better than at any time during the 1980s. Demilitarisation was organised by teams of senior officers, and the newly set up Yemen Company for Investment in Oil and Mineral Resources was negotiating with a consortium of Western, Arab, and Russian companies. The oil fields in Hadhramaut appeared more promising than those of Marib. The people were very happy with the decision to allow freedom of movement, and more than 250,000 PDRY citizens visited the North and found that, contrary to the anti-North propaganda they had been fed over the years, it was prosperous and stable, unlike the South. This prompted tens of thousands of Southerners to emigrate to the North. The PDRY's leadership was alarmed and became more convinced of the need for unity, which came much sooner than its leaders expected. The YSP had politically and emotionally charged the psyche of the population in favour of unity as one of the main objectives of the 14 October revolution. Most Southerners wanted Yemen unity at any cost.

The first meeting of the Joint Committee for a Unified Political Organisation was held in October 1989 in Aden. The Northerners proposed the merging of five ministries including Defence and Foreign Affairs. There was a disagreement about what form unity should take, with the North wanting to preserve the separate governments even when the ministries were joined and the Southerners proposing confederation. The talks were tense, and Salih threatened to return to Sanaa.

The impasse was resolved when the two presidents went on a car journey together. Al-Beidh proposed that an agreement should be reached based on the constitution agreed in Kuwait in 1980, which proposed a union rather than a federation or confederation. Salih agreed, and an agreement was drawn up on a small piece of paper on this basis by the ministers of Unity Affairs.

The YSP politburo members objected to the speed in which unity was driven by the two leaders but in the end agreed to what the two Alis decided. Those who objected to this form of unification within the YSP were quickly silenced, and Al-Beidh used the sympathetic political emotions of the Southerners to help him take unification of the two Yemens forward.

When Al-Beidh returned to Aden, the politburo wanted to know how he signed the unity agreement without their consent and that of the party's central committee. Some said the agreement was not legal but accepted it in the end, insisting that none of Nasser's men should be ministers in the unity government. In the unity agreement, the South was supposed to be treated as an equal despite its smaller population and weaker economy. A referendum on the draft constitution was scheduled within six months and took place on 15–16 May 1991 to ratify the new constitution. Numerous meetings were held to work out the details of the union, and the PDRY began a major political reform programme which included the passing of laws which gave the press greater freedom. New political parties were allowed, and many of the restrictions on freedom of expression were removed.

The rhetoric of the South had changed. Al-Beidh was no longer a hard-line leftist. Speaking to Abdul Galil Shaif, author of the PhD thesis "Revolutionary Politics in South Yemen 1967–1986", in 1990, he said,

> It is imperative to open a new page in our history in which we have to allow people to participate in both political and economic life. Democracy is the only alternative we have to enable our society to develop. We have tired all the means available to us to rule Yemeni society but unfortunately these means have had their limitations and in more cases than one, have resulted in a failure or in a crisis. It was wrong of us to assume that we could govern on the basis of no criticism or labelling people to different political positions - we have to learn from our mistakes in order to build a future but we must not continuously repeat those mistakes internationally. If our party is to succeed in the future than it has to do so by the wish of the people rather than by our wishes as leaders. The struggle before us is no longer a struggle based on force but a struggle based on political democracy. Our party will have to learn to enter elections and compete for positions and if other parties were to do this better than us, then we have to accept that fact and live with it until such time as we can convince the majority of the population of our credibility.[12]

The North was also liberalised, and it was agreed that multi-party elections would be held. Aden would continue in its historical role as the country's commercial capital.

The final unity agreement was known as the Sanaa Accord with the following key features.
- The date of the union was brought forward six months to May 1990.
- It would take the form of a full merger into a unitary state with a thirty-month transition period to enable ministries and other institutions to complete their mergers.
- The elections would take place in November 1992. They would produce a parliament that would elect a new five-person presidential council, which would invite a new prime minister to form a government.
- There would be a Chamber of Deputies, made up of members of the YAR Consultative Council and the SPC, as well as thirty-one appointed members.

---

[12] Abdul Galil Shaif, *Revolutionary Politics in South Yemen 1967–1986*, PhD thesis, University of Sheffield, 1990.

- The current cabinets would be merged into a thirty-nine-member cabinet. There was a division of posts at lower levels, which was greatly in favour of the PDRY given that its population was only a fifth of that of the ROY.

On paper the agreement was short on details but looked fine, but in implementation the devil was in the detail. What was easily agreed between the two Alis was not so easy to put into practice even though the people of the North and South were behind the agreement and respected their leaders for reaching it.

PART TWO:

Unity, War, and the End of the Partnership

Chapter 6

The Unity Experiment (1990–94)

On 22 May 1990, the Yemen Arab Republic (YAR) and the People's Democratic Republic of Yemen (PDRY) united, forming the Republic of Yemen (ROY) with Ali Abdullah Salih as president and Ali Salim Al-Beidh as vice president. The ROY's constitution was the most democratic in the Arab world and made provision for universal adult suffrage, freedom of expression and association, and legal rights for defendants. The people of the North and South were overjoyed, their leaders were heroes, and unity was seen as a dream come true which would solve intractable problems.

Before the 1993 elections, during the transition period the country was governed by a five-member Presidential Council headed by President Ali Abdullah Salih with Al-Beidh as vice president. There was a 39-member cabinet made up of ministers from the two Yemens and a 301-member Council of Representatives.

A Positive Beginning

The two main political parties involved in unity were the Yemeni Socialist Party (YSP) in the South of Yemen and the General People's Congress (GPC) in the North. Many expected that a united Yemen would be economically viable in a way that the North or South on its own could not have been. It was thought that the nation's combined resources and human energy would gradually lead to a better standard of living. The combined population of the country would be close to fourteen million. The speed with which the two leaders announced the unity agreement surprised most people, including their close colleagues. They were afraid that opponents of the merger would grow in strength as time passed and simply pre-empted them by making unity a fait accompli.

The YSP leadership believed that unity was achieved on the basis of a power-sharing arrangement between it and the GPC, roughly on an equal basis. The unification process was managed without rancour, with each separate state willingly giving up its individual sovereignty. This was viewed by most Yemenis as a significant political achievement which they hoped would lead to economic prosperity, greater democracy, and political stability in a country in which poverty and wars were endemic. The leaderships of the two states decided to embark on unifying the country and experiment with democratisation in the form of a liberal democracy. The political unification of the two states was perceived as a major triumph for Yemenis and a turning point in their history.

The leaders referred to the benefits of freedom and spoke of democracy providing the stable foundation for unity.

Soon after unification, there were around fifty political parties and hundreds of new publications. In the South, the old South Arabian League reinvented itself as the League of the Sons of Yemen, led by

Abd Al-Rahman Al-Jiffri. Aden intellectuals set up the Yemen Unity Gathering. The Yemeni Reform Rally (Al-Islah) represented a tribal-commercial-religious mix. Its leader was Sheikh Abdullah Al-Ahmar, the head of the Hashid tribal confederation. There was also the Baath Party, the Nasserists, and Al Haq from the Zaydi Islamic School.

It was strange that government-produced posters in support of unity showed the two Alis in separate photos next to each other but not shaking hands. It soon became clear that Al-Beidh was no match for Salih when it came to surviving political intrigues and negotiating the quagmires of Yemeni politics. In the face of disagreements or serious problems, he retreated to Aden and behaved as if South Yemen was still independent.

Describing the situation in the early 1990s, Carapico wrote, "The expansion of the civil space was palpable as the many barriers to assembly, publication, speech, travel, investment and open partisanship were lifted. A discernible, diverse realm of public opinion dealing with broad issues concerning the constitution, the judiciary, education, the very conception of the public arena, was debated in the press, symposia and conferences, replete with references to the full range of recent political experiences."[13]

According to Joseph Kostiner, "In the late 1980s the end of the Cold War and the demise of the Soviet bloc, together with an inter-Arab atmosphere of pacification after the end of the Iran-Iraq war, brought a new geopolitical environment, generating sympathy for Yemeni unity from regional, Western and Eastern bloc states. Moreover, in this period, neither Yemeni state was involved in any external disputes, and both were left to their own devices."[14]

Iraq wanted a united Yemen to attend the Baghdad summit in May 1990. Saudi Arabia was also supportive of Yemeni unity as the leaders spoke of a peaceful and development oriented future state.

The End of the Honeymoon

Despite the initial euphoria that unity had been achieved, and despite great expectations and good intentions, it soon became apparent that turning two totally different states into a single functional entity was easier said than done.

Unity was decided on by the leaders and came quickly without institutional preparation, which was most evident in the economic sphere. It was hoped that the two economies would mesh naturally even though the North had a mixed economy and the South had a socialist economy in which central planning featured prominently. A return to the precolonial subsistence economies based on small-scale agriculture and industries was expected with improvements brought about by the introduction of a better transport system, technological infrastructure, and less bureaucracy for investors. Increased oil revenues from the Shabwa-Marib region were also expected, and no attempt was made to diversify the sources of revenue based on remittances from Yemenis overseas and the fledgling oil industry.

The people were not given a chance to participate in unity and were given no guidelines on how to adapt to the reality of a greater Yemen. The governments of the North and South simply relied on friendships and contacts to generate a spirit of unity, which was enhanced as movement across the former borders was facilitated.

The South had a well-organised government structure, a clear political ideology, and an impressive record of giving rights to women. The North was a patronage system built up by Ali Abdullah Salih, whose General Peoples Congress, in theory a party to include all political views, was in practice a vehicle for

---

[13] S. Carapico, *Civil Society in Yemen: The Political Economy of Activism in Modern Arabia* (Cambridge University Press, 1993).

[14] Joseph Kostiner, "Yemen: the Tortuous Quest for Unity 1990–1994", Chatham House papers, London, 1996.

arranging deals between businessmen and local elites. It did not have an ideology and was characterised by a traditional and tribal way of doing things.

The Islamists were growing stronger in the North, and the Muslim Brothers were given sanctuary in the YAR. Yemenis studied in Saudi Islamic schools and returned with Salafi and Wahhabi ideas. Sheikh Abdullah Al-Ahmar, leader of the powerful Hashid tribal confederation, was influential in setting up the Yemeni Congregation for Reform (YRG or Islah). Muqbil Al-Wadi, one of the less moderate Islamic leaders, argued for fighting the regime in the PDRY, and Al-Zindani stated that sharia should be the only, not just the main, source of legislation in Yemen. The GPC and Islah tried to establish themselves in those areas of the South where the YSP lost popularity. The YSP also tried to gain a foothold in the North, especially in areas of the Bakil tribal confederation.

The Southerners had great hopes of modernising the North, but in reality Northern practices like tribalism and making use of tribal connections began spreading South. The progressive Personal Status Law, a hallmark of the PDRY, was amended by a Republican Decree No. 20 in May 1992 without the prior approval of parliament. A woman's right to sue for divorce in the former PDRY was removed unless she could prove that her husband was abusive. The restrictions on polygamy and the ceiling on dowries were also removed. The Islamists also tried unsuccessfully to close the Seera Brewery in Aden, one of the few profitable enterprises in the city.

The qat chewing habit returned to the South. The cultivation of qat was forbidden on state-owned land but was now possible owing to privatisation. After unity, most of the state-owned land was privatised. Institutionalised corruption spread, and several Southern projects such as the Aden Free Port Scheme were transferred to the North, often with disappointing results. The Northern port of Hodeidah received more favourable treatment.

There were four different visions of the united Yemen: The GPC wanted to combine existing traditional social patterns and values with modern government methods and an economic policy of oil-based development. The YSP wanted to see a national programme for reform, a state planned economy, and carefully structured institutions staffed by honest officials. The YRG wanted to turn Yemen into a tradition-minded society governed by tribal values and sharia law. The old South Yemeni elite advocated a pro-Western, mercantile Yemen.

The newly united country faced serious economic problems. Yemen's support for Saddam Hussein when he invaded Kuwait on 2 August 1990 resulted in the expulsion of eight hundred thousand Yemenis from the Gulf states. When the expelled workers could no longer send money home, the economy lost $3 billion. Saudi Arabia also halted its annual aid allotment of $500 million, and the United States cut its aid programme by nearly 90 per cent from $42 million in 1990 to less than $4 million in 1991 and then $6 million in 1992. Another 120,000 Somali refugees added to the economic problems. Assistance from the Soviet Union came to an end, and the West lost interest in Yemen. With the exception of Oman, the YR was surrounded by hostile neighbours.

The current account deficit in 1991 was $216 million and more than doubled to $500 million in 1992. Oil was a temporary lifesaver with the government selling rights to eighteen companies early in 1991, but it was less successful during the rest of the year. Production from the new oilfield in Hadhramaut rose to three hundred thousand barrels a day but did not reverse the general recessionary trend.

The economic problems led to demonstrations and strikes in both North and South. When Salih visited Aden in early 1992, he was greeted by protestors calling for the Zaydis to go home and for Nasser to return. In North Yemen the demonstrations were a form of popular uprising in different cities through which ordinary people showed their anger about the economic situation and expressed a distaste for the leadership. The protests were a clear sign of discontent with Salih's regime, and the press gave coverage to many of the complaints of the ordinary people. It appeared that Salih was losing popularity and his grip on the opposition.

During and after the protests, the YSP failed to use them as a vehicle to influence change by mobilising people around issues which concerned them. Instead, the YSP leadership locked itself in the struggle for political power, confining the party to narrow political objectives. It is reported that North Yemenis who participated in the protests criticised the role of the YSP and blamed it for siding with the establishment against popular demands. Amnesty International reported that hundreds of people were arrested during the riots, and fifteen were killed.

The South had its special economic problems. Housing was scarce, and many South Yemeni cities had not recovered from the destruction of the 1986 conflict. Subsidised food came to an end, and there were sharp price rises and lack of medicines. There was an attempt to reverse the nationalisation of land, and several alleged owners tried to claim the same property. Ex-Southerners were not well treated and faced discrimination. In January 1991, a joint meeting of the Presidency Council and the cabinet was held in Aden, but it did little to solve the problems of the South.

In 1991, assassinations of Southern leaders started. According to the YSP, 150 of its members were killed during the first four years after unification. YSP members criticised the security arrangements, which were clearly not adequate to protect them. Evidence suggested that Afghanistan veterans were responsible for the killings, but cynics in the North attributed them to vendettas within the YSP and members of Nasser's faction. Islah and Salih's inner circle were also accused.

Law and order was also an issue and showed how North and South differed in the way they dealt with conflict. In the North, the tribes had their own arsenal of weapons, and influential tribal leaders had their own prisons and were responsible for the administration of justice. Yemen had less than one police station for every one hundred thousand people, compared with a station for every twenty thousand on average elsewhere in the world. The police were poorly paid and often resorted to bribery and turning a blind eye to offences to supplement their incomes. Hostage taking was common in the North, with the tribes negotiating with the government, and in 1993 and 1994 the growing community of expatriate workers in the oilfields were frequent targets. In early 1993, tribal lawlessness in the Marib-Shabwa area prompted the minister of oil to warn the US-based Hunt Company that the government could not guarantee the safety of its employees, and they advised evacuation to Sanaa.

Al-Qaeda in the Arabian Peninsula (AQAP) and the Afghan Arabs

The years 1990–94 were a period when Salih, with the support of Ali Mohsin, began the process of recruiting the Afghan Arabs returning from Afghanistan with the tacit support of Western states. These Afghan Arabs, mostly Yemenis, were seen by the United States and the United Kingdom at the time of fighting against the Soviet Union as freedom fighters—as they were widely known. They arrived in the South under the leadership of Ali Mohsin with numerous leaders, including Tariq Al Fadhli, and became a useful military tool for Salih against what they perceived as Southern communists closely connected with the Soviet communists.

Some members of this group later developed into the AQAP branch in Abyan in South Yemen with other members, spreading widely around the country but mostly settling in South Yemen.

In his book *The Last Refuge*, Gregory Johnsen addressed the discrepancies between Yemen and other Arab governments in their support for the jihad in Afghanistan against the Soviets, especially as more Arab fighters travelled to Afghanistan in the mid-1980s. In contrast, the Northern Yemen Arab Republic sent many of their fighters, including a good number from the South, to the front lines, with the journey becoming a rite of passage for many.

After the "Mujahidin" returned to a unified Yemen in the early 1990s, they were welcomed as heroes by Northerner President Saleh's government—with some even receiving official military positions. During this period, Ali Mohsin and his close connections with these mujahidin were working very hard to indoctrinate the men to fight in support of Salih and the unification of the republic. Much of the finance to support these mujahidin was channelled through various networks but mostly through the ministry of defence. There was no diplomatic or military resistance to the mujahidin engagement in Salih's forces mainly because at the time, these mujahidin were not perceived as enemy combatants.

Summer Ahmed, working for the United Nations on woman's issues, described the situation during the first years of unity. She said that this deep rift in ideology would play a role in "returning Afghan Arabs'" attitudes towards the South. When civil war broke out in the summer of 1994, the northern jihadis overran South Yemen armed with a religious fatwa, justifying the killing of socialist infidels in the south. The fatwa came from the Northern Yemeni Justice Minister Abdul Wahab Al Daylami and the religious cleric Abd Al-Majid Al-Zindani, now on the US Global Terrorist list.

As the International Crisis Group notes, Salih and his general, Ali Mohsen Al-Ahmar, relied on these forces as proxies, rewarding some of these men afterwards. After Northern groups defeated the Southern military forces, the "Afghan Arabs" never left. Instead, they became the arm of the Northern government in Southern Yemen and were used to defend and protect the Yemeni union.

The government's attitudes towards extremists in the country were called into question through a series of government appointments, the most famous of these being the "returning Afghan Arabs", including Tarik Al-Fadhli and Jamal Al-Nahdi, as well as current vice president Ali Mohsen al-Ahmar. Tarik Al-Fadhli, considered one of the founding members of AQAP, served in the Majlis al-Shura council and Salih's General People's Congress party. Al-Nahdi was also on a permanent committee of the General People's Congress—despite his role in the 1992 bombing of the several hotels under the direction of Osama bin Laden. Moreover, Ali Mohsen al-Ahmar, who also played a major role in Saleh's government, is widely seen in the South as a man with deep connections to the South's extremist elements. Ultimately, through empowering men such as these and through a variety of restrictive policies, the Northern-based government took full control of the South, implementing unity by force.

Aden Hotel bombing. Source: Qais Saeed.

Jihadist groups, including Al-Qaeda, were responsible for a number of terrorist attacks, including the Aden Hotel bombings in 1992, which unsuccessfully targeted US marines who left the hotel when the bomb went off. It looked as if Shaykh Tariq, who surrounded himself with Afghan war veterans and members of his own tribe and religious opponents of the YSP, was responsible. Salih brought him to Sanaa, knowing that arresting a prominent local leader would cause serious law-and-order problems, and portrayed the incident as a tribal dispute in which Tariq was in dispute with another tribe; the YSP was described as a tribe by Salih. Needless to say, the Southerners did not agree with this way of dealing with the matter and accused Salih of sponsoring terrorism. But this incident eliminated Tariq as a cause of trouble in the South, drove a wedge between his tribe and the religious extremists, and ultimately turned him into an ally of Salih.

Yemen was attractive to terrorist organisations as both a safe haven and a training ground, because it was a country where weapons were easily available, the terrain was remote, and the government did not exert much control outside the cities.

Crime was another problem. It began to increase owing to economic upheavals such as the introduction of the free market in the South and increasing unemployment among the workers expelled from Saudi Arabia. The Saudis also "exported" some criminal elements and drug users across the border.

Union without Unity
One of the most serious shortcomings of unity was the failure to merge the institutions and bureaucracies of the two Yemens, which happened very slowly or not at all. The leadership on both sides intended to integrate the two separate establishments into one structure. But the intention was not sincere, and both sides became increasingly suspicious of each other and paid only lip service to military integration. By not integrating the military, it became obvious that both sides were preparing contingency plans to use in the event of conflict. The mechanisms and technical details for sharing power were ignored, and as a result, the concept of sharing power gradually became meaningless. From their refusal to integrate the military, it became clear that little trust if any at all existed between the two leaders, who were partners more in theory than in practice. Less than a month after unity when military equipment, including tanks, ordered by the PDRY arrived, Al-Beidh insisted that it was delivered to Aden.

Following the unity agreement, the new state and its apparatus were completely in disarray, and the leadership showed no clear sense of direction. The strategic priority for each side was to build as much power as possible for that side; the existence of two separate military establishments within one state was proof of disunity in the new republic.

It was argued that the army should be moved outside the cities so it could protect the country and did not interfere in civilian affairs. Some units did leave Sanaa and Aden but quickly returned when there was a crisis. It was difficult to keep the army out of politics because Salih's relatives and fellow tribesmen held key military positions, and many Southern soldiers were members of the YSP. It was also difficult to amalgamate the security service because the Southerners felt marginalised and sought to revive the former security service of the PDRY.

The currencies were not amalgamated, and the Southern and Northern leaders continued to use Aden in the South and Sanaa in the North as their political bases. The 1990–94 period was characterised by a sustained power struggle between Salih and Al-Beidh and their colleagues. This power struggle was largely about political control of the state rather than ideological or policy differences.

Yemenia in its heyday.

In his dissertation *The Politics of Survival and the Structure of Control in the Unified Yemen 1990–97*, Ahmed Abdel-Karim Saif wrote, "Forty-six laws were approved regarding unified procedures for customs, taxation, the issue of passports, banking and diplomatic representation, but in practice, banking, currency and other key functions remained separate. The army commands of the two states were amalgamated, but the units remained separate. In similar fashion, such major national bodies as trade unions and the militias were only united at the top, while retaining their previous composition in the middle and lower levels of ranking."

The two national airlines, Yemenia and Alyemda, continued to operate separately at first but were later merged to form Yemen Airlines. Alyemda, South Yemen's airline, was very successful in its own right and did not benefit from the merger.

Saif also points out, "The building of the state was a rather conflictual matter, with the YSP calling on the government to implement a national programme for reform, which it adopted in principle and to take responsibility for mistakes and negligence. These reforms would lead to comprehensive administrative and institutional changes, to reform security measures, education, the health system and price control. These improvements must of necessity be accompanied by strict moral behaviour at the top, and include a readiness on the part of officials to resign over past mistakes." This programme was absolutely refused by the GPC and Islah. In response, Al-Beidh withdrew to Aden in September 1992 to express his disagreement.

The transition period from the announcement of unity to the elections was a time of inaction rather than transition. The fact that elections would be held was used as an excuse for failing to develop mechanisms to resolve disputes democratically. There was an expectation that elections would bring change and that this change would be for the better.

But the two leaders realised they would have to cooperate in certain key areas to maintain a façade of unity, and the approval of the constitution and the establishment of electoral procedures were agreed upon. Continual infighting continued about everything else related to the nature of the united Yemeni state.

During the three years of power sharing, there was a difference in outlook. The YSP believed it had a monopoly on *nidham* (order and discipline), a shorthand for its way of doing things, whereas it said the North was characterised by *fawda* (chaos): lawlessness, tribalism, favouritism, and ineffective government. In reality both sides had their fair share of *nidham* and *fawda*, and it was clear the North was never going to accept the South's way of doing things.

The 1993 Elections and the Ensuing Crisis

In the run-up to the elections, the GPC and the YSP tried to establish firm power bases in public and governmental administrative bodies.

Brehony wrote,

> The parliamentary elections of April 27, 1993, although delayed six months beyond their appointed date, were nevertheless a milestone in Yemen's political development: the first popular expression of the new pluralism. Beyond that, the fact that Yemen became the first state in the peninsula to hold competitive elections on the basis of universal suffrage was, for all the flaws and problems, no mean achievement. More subtly, the elections reaffirmed the constitutional axiom that 'the people of Yemen are the possessors and source of power' and helped to implant the idea that ordinary citizens can hold their leaders accountable to public opinion, even if the leaders themselves do not always heed it. This is not to suggest that everyone in Yemen valued the exercise or even approved of it. Attitudes among the public ranged from excitement to apathy, while expectations varied between those who hoped for dramatic improvements and those who saw the process as little more than window-dressing.[15]

When elections were held, the economy was not in good shape. Per capita income was 10 per cent lower than in 1989, unemployment reached 25 per cent, and inflation reached between 30 and 50 per cent. Inflation was increasing so rapidly that ordinary families could not afford some essential foods. The high price increases, particularly for essential goods and services, adversely effected those who were paid low salaries by the government and the private sector, and this in turn led to widespread corruption, which by 1994 had become an accepted norm of everyday life.

---

[15] Noel Brehony, *Yemen Divided—The Story of a Failed State in South Arabia* (London: I. B. Tauris, 2013), 192.

The national currency was valued at an all-time low, and a flourishing black market emerged. Essential services like schools and hospitals deteriorated in quality. The regime's failure on the political front, its mismanagement of the economy, and the continuous decline in the standard of living resulted in economic hardship and increasing disenchantment.

The leadership of the state was too far removed from the concerns of ordinary people and thus was unable to take appropriate action. The two leaders were too busy plotting against each other to concern themselves with real problems. The fundamental inability of the YSP leadership to remove itself from the vicious circle of power struggle, grasp issues which were relevant to the people, and raise demands which were of immediate interest to them eventually inflicted maximum damage on the party. The unwillingness of the leadership to resolve the dispute between themselves threatened to break up the recently found state of national unity and, to a large extent, paralysed the functions of the government led by Prime Minister Haider Abubakir Al-Attas.

There were also disagreements within the YSP itself, which led to the emergence of two factions. The pragmatists were led by Mohammed Salim Salih, a member of the Presidential Council, and Yasin Said Numan, the speaker of Parliament. They were eager to see greater cooperation with the GPC and agreed with President Salih that only a unified GPC/YSP would create the political conditions needed for economic prosperity and a meaningful unification of the political and administrative structures of the YAR and the PDRY. The Southern hardliners were led by Omar Jarallah and the minister of local administration, Mohammad Said Abdallah, who wanted the YSP to distance itself from the GPC and align with the opposition. Al-Beidh, the YSP secretary general, sided with the hardliners until the elections of 1993, when he switched allegiance to the pragmatists.

The Southerners had good relations with the Bakil tribal confederation which had been marginalised by the Northern regime. The lower North Yemen areas of Hujaryya which represented the urbanised and intellectual strata in the YAR and were historically deprived were also sympathetic to the South. The YSP, with its progressive family code, extensive legal rights for women, and encouragement of women's education and access to work was able to mobilise most gender organisations in Yemen.

Civil society organisations flourished and showed the leaders how a democracy should function. They organised nation-wide conferences which brought diverse groups together—tribesmen, urban intellectuals, journalists, and professionals—and advocated many essential reforms such as the merging of the armies, judicial independence, fiscal restraint, and management and peaceful resolution of tribal disputes.

The tribes also organised important conferences which Salih and the government disregarded. Abu Luhum from the Bakil confederation organised a nine-day conference in December 1991 called Cohesion (*talahhum*), which ended with thirty-three resolutions which the South supported. This conference also stopped a number of perennial disputes amongst several tribal groups. Another tribal gathering took place in September 1992 at Wadi Dhannah which aimed to stop feuding and bloodshed and encourage responsibility in society. In March 1993, a Higher Council of Yemeni tribes was established after tribal battles, killings, and abductions were affecting the streets of Sanaa. The government tried to ban the ownership and purchase of arms by tribal groups and issued a law in 1992 to that effect, but it was never enforced.

As Saleh Yafi, an anti-war activist, explained during an interview with the author in London in 1994, "The number of weapons available on the black market was unbelievably high and to no one's surprise, sold openly, encouraged by government officials and wealthy businessmen. Most weapons you could think of were for sale and to be honest even young children were buying and selling. The leadership made no effort to stop this madness and in fact they encouraged it. The country is full of weapons and no controls are in place as yet, weapons are more accessible to young kids than sweets and ice cream."

The "Afghans" were another problem. The South Yemenis accused the YRG of organising training camps for some three thousand Afghanistan war veterans in the Maraqisha Mountains in Abyan Governorate so they could strike at Southern targets.

It was agreed by the leading political parties that the first Yemeni elections should take place by the end of 1992, but because of internal conflict, they were not held until 27 April 1993. The election manifestos showed that the policies of the main and smaller parties were very similar, and differences tended to be those of emphasis and personalities. The GPC described itself as democratic and reformist while upholding Islamic tradition. The YSP gave up most of its Marxist ideas and adopted a social democratic stance, calling for democratisation. For Islah, restoring Islam to a central position in Yemeni society was the main issue, but its rhetoric was subdued. There was a lot of agreement on actual policies in the fields of economics, foreign policy, health, education, decentralisation of government, and freedom of speech. This was to be expected because the GPC and YSP were expecting to merge. In an attempt to shed labels like "atheistic", the YSP proposed the setting up of an Islamic University, and Islah, eager not to be considered fundamentalist or reactionary, included proposals on women's rights.

In the choice of candidates for all the parties, popular appeal was more important than party affiliation. Individuals who were key regional political figures, such as the scions of leading families, tribal sheikhs, religious figures, important merchants, and university professors, were chosen.

The GPC won 123 seats, Islah won 62, and the YSP won 56. The remainder of the seats were won by other political parties and independent personalities. The election resulted in a tripartite ruling coalition between the three leading political parties. The South supported the YSP, with which the Southerners identified. The GPC won, the results reinforced the sense of division prevalent in the country as the GPC and Islah gained almost full control of the North. The seats the YSP won in the South were not enough to take any effective political control in parliament, and losing in the North relegated the YSP into overall third position. Islah gained some support in the South thanks to the social services it provided through its own networks, including health care, emergency relief, post-secondary vocational training, religious education, needlework classes, summer camps, and group marriage ceremonies for those who could not afford a traditional wedding.

Around thirty-five thousand security guards kept order at polling stations. There were three hundred European and US observers plus foreign diplomats, journalists, and interested individuals.

Fruitless discussions about a merger between the GPC and the YSP delayed the election of the five-person Presidential Council. Discussions about a merger resumed on 10 May 1993, and Salih and Al-Beidh did in fact sign a "merger agreement". But instead of agreeing to an immediate merger, they promised only "to initiate deep and extensive co-ordination leading to a unified political organ". The YSP said the talks failed because the GPC had made a secret deal with Islah. Many in the YSP totally rejected the merger once the party had secured its power base in the South. It seemed as if Al-Beidh was willing to countenance a possible merger before the elections only to secure the best possible deal for his party in terms of electoral cooperation with the GPC.

Noel Brehony described how the coalition government was finally appointed by Salih in October 1993. Al-Attas remained prime minister with a cabinet consisting of fifteen from the GPC, nine from the YSP, and four from Islah. One of the new ministers representing the GPC was Muhammad Ali Haytham, a former prime minster of the PDRY. There were deputy prime ministers from all three parties, with

Muhammad Haydarah Masdus representing the YSP, which retained the portfolios of defence, fishing, minerals, industry, electricity, transport, and housing.[16]

The government was a broad coalition, embracing everyone who was someone in Yemen's broad political spectrum: left and right, religious and secular, modernist and traditionalist, pro-Saudi and pro-Iraqi. It was agreed that no party would be allowed to leave the coalition during the first twelve months of the new government or during the six months before a general election.

The results of the elections had a major impact on the partnership between the YSP and the GPC. The theory of partnership between the two parties and the two leaders who had made unity possible began to come to an end. YSP members found themselves trapped and absorbed into a state machinery now almost totally led by the GPC and Islah leaders.

It was clear that the election results were inevitable in view of the population make-up: the North had a population of twelve million and the South had just two million, even though the South was much bigger than the North in area.

Senior YSP officials claimed that because of their election failure, differences clearly emerged within the politburo about election strategy. Al-Beidh and others were blamed for having neglected the broad-based support the party had in North Yemen and concentrated too much on the South. Some within the politburo, particularly those of Northern origin, felt that the election strategy should have prioritised gaining of votes and increasing party membership from the North. The YSP's policies differed little from those of the GPC, and it was not able to develop a different political agenda to attract voters.

Following the elections, the YSP as a political party was no longer a leading ruling party. Its leadership had neglected the structures of the party at national and local levels, which were disorganised and in most cases inoperational. YSP members and army officers were confused about their role and carried out their work for the party as a secondary task and not as the principal task it was before unity. The party cells gradually became very weak and most of the time remained without any specific tasks.

The YSP's political weakness throughout the country was exploited by Islah, which gained more seats in parliament, increased its ministerial portfolios at the expense of the YSP, and tried to remove the socialists. Salih and the GPC took advantage of Islah's growing popularity and brought it into the new coalition as a major partner, further reducing the power of the YSP. The three main parties started a vicious smear campaign of hatred against each other, and each shifted the blame for the country's dire economic situation onto the others. Individual tribes and opportunists were waiting in the wings to take over the divided state.

Sadly the ordinary people who were initially jubilant about unity began reproducing the crisis at the leadership levels through their actions. It no longer became a question of who was right and who was wrong but rather of who supported which faction, a scenario which was defined in terms of allegiance to the South or the North. Salih and Al-Beidh, rather than the welfare of the country and its economy, education, and health services, became the main topic of public discussion. Yemen was sliding from a fledgling democracy into a dictatorship.

After losing the elections, the YSP had to rethink its strategy. During the summer of 1993, it was faced with demonstrations and strikes in Aden and Mukalla sparked off by food shortages and rising prices. Al-Beidh's strategy was to weaken the power of the GPC, first by suggesting the entire electorate took part in direct elections for the president and vice president. The GPC did not agree to this. Al-Beidh also presented an eighteen-point letter which advocated a Consultative Council with equal representation

---

[16] Brehony, 192.

for Yemen's eighteen governorates, a new presidential format, the reorganisation of the police and armed forces on a national basis, recognition for personal qualifications and merit, the reorganisation of the provincial governorates to eliminate their pre-unification divisions and prepare for local elections, limits to the government's interference in implementing laws and ordinances pertaining to society, and the development of plans for the economy that would pay greater attention to the free trade area of Aden. A more reasonable time to present these claims would have been during the unity negotiations, and they were seen as a strategy to weaken the GPC. The GPC responded by issuing an alternative list of nineteen points, and the smaller political parties also added their list of points. Many of the issues raised were later incorporated into the discussions of the Political Dialogue Committee.

The YSP was also worried about having to share power with Islah and tried to spread its authority over the military. When these efforts were aborted, it turned to cultivating underground YSP militias in the South.

The GPC was able to dominate the political scene owing to a number of miscalculations on the part of the YSP. It agreed to unity because it was under pressure owing to the disintegration of the Soviet Union, its main supporter. There was no provision for the successful integration of the institutions of the two Yemens, which never happened. The YSP stuck to its radical ideology and insisted on its anti-Islamic and detribalisation policies which alienated the Northerners who were largely illiterate, conservative, and of tribal origin. Ex-Southerners were also alienated and gravitated towards the GPC or Islah. The YSP concentrated on urban areas in a country which was dominated by the rural countryside and put its faith in an uprising by the Bakil tribal confederation, which did not happen. The YSP was also weakened by endless internal debates and disagreements.

The GPC worked step by step to eliminate the YSP by keeping the military and security organisations out of its control and successfully mobilising people through rewards and sanctions. Islah mobilised the ancient religious centres which were revived after unity. The GPC and Islah launched a massive propaganda campaign against the YSP, accused it of being anti-Islam, and called on all Yemenis to be loyal to the mother country against a party that was mortgaging its policies to foreign interests.

The South formally abandoned Marxism and faced many of the problems experienced by Eastern European states in the transition to a free market. At first there was nothing in the shops; afterwards, there was plenty in the shops, but the people did not have the money to buy. Mass unemployment was avoided because many unnecessary civil service jobs were maintained. Some of the positive aspects of Marxism were abandoned, namely the free health service and social planning, especially in education, where significant progress had been made in the elimination of illiteracy.

Sheila Carapico summed up the political problems facing Yemen in this way: "In the end it boiled down to both military leaderships' rejection of pluralism and dialogue. Simply put, each side wanted its maximum domain: for the southerners, either a full half of the power in a unified government or an effectively independent administration in the south; and for the North Salih's control of the whole country." Despite the problems, the ordinary people still supported unity because it brought freedom of movement between North and South.

The Dialogue Committee

In 1993, the coalition government was in crisis and no longer functioned as a government. The government departments in the North and South operated independently of one another, and the YSP was conducting its own foreign policy and acting as if it was an independent state. Trade union leaders demanded remedies for unemployment, food shortages, and high housing rents. The political parties urged the people to come out on the streets and protest about the government's performance, which they did. But the protestors did not have any ideological common denominator apart from dissatisfaction with the government, and they never formed a unified political body.

Throughout the political crisis, many attempts were made to find a peaceful outcome, including the formation of several peace committees, the most notable being the Dialogue Committee (Lajnat Al-Hiwar), established in November 1993—one of the most remarkable achievements in Yemen's political history. It was the brainchild of the minor parties and was led by two prominent politicians who were respected for their attempts to establish an independent republic in the 1960s: Mujahid Abu Shawarib and Sinan Abu Luhum. Abu Shawarib, the Ba'athist leader with Hashid connections (he was distantly related to both President Salih and Shaykh Abdullah Al-Ahmar), had been made a deputy prime minister after the elections. Abu Luhum was a leading shaykh of the Bakil tribe. The committee was made up of representatives of all political parties and regions and also consulted lawyers and academics.

The committee met in almost continuous sessions in Sanaa and Aden between 23 November 1993 and 18 January 1994. It produced a seven-thousand-word document. Part one dealt with preventing terrorism, controlling the military and security apparatus, and limiting the powers of the Presidential Council. The eighteen points in Al-Beidh's letter were addressed, and it was suggested a new intelligence service be established. The military was not to interfere in the affairs of the citizens or local authorities, and the setting up of militias was forbidden.

Part two, entitled "Foundations for Building a Modern State", was a plan for the future, with proposals for the reform of central government, the creation of a democratic system of local government, reorganisation of the armed forces, and economic and financial reform. The Presidential Council would have no real power and would act like a constitutional monarchy.

Local government would be empowered as Yemen was to be divided into regions known as *makhalif,* based on the principles of "administrative and financial decentralisation in a unified state, and on the broad-based popular participation in government and on the principle of democracy". Local councils would be elected. Concern was expressed that this system could enable the establishment of a Southern state by stealth, but central government was provided with a constitutional means to assert control if necessary.

The armed forces, the document said, "must serve as a model for national cohesion based on qualifications and experience, not influenced by factors of politics, familial and tribal ties, sectarian or geographic affiliation". The fact that two separate armies existed contributed largely to the political crisis. Unfortunately, the document did not put forward a plan to merge the armed forces.

Carapico commented,

> After meeting in virtually continuous session for three months, the 30 most respected men in the country produced in early 1994 a document (wathiqa) of Contract and Agreement spelling out comprehensive reforms. Among the most important of these was the delineation and limitation of presidential and vice-presidential power; depoliticization, merger and redeployment of military and security forces, starting with the removal of check points from cities and highways; administration and financial decentralization to elected local governments starting with development budgets; empowerment of an independent judiciary to enforce the letter of the law, starting with the arrest of assassins; election of an upper house of parliament modelled on the US senate; stricter auditing procedures; abolition of the Ministry of Information and a comprehensive list of other reforms.

The YSP could not reject the accord because its eighteen recommendations had been included. But acceptance would mean losing the political leverage it had during the crisis. The challenge for the YSP was to extricate itself from the accord without rejecting it.

The GPC had a lot to disagree with in the accord, but unity was vital to ensure the survival of Salih's regime, so it was forced to accept it even though it was afraid the YSP would exploit the changes to further its own agenda.

Several incidents heightened mistrust between the two parties. Al-Beidh was invited by Yemeni religious leaders in Taiz to meet Salih in January 1994. He did not show up and gave no explanation or apology. This was interpreted as a calculated insult, but his house was raked by machine gun fire before the meeting, and he was afraid that if he went to Taiz, an attempt would be made on his life. Haydar Al-Attas, the socialist prime minister, cancelled the first national census, claiming it was not being conducted in a professional manner, but it seems likely he was more concerned about the results drawing attention to the huge population disparity between North and South. Northern authorities forced a Ugandan aircraft carrying military equipment to the south to land in Sanaa, with the defence minister in Sanaa insisting that the purchase of the equipment had not been approved. Prime Minister Attas appointed a new governor for Abyan to prevent corruption in the province, but this appointment was annulled by Salih.

The Dialogue Committee's document (the accord) to some extent reflected many of the concerns expressed by the YSP. Its clauses were not implemented despite its attempts to satisfy all sides—attempts which in some cases were genuine, but all came to no avail mainly because neither side showed any flexibility in shifting from its position. The public responded positively to the document, and many believed it provided both sides with an opportunity to reduce tensions and avert war. It later became obvious that the leaders themselves did not believe in the document they signed, nor did they care about their people's response to it.

As soon as the accord was finalised on 18 January, Salih agreed to sign it, but the YSP delayed, and Al-Beidh said he wanted to be briefed on security arrangements for the signing ceremony. He also sought guarantees from Salih that the accord would be implemented. YSP politicians were also not convinced it was necessary to return to Sanaa straight after the signing.

When the YSP refused to sign the accord in Yemen, King Hussein of Jordan extended an invitation for it to be signed in Amman. This happened on 20 February. The two Yemeni leaders sat on either side of King Hussein surrounded by flowers and staring in opposite directions.

A leading GPC figure who wanted to remain autonomous argued, "The document signed and agreed upon in Jordan will if implemented strengthen our democratic institutions by taking power away from the president and vice-president. The document is designed to increase democratic participation both at the local level and nationally, reduce corruption and improve security for those who are most vulnerable. Our biggest problem now is to commit the leadership to the document and I doubt this will happen."

There were ominous signs both before and after the accord was signed. *Al Hayat* claimed that there was a plot to shoot down the plane taking Al-Beidh to Amman. Instead of going straight to the Jordanian capital, he flew to Cairo to discuss issues of concern in Yemen with President Mubarak. He also visited Syria, where he met the vice president.

During the ceremony, Salih promised "to break with all past pages". Al-Beidh said, "Our sincerity and seriousness will be tested tomorrow, when we return to Yemen," and he flew first to Saudi Arabia and then to Oman, refusing to return to Yemen on the same plane as Salih. These visits were made without the knowledge of the presidency or the Foreign Ministry.

The economic situation was bleak and the prospect of economic rehabilitation looked bleaker than ever. Attempts to find new sources of oil were not successful, the currency depreciation rate reached YR78=$1 and the inflation rate reached 100 per cent. The GNP per capita was at an all-time low of $300-400, with unemployment at approximately 36 per cent. The budget announced in February 1994 showed an anticipated deficit of £3.5 billion. The government's spending did not reflect any organised policy; funds were allocated sporadically in response to crises as they arose, and Aden was not turned into a free zone.

The Road to War

As soon as the accord was signed, fighting broke out for a brief period in Abyan. The clashes were a continuation by military means of a dispute about the replacement of a Northern governor with a Southerner. The Political Forces Dialogue Committee attempted to bring the fighting to an end. There was also a sit-in movement which started in March 1994 in Taiz and spread quickly to other cities. During the whole day, qat-chewing sessions sought to bring Yemenis together. On a white piece of cloth pinned to the chest of the participants were three slogans: "No to fighting", "No to separation" and "Yes to implementation" of the accord document.

Several states in the region—Egypt, Jordan, the United Arab Emirates, Morocco, and Eritrea—tried to find a solution to the ongoing crisis. Even the United States got involved. In Oman, the two Alis agreed on measures to avert the threat of civil war but failed to agree on a joint communiqué; Sultan Qaboos became frustrated and stopped mediation attempts. The other countries tried to find a federal solution which would give the South a degree of autonomy while maintaining unity.

The task of mediation was made increasingly difficult by the partners' refusal to cooperate. At this stage of the conflict, however, many people still supported the YSP's position of immediate reforms. Salih was able to create division within the YSP leadership through divide-and-rule tactics. He was partly correct when he accused Al-Beidh of being too emotional and having an ability to run away from problems, but he failed to acknowledge that he wanted to rule Yemen alone.

The YSP leadership, in an attempt to explain its position, drafted a report on 3 March 1994 for the benefit of its members and clearly placed the blame for the deteriorating political situation on the GPC leadership. It accused them of refusing to immediately implement the Dialogue Committee document agreed upon by all parties.

Furthermore, the report accused the GPC leadership of preparing for war while pretending to speak about peace. The YSP leadership indicated in this document that a war in Yemen would have severe implications for all concerned. It explained that the YSP leadership made a commitment on its part to remain loyal to the unity of the nation and appealed to all Yemenis to expose those it labelled as working against unification.

But the report came too late to convince party members about what was happening, and furthermore the party organisations were too disorganised and demoralised to provide any effective support for the leadership. Many in the North sympathised with the concerns raised by the YSP leadership, but they opposed the tactics of Vice President Al-Beidh.

Cabinet meetings resumed on 27 March 1994. At the first meeting held in Aden, ten committees were set up to discuss plans for implementing the accord. The next cabinet meeting was held in Taiz on 6–7 April. Ministers reviewed a final formula for implementing the accord and approved a plan concerning the trial of suspected terrorists. While the meeting was taking place, there was a clash in Dhamar, 125 miles South of Sanaa, between the camp of the Southern Ba Suhayb brigade and Northern forces. The conflict was resolved after the Joint Military Committee talked to commanders and soldiers on both sides.

The YSP now had to return to Sanaa for the third cabinet meeting. It failed to provoke the GPC into rejecting the accord, and it no longer had an excuse for not attending the cabinet meeting scheduled for 12 April. On the day of the meeting, Prime Minister Attas, whose duty it was to convene the cabinet meeting, left Aden for medical treatment aboard.

President Salih's speech on 27 April 1994 strongly accused the Dialogue Committee of sympathising with the YSP and openly called for the nation to rise against the secessionist tendencies in the YSP. Many observers perceived this speech as a declaration of war. The YSP, in a communiqué two days after the president's speech, accused him of having planned for the war against the YSP and other progressive forces. Both leaders were allegedly negotiating a settlement while keeping the military option open to safeguard their own interests. Whereas the unity agreement of 1990 surprised most people, the war of 1994 did not. The structure of the government in the new republic was not sufficiently institutionalised to survive a political crisis.

Leading and important figures involved in the mediation process, including Sheikh Sinan Abu Lahum and Brigadier Mujahid Abu Shawrib, ultimately gave up and fled the country immediately before the war broke out, signalling that the positions held by each side were irreconcilable, and in a joint statement they warned that the Dialogue Committee was no longer effective and a bloodbath would occur.

Sadly, Yemeni unity, a dream of both the North and the South, was not achieved because of the inadequacy of preparation. Yemen's pro-Iraq stance during the first Gulf War isolated the country from both the Arab and Western worlds and resulted in an economic crisis with high unemployment and spiralling inflation. Major development projects could not be financed, and the country's revenues were not boosted by the slowly developing oil industry. This resulted in disillusionment on the part of the people and a reluctance to relinquish their Northern and Southern power bases on the part of the two leaders. The states were unable to merge their administrative, military, and social establishments, and the leaders and elites were suspicious of each other. The Yemeni people, although supportive of unity, were not involved in it, and the North and the South were not able to reconcile their visions for a united state. The North (the GPC and YRG) advocated a traditional lifestyle underpinned by Islamic principles, whereas the South (YSP) wanted to build a modern state. During 1993–94, different perceptions of state-building and power sharing made the gap between North and South unbridgeable, and war became inevitable when Salih adopted the role of a vigorous unifier determined to maintain Yemeni unity through the use of crude power.

Yemen is not the first country to unify, and its unification in 1990 was the first time in its history it was united as one big state. The United States fought a bitter civil war but united afterwards. West Germany and East Germany reunited after the fall of the Berlin Wall in 1989, and they now constitute one of the world's foremost powers. It has been the opposite in Yemen. Unification has, if anything, exacerbated regional and internal conflict and divisions. The answer to this issue lies within the framework and false foundations of that very unification. The unification of Yemen in 1990 was developed to fail, and consequently the persistence of the North–South divide is due to the unification of Yemen never being properly completed. Reconciliation after the many internal struggles in both states and the 1994 civil war never materialised to resolve the problems of power struggles and the ambiguous relationship with the region.

After all the struggle to build a socialist state in the form of the PDRY, some are still of the opinion that things were much better then than they are now. The YSP and the PDRY collapsed as a consequence of pointless internal political power struggles. The Soviet Union withdrawing its support in 1989 had a devastating effect. The South then entered into a "union" with a tribal state in the North without any analysis of the future and the obstacles it could face. In reality, Al-Beidh rushed into unity without proper consultation or any study of the possible success or failure of the project. There was an annexation of the South on the part of the political class in the North.

CHAPTER 7

The 1994 War of Secession and the Withering Away of the Yemeni Socialist Party

In 1994 war broke out between those leaders who made unity possible—a national unification triumph became a national tragedy. As was often the case throughout Yemen's troubled history, instead of settling their differences peacefully or continuing to live with them the opposing parties, the leaders of the North and the South and their followers, resorted to the gun without thinking through the consequences.

Despite the unity agreement, both leaderships maintained their own separate military establishments with the intention of destroying any possible chance of genuine unity for the people of Yemen, dashing the hopes of millions of Yemenis. This regrettably happened on 4 May 1994, when the two sides resorted to violence to resolve their differences.

The Northern political class was clear about what it was fighting for and had three military objectives: to secure the North (i.e., eliminate the Southern forces in the North and prevent tribal or public disturbances), to separate Aden and Hadhramaut by driving a wedge southwards though Abyan to the sea, and to besiege Aden and force its surrender.

The socialists, still suffering from the scars of division, kept coming up with an ever-growing list of things they were fighting against, but without a clear public policy objective to gain mass support. When the political process failed, the Southern leadership had two options: take power by bringing down Salih or withdraw from the union. Not all Southerners initially supported secession, but most Southerners were unhappy with the way unity had materialised, and many grievances were aired; Al-Beidh belatedly began to make moves towards secession with his supporters, including Al-Siyali, then governor of Aden. Some Northern leaders speculated that the war broke out earlier than the Southerners had anticipated. Weapons started arriving in Aden at the end of the conflict, and there were weapons stores in Sanaa which the Northern security forces seized when the war started. It is possible that the Southerners, expecting fighting to be concentrated in the North, planned to attack the presidential palace and get support from socialist-controlled battalions. The Southerners were also expecting support (which never came) from tribes sympathetic to them in the North and from their old partner, the National Democratic Front, a Northern political group absorbed into the YSP before and after unification.

Pre-war Skirmishes

In the North, the Southerners stationed five brigades: the Third Armoured at Amran, thirty-eight miles north of Sana'a; the Basahib at Dhamar, sixty miles south of the capital; the First Artillery at Yarim, a few miles farther south; the Fourth Infantry at Kawlan; and the Fifth Infantry at Harf Sufyan. The Northerners stationed three brigades in the South: the Amaliqah Brigade at Lawdar, in Abyan province; the Second Armoured Brigade at Al-Raha, in Lahij province; and Central Security near the Aden airport.

The exchange of troops was a confidence-building measure which was to be followed by the merging of the two armies, but this never happened. The Southerners felt threatened by the Northerners, and vice versa. Tactical military manoeuvring was a trademark skill of President Salih that would later prove to be decisive in the military confrontation.

There were a number of skirmishes which preceded the outbreak of an all-out war. They were instigated by the commands of both factions to test each other's strength. The opening shots were fired on the day the accord document was signed, when each side accused the other of military manoeuvres. The GPC deployed troops near the northern Amaliqa brigade's camp in Abyan in breach of earlier agreements. Politically, the clashes were a continuation of a dispute about the appointment of the governor of Abyan. Prime Minister Attas belatedly replaced the Northern governor with a Southerner, Muhammad Ali Ahmed, a former YSP member who was on the losing side of the 1986 massacre and one of Ali Nasser's strong supporters. The GPC and Islah viewed his appointment as an attempt by the YSP to secure Abyan by wooing back the supporters of Ali Nasser. They consisted of up to twenty thousand soldiers in the PDRY's seven brigades who fled to the North and provided Salih with intelligence and fighters. This move was not substantial enough to turn the losing side in 1986 against Salih; many of that group remained staunch supporters, including the current president of Yemen, Abdroba Mansur Hadi.

Taking Abyan was of great strategic importance because by controlling a small amount of territory, it was possible to isolate Aden from Hadhramaut and the oilfields and separate the east from the west if war broke out. The North was warning the South it could do this. At the time of unification, the Northern regime strategically placed the Amaliqa brigade in Abyan while the South placed its finest troops in the North in Dhamar on the main Sanaa-Aden road and Amran, close to Sanaa but in Bakil territory.

Reuters reported that the YSP dispatched tanks and armoured equipment to the Shabwa oilfield. Travellers were also quoted as saying that Russian-made tanks which had previously been stationed along the frontiers with Oman and Saudi Arabia had been moved to support four Southern army units which were being rushed to Sayyun in Hadhramaut.

Substantial troop movements were taking place throughout the country, with the Northern Second Armoured Brigade redeployed in Lahij, forces from another Northern brigade taking up positions in a former border area, and Republican Guard and riot police units from the North occupying an area in close proximity to Al-Dalih province. The Southern forces moved tanks, long-range guns, and ground-to-air missiles to positions near Ataq, the capital of the oil-producing Shabwa province about one hundred miles north-east of Aden.

All-out War: 4 May–7 July 1994

The war was brutal and vicious and carried out by modern, sophisticated weapons. Initially it was between two armies, but the weapons were soon directed at the civilian population. The indiscriminate bombing of innocent civilians in Aden and the launch of Scud missiles into Sanaa were irresponsible acts which shocked public opinion at both national and local level.

When the war started on 4 May 1994, the Northern regime forces quickly demonstrated their tactical and preplanning military superiority, and the Southerners were on the back foot in most of this military adventure, unable to force back this relentless, calculated military offensive. The Southerners were keen to demand changes to the political system and threatened secession, but when it came to military conflict, they took a defensive posture and generally did not initiate hostilities except at the start of the war, when they attacked Northern airports at Sanaa, Ta'iz, and Hodeidah; the presidential palace in Sanaa; the country's two main power stations; Hodeidah port; and oil storage and pipeline facilities at Marib, aiming to prevent retaliatory strikes by the Northern air force. The Southern leaders did not pay sufficient

The war of secession broke out only four years after unity. Source: Wikipedia.

attention to military strategy because they were preoccupied with internal debates and negotiations with the North. They also overestimated the strength of their army, and Al-Beidh was somehow convinced they would win, as in the previous conflicts with the North in the 1970s. They also held out false hope that the Gulf states would apply pressure on Salih, now seen by many of those states as the arch-enemy, and provide them with assistance.

When the war started, Salih declared a thirty-day state of emergency, including a night curfew. Al-Beidh, At-Attas, and all YSP cabinet ministers were dismissed. Salih portrayed himself as the defender of unity against the secessionists and described the Northern troops as "the forces of constitutional legitimacy". He projected a message of moral superiority and political self-legitimacy, and he repeated the often-voiced criticisms of the South: it was a Soviet bloc state armed by Eastern Europe, its leaders were big spenders whose financial policies badly damaged the economy, and now the socialists were allied with conservative elements like Al-Jiffri and were establishing a sheikhdom, not a modern state. Unlike Al-Beidh, Salih spoke directly to his supporters and frequently visited his troops to boost their morale.

Many Southerners saw this Northern military campaign as a crime against humanity. They were attacked and had no choice but to defend themselves. They believed that unity had not benefited them and that they had every right to break away from the partnership. Some Southerners were surprised by the failure of their leadership to resist a Northern invasion.

According to Western estimates, the North had approximately 40,000 troops and 40,000 reservists. It could call up a tribal militia, drawn mostly from the Hashid confederation, of up to 100,000 men. It had 700 tanks, 300 artillery units, and 80 aircraft. The South had 27,000 soldiers, 45,000 reservists and a tribal militia of 20,000, 400 tanks, 200 artillery pieces, and 90 aircraft.

In Abyan and Shabwa, the North had the upper hand. Some of the Southern units in those areas were given money and promised positions, so they allowed the Northern troops to pass through unopposed.

Northern units attacked Aden to isolate it and cut off Hadhramaut from Aden. Southern forces regrouped to try to defend Aden. The Southern brigades in the North were quickly immobilised. Northern forces used three columns to attack the South and capture Aden.

During the first weeks of fighting, the Southerners were able to prevent the North from achieving significant breakthroughs. They did not launch any major offensives but mounted a tenacious defence between Ataq and Hadhramaut. With a well-developed air force and navy, the South was encouraged not to give in, especially when it succeeded in blocking the main thrust of the Northern attack. Scud missiles were fired at Sanaa and Taiz, causing major havoc and destruction. Throughout the 1970s and

1980s, the Soviet Union provided the South with military equipment, but during the 1994 conflict, it did not provide any maintenance or support for the equipment it had previously supplied, and it did not provide any further equipment.

Al-Beidh was nowhere to be seen as a leader in battle, and this issue alone demoralised the fightback. The Southerners were aware of their military strategic weakness and, to avoid huge loss of lives, called for a ceasefire to be mediated by Arab states. The North agreed, but because it was having initial military successes in the war, it preferred to continue hostilities unless, they said, the Southern leaders changed tack completely and agreed the continuation of unity on their terms. Ceasefires were brokered but were routinely violated by both sides. Much of the fighting took place in sparsely populated remote areas, so the claims made by both sides could not be verified by independent observers.

The North fought on several fronts to wear out the South but did not concentrate large numbers of troops in one area, to prevent the Southern air force from targeting them. Aden was the jewel in the crown. Between 27 May and 2 June, Lahij was occupied, and four assault columns headed for Aden. The oil refinery was bombed, and the Northern forces headed to Shabwa on their way to Hadhramaut, where the rich Masila oilfields were located. Through the use of air power, the South blocked the move on Aden, and the North observed a ceasefire but then resumed its attack on 10 June.

The war was now centred on Aden and the Hadhrami port of Mukalla, four hundred miles farther east. Defeat was staring the South in the face, but they hung on in anticipation of foreign assistance, which never came.

When it came to the capture of Aden, the North had two options: storm the city or lay siege to it. Storming the city would result in large numbers of casualties and international condemnation. The Northern forces chose to lay siege and wait for the Southerners to surrender. The shelling often resulted in civilian casualties and gave the South time to try to rally support through diplomatic means.

Aden's civilian population, its infrastructure, and its supply installations were targeted. The South refused to take part in ceasefire negotiations because the North refused to hold an interstate dialogue between the YAR and the state newly declared on 21 May 1994, called the Democratic Republic of Yemen, insisting it should be a YAR dialogue. The North was accused of using the negotiations to buy time so it could strengthen its siege of Aden.

On 23 June, the Northern forces reached Aden's suburbs of Shaykh Uthman, Bir Na'ma, and Little Aden. At the same time, the Northerners were able to move through the mountains, avoiding air raids, and occupied a number of Southern towns including Mukalla, the capital of Hadhramaut.

On 24 June, Northern and Southern ministers were scheduled to hold their first face-to-face meeting at the United Nations. This was when Northern forces launched their heaviest bombardment of Aden since the war had begun. The US State Department responded with a strong warning: "We view these attacks as a clear violation of UN Security Council resolution 924," a statement said. "Northern forces should cease their bombardment of Aden immediately, avoid ground action against the city and pull back their rocket launchers and artillery. Further military operations will require urgent Security Council consideration." But the United States never stated what kind of action it would take if the Northern forces did not stop their attacks.

Most of Aden was deprived of basic amenities including water, electricity, and health provision. On 28 June, Salih's forces made a direct attack on Aden's water-pumping station, cutting off essential water supply, which in turn crippled life-sustaining services. It appeared at that stage of the war that the longer it continued, the more the civilian population would bear the brunt of it.

A young schoolgirl named Waila quoted in the author's booklet *The Yemen Civil War 1994* described what was happening:

> The shelling and the bombs were terrible. There were explosions all around and aeroplanes overhead, just like I imagined the Second World War was like. People were screaming and running all around and some were hit by the blasts and pieces of exploding buildings. There was blood in the streets and suddenly the buildings were looking like ruins. Everything changed—even the weather changed too and it became much hotter and more sticky. So I went to help in the hospital, bringing water from the tanks to the old people who couldn't walk. There was no water in the taps and we had to bring the water back to the hospital in big bottles. There were not enough doctors and not enough beds. People were lying on the floor and some of them were dying and bleeding. Some were groaning and crying for their lost children, only thinking about their families and those they loved.

Mukalla fell a few days before Aden. Battles on 2–3 July at Buroum, west of the city, left it exposed. The city's inhabitants knew that defeat was inevitable and requested the Southern leaders and fighters to leave before Mukalla was reduced to rubble. They fled en masse to Oman and other neighbouring states, mainly by sea. Al-Beidh, politically and militarily defeated, was nowhere to be seen. He later fled to Oman.

Aden was besieged by Northern forces in June and fell on 7 July. The government forces entering the suburbs of Aden came with trucks carrying bread, water, and qat for the population. The socialist troops retreated to the central Crater district, a natural citadel of volcanic rock, and appealed the people to join them in the "positions of honour". The United States helped in negotiations to ensure the peaceful surrender of Aden. Abdul Rahman Al-Jiffri, a leading member of the secessionist government, stayed behind until he fled on a boat for Djibouti.

With regard to the shelling of Aden, Human Rights Watch reported that Aden, whose population swelled with displaced persons during the war to an estimated five hundred thousand, was bombed and shelled by government forces from 4 May until 6 July. The government intensified its attack after 19 June when the separatist army withdrew many heavy weapons inside the city. Shelling, once fairly limited to the area of the airport in Khor Maksar and other obvious military targets, began to regularly hit civilian areas as the siege of Aden tightened. After 19 June, admissions to the largest Aden hospital, Al-Jumhuriyya, averaged 150 war-wounded a day, with about fifteen to twenty deaths daily. The Aden casualties, unlike those in other regions, were predominantly civilian, and one informed source estimated that this hospital's admissions were at least 75 per cent civilian. Most military casualties were treated at Aden's military hospital.

By 23 June, about 1,500 war-wounded persons had been admitted to all of Aden's hospitals, according to the ICRC. The worst days were later, on 23–25 June, when, with more intense shelling over wider areas of Aden, the estimated average was two hundred wounded and thirty dead per day. On 30 June, Al-Jumhuriyya Hospital estimated that its total war injury–related patients (including outpatients) had climbed to 2,900, plus 400 dead. From these figures, the number of 405 killed and 2,707 wounded civilians in Aden may be roughly extrapolated. Artillery pounded Aden each morning and from 5.00 to 10.00 p.m. nightly. During over three weeks of daily shelling, and especially after government troops overran Bir Ahmad north of Aden on 24 June, many high-rise blocks and other buildings in outlying suburbs such as Dar Saad, Little Aden (Barakah), Khor Maksar, Mansour, and Shaykh Othman suffered damage ranging from slight shrapnel marks to complete destruction. Residents of these districts fled into the Aden inner city districts of Crater, Ma'alla, and Tawahi (Steamer Point). Despite a government promise broadcast on Sanaa radio not to hit the densely populated Crater and Tawahi districts, shells did fall there.

Examples of events causing civilian casualties included the bombing of three houses in Khor Maksar near the airport, crushing about ten sleeping people according to neighbours; the bombing of the crowded vegetable suq (market) in Crater towards the end of the war; and the shelling of the Hotel Aden Movenpick on 5 July during fighting at the airport, when a French medical volunteer from Médecins Sans Frontières, in the MSF office in the hotel at the time, was seriously injured. The proportion and number of civilian casualties in Aden and the pattern of intensive shelling of urban areas crowded with displaced people as well as residents indicate that, especially after 19 June, government forces were not complying with their duty to take measures to avoid civilian casualties and that this attack on Aden was indiscriminate.

Aden was ransacked by the Northern army, and Islah militias and even some Southerners joined in the looting. During the war, a fatwa was issued by Dr Abdul Wahab Al-Daylmi, one of Islah's influential leaders, who declared the war on the socialists as a duty of all Muslims. He branded the socialists *kuffar*s (infidels), and as the troops marched into Aden, he reminded everyone that the Prophet Muhammad sanctioned the looting of a defeated enemy's property and the auctioning of their women and children as slaves. Al-Daylmi's strategy during the war was to use religious opportunism to justify the physical elimination of YSP members.

Human Rights Watch reported that at the end of the fighting, first the separatists and then government forces engaged in and permitted extensive looting and vandalism of Aden; during the war, government army attacks on Socialist Party offices in non-conflictive, government-held areas were followed by looting and vandalism that was organised or permitted by the authorities. Ironically, the government looked to the international community for millions of dollars in assistance to repair damage that could have been prevented if a modicum of military discipline had been exercised in this direction.

In his book *The Birth of Modern Yemen*, Brian Whitaker gave seven reasons for the humiliating defeat of the South.[17]

1. The socialists' initial disposition of forces placed them at a disadvantage; they stood to lose one-third of their army in the opening stages of the war.

2. The North struck pre-emptively, before the Socialists were ready. Large supplies of weapons were still en route to the South when war broke out, and some of the equipment was left unused through lack of trained personnel. The destruction of the battalions at Amran and Dhamar threw the socialists off course from the beginning.

3. The socialists' plans were over-reliant on help from their supposed allies amongst Arab states and Northern tribes. In the later stages of the war, the socialists were relying on Arab neighbours to recognise the new state and apply international pressure to stop the fighting.

4. Whatever value the Southern leaders placed on discipline counted for little against battle experience. Sections of the Northern army had fought for Iraq against Iran during the 1980s and had learned tactics which the Southern forces had never encountered. Towards the end of the war, a number of Northern tanks succeeded in entering Aden unchallenged simply by displaying posters of Ali Salem Al-Beidh on their sides.

5. The Northern forces were more highly motivated because their goal was simpler and more readily understood: they were fighting for "unity". Once the Islah leader, Shaykh al-Ahmar, had declared

---

[17] Joseph Kostiner, *Yemen: The Tortuous Quest for Unity (1990–1994)* (London: Royal Institute for International Affairs, 1996).

the war a jihad (something his party later retracted), it acquired a clear religious dimension as well. The Southern forces, by contrast, were being asked to fight over a somewhat nebulous collection of grievances and, later, for the creation of a state that not all the people of the South wanted.

6. Because of the events of 1986, the socialist army did not represent the South as a whole; it was drawn mainly from Radfan, Dali', and Yafa'i—three parts of the Lahij province. Ali Nasser Muhammad, the socialist president ousted in 1986, had come from Abyan, and seven Southern brigades from Abyan and Shabwa, which had fled to the North during the coup, fought on Salih's side in Shabwa during the 1994 war, with the result that Southern defenders were confronted not by "invading" Northerners but by returning Southerners.

7. The benefits of Southern air superiority were grossly overestimated. Although the Southern air force did succeed in hitting several important targets, its superiority was relative: it was incapable of mounting huge, sustained attacks of the kind employed by the United States against Iraq in 1991.

When it was clear that the South was losing the war, both Riyadh and Sanaa agreed that there should be a link between the war and the Yemen-Saudi Arabia border dispute if the Saudis supported the unification of Yemen. Salih wrote to the Saudis promising a quick resolution to the border issue and sought better relations with the Saudis. By then, Salih saw himself as commander in chief with no opposition.

The Northern regime's victory was clearly not in the Saudis' interests, and less than six months after the end of the war, Yemenis and Saudis clashed on the border with minor skirmishes. Salih was now in a position to impose himself on the international stage with no competitor. The Northern regime and Salih loyalists were in complete control of the whole of Yemen. The partnership engineered in 1990 by the two Alis ended up in a brutal divorce, with Ali Abdulla Salih taking all the spoils of a military victory. Unity as a partnership voluntarily entered into was now to be a unity by force with one leadership in charge.

The Short-Lived Democratic Republic of Yemen (DRY)

The Southern leaders made many mistaken calculations. They did not expect a full-scale serious war, believing the fighting would be confined to border clashes which would persuade Arab mediators and international powers to intervene and prevent further fighting.

On 21 May, Al-Beidh proclaimed the creation of the Democratic Republic of Yemen (DRY) with Aden as its capital. He described it as an alternative regime for Yemen as outlined in the accord, not a secessionist state. The DRY was recognised only by Somalia, but the Gulf Corporation Council (GCC) states, with the exception of Qatar, issued a statement that implied recognition. The DRY did not have the support of the full leadership of the YSP, and some of its ministers were not in Yemen when they were appointed.

The declaration (see appendix 2) was an attempt to internationalise the conflict which would now become a war between two states. The Southerners hoped for international support and were also careful not to alienate supporters who were willing to bring down Salih but did not agree with secession. The declaration document focused on justifying secession and consisted of sixteen points outlining constitutional arrangements. Yemeni unity was stated as an objective, and the document was written in such a way that it could be interpreted as proclaiming an alternative state rather than two separate states.

On 24 May 1994, Al-Beidh stated at a rare press conference in Mukalla, "We found ourselves compelled in overwhelming circumstances to announce the formation of our new system of the Democratic Republic of Yemen, which we consider to be a nucleus for a unified Yemen, because it was erected on the firm foundations of the Document of Pledge and Accord, this being a document of national consensus."

The declaration of the independent state certainly did not have the support of all YSP members and caused major rifts and conflicts within the party. On the same day as Al-Beidh gave his press conference, three members of the YSP Central Committee, Abd Al-Bari Tahir, Abdullah Hamid Al-Ulufi, and Abdullah Baydar, issued the following statement broadcast on Sanaa radio, condemning the secession:

> We, along with our people, were surprised by the declaration of secession made by the secessionist elements in the YSP leadership. We, along with our people, realise that the YSP's elements, cadres and many of its leaders reject, absolutely and in principle, this declaration, which does not express our party's spirit, principles and lengthy struggle designed to effect both the September and October Yemeni revolutions and Yemeni unification on the great 22nd May (1990).

Abd Al-Rahman Al-Jiffri. Source: Wikipedia.

Al-Beidh was head of the newly declared state in a presidential council made up of Abd Al-Qawi Makkawi, the former leader of FLOSY; Abd Al-Rahman Al-Jiffri, secretary general of the League of the Sons of Yemen (and vice president of the DRY); and Salim Salih Muhammad. The government was announced on 2 June with Hyder Al-Attas as prime minister. There were five deputy prime ministers. The ministers retained the portfolios they held in the government after the 1993 elections; Muhammad Ali Ahmad was appointed minister of the interior. Soon after announcing the DRY, Al-Beidh left for Mukalla with his supporters, and Al-Jiffri and Haytham Qasim ran the government from Aden.

The DRY brought in parties that were outlawed by the PDRY, including the Nasserists and Baathists, because its leaders were afraid the war would split the YSP and the Southern community. Hadhramaut was cut off from the rest of the South and there were fears it might join the North or form its own state. The Southern leaders wanted to ensure they retained control of the oil wealth in Hadhramaut and did their utmost to prevent the fragmentation of the South. Having brought conservative elements into the government, the DRY made some major concessions, including the declaration of Islam as the state religion and the basis of state legislation. The new state was not supported by some South Yemeni tribes but had the support of the Awatifah, Ba Wazir, Jayd, and Haddad clans in Hadhramaut and the prominent Farid family of Shabwa. Most of the Islamists remained neutral, and the former Afghanistan volunteers, mainly from the South, were totally opposed to the DRY. The people of Aden gave the DRY their unqualified support. They were non-tribal and hated the tribalism and religiosity of the North. Salih was seen by Adenis as Yemen's Saddam.

The announcement of the DRY took the North by surprise and prompted Salih to preserve unity at any cost. He became determined to inflict a total defeat on the South, and occupy Aden, which he did successfully in line with the three goals he set at the beginning of war.

As soon as he declared the new state, Al-Beidh left for Mukalla, where he stayed until the end of the war. Only Jiffri and Defence Minister Haytham Qasim Tahir remained in Aden. The other members of the government were either in Mukalla or abroad. It was not clear why Al-Beidh left for Mukalla and didn't remain in Aden with his comrades, but it was a logical choice because it became increasingly difficult to communicate with the rest of the South from Aden, and any shipment of weapons for the socialists would come into South Yemen through Mukalla.

Al-Beidh and some of the DRY leaders stayed in Mukalla until 2 July, when the Northern forces were on the outskirts of the city. They left at the request of the people and took Scud missiles with them on their way to Oman. Al-Beidh was granted asylum and nationality in Oman, which he lost when he decided to return to politics in 2009.

Mediation and Foreign Support

Arab support for the North or the South replicated the divisions of the 1990–91 Gulf War. Saudi Arabia and Kuwait were hostile to Salih because of his support for Iraq and hoped that by supporting the South, they would help to bring about his downfall. Oman, Bahrain, the United Arab Emirates, Syria, and Egypt were weary of Saddam Hussein and supported ceasefires on terms favourable to the South. Egypt may have been influenced by the South's claims that the North was exporting Islamic fighters.

The North was supported by Iraq and by those countries which were not on good terms with the Saudis, like Jordan, which was perceived to be pro-Saddam. The North was also supported by Sudan, which had a connection with Al-Zindani, one of Islah's leaders. Eritrea was returning a favour because Yemen had allowed its fighters to use Hunaish island as a base before it gained independence. It allowed Northern aircraft to operate from its territory.

When war seemed inevitable in April 1994, both sides were willing to accept mediation from Oman, Jordan, and Egypt. King Hussein invited Salih and Al-Beidh to Amman to sign the accord just before the outbreak of the war. Oman was keen to maintain stability on its western border, and Jordan needed to salvage its reputation in the Arab world after being portrayed as Saddam's ally. But when the Amman Accord and talks in Salalah failed, the mediation was left to Egypt and the Arab League. The North wanted to ensure there was no real intervention in a war that it was winning, and by now it wanted to occupy the South; it ostensibly agreed to the ceasefires proposed but had no intention of stopping fighting until its aim was achieved. Salih's clever manoeuvring and appeasement gave him time to complete his mission of defeating the Southern army and eliminating the YSP in its current form, eliminating the opposition. His strategic approach during the war was intended to eliminate his opponents while at the same time discussing peace with the United Nations, the Arab League, the French, the Egyptians, the British, Americans, and more. He skilfully and artificially constructed a number of ceasefires during the fighting to buy time and consolidate his position, and then he continued the hostilities.

Egypt focused its efforts on securing undertakings from both sides to avoid the use of force and to resume discussions based on the Amman Accord, but the efforts of its special envoy, Badr Hammam, were frustrated when hostilities began.

The Arab League tried to send mediation missions to both Sanaa and Aden, but the fighting aborted the mediation attempts. Egypt's proposal to send an Arab peacekeeping force was accepted by the South but rejected by the North.

America gave its support to the mediation efforts, stressing there was no military solution to Yemen's problems. The Americans believed that the North was responsible for the war. Kostiner summarised American's concerns: "The build-up of weaponry in both Yemens; the fears of Saudi Arabia and the

Gulf States about a triumph by the North; the strengthening of the Islamic fundamentalists evident in the YRG in North Yemen and the support of North Yemen from radical regional states."[18] The Americans supported the pro-Western coalition of Arab countries which emerged when Iraq invaded Kuwait, and they even threatened to recognise the DRY and impose sanctions on the North. Above all, the Americans were concerned about regional stability.

Like the United States, Britain supported the mediation attempts, but Western states did not get involved in the conflict. The British minister of state at the Foreign Office, Douglas Hogg, told *Al-Hayat* that the war was confined to Yemeni territory, did not endanger the Gulf states, and did not alarm the West. Russia's foreign minister, Andrei Kozyrev, urged both parties to settle their differences through dialogue as the Arab League had done, hoping through its mediation efforts to regain some of the international prestige it had lost.

It was easier for the South to influence Western diplomats and mediators. In the past, the South had more contact with the outside world as it was colonised by the British and later assisted by the Soviet Union. Westerners were used to dealing with Southerners, whereas Northerners were viewed through the lens of the tribal stereotype as disorganised and devious. In an interview with Reuters, a so-called expert said the North could not win the war because when Sanaa received four helicopters in the 1970s from the Saudis, within a week, one crashed on landing, two collided during take-off, and the fourth hit a building in Sanaa during a low-flying routine. Western observers didn't realise that Salih was a military man with tactical abilities and was a political manipulator, and the Northern regime he led had become much more sophisticated and much more ambitious about Yemen's place and his place in the international scene.

The Arab League's mediation was not successful because it focused on a ceasefire and resumption of negotiations rather than proposing any new initiatives. The North wanted the mediation to maintain the status quo and lead to the South's acceptance of the Republic of Yemen. The South accepted ceasefire proposals, but they were not followed up by any lasting guarantees. The mediators were concerned with restoring the prestige of the Arab League as a successful mediator because it had failed to mediate in the Kuwait–Iraq dispute in 1990–91. In trying to get the consensus of all Arab states for their proposals, they focused only on a ceasefire and subsequent negotiations.

When the war broke out, Saudi Arabia and some GCC states sided with the South and were reported to have sent money and arms to Aden. Many questions remained unanswered as to where such money was sent. It is likely that Saudi families of Hadhrami descent made private contributions to the South's war effort. The North received aid from Iraq in the form of training. The South captured several Iraqi pilots who fought with the North. It also purchased weapons and aircraft from its former allies in Eastern Europe.

The Saudis were not comfortable with a strong Yemeni state on their border and were concerned the Yemenis might claim the entire Asir zone south of the Hijaz. A client state in the South would weaken Salih, and that is why the Saudis did not officially oppose secession. The Saudis portrayed Salih as a little Saddam who had to be stopped, and they tried unsuccessfully to recreate the atmosphere of the Second Gulf War. They referred the Yemen issue to the UN Security Council, but UNSC No. 924 of 1 June condemned the war but proposed only to send a fact-finding mission to Yemen; it did nothing to stop the Northern army encroaching into the South as the Saudis had hoped. It made no reference to Yemeni unity, to the dismay of the North. The resolution was accepted by the South, and its leaders urged the

---

[18] Brian Whitaker, *The Birth of Modern Yemen*, e-book, 181–82, available on www.al.bab.com.

Arab states to recognise the DYR and bring the fighting to an end. The North opposed the resolution but adhered to the ceasefire declarations so it could reinforce its troops with Nasser's men.

On 4 June, GGC foreign ministers held an emergency meeting on Yemen and stressed that Yemeni unity could only continue by mutual consent and could not be imposed by military means, but the Gulf states did not recognise the DRY, and no soldiers were sent to fight alongside South Yemeni forces.

Another UN Security Council resolution (No. 931) was passed on 29 June allowing regional parties acceptable to both sides to help implement a ceasefire. Adopted unanimously, after recalling Resolution 924 (1994) on Yemen, it considered the findings of the fact-finding mission deployed to the country and demanded a ceasefire. The council supported the call of Secretary General Boutros Boutros-Ghali for an immediate cessation of the shelling in the city of Aden, condemning the failure of the parties to heed the call. It was also disturbed at the lack of a ceasefire despite several declarations by the Yemeni government and supporters of the Yemeni Socialist Party. Concern was expressed over the deteriorating situation in Yemen, in particular the humanitarian situation and the provision of arms and other materiel, whose immediate cessation it demanded. A ceasefire was then demanded, with emphasis on the importance of an effective ceasefire and its effective implementation. The resolution deplored the continuing military assault on Aden, calling for heavy weapons to be moved out of range of the city. The secretary general and his special envoy were requested to continue negotiations with both parties on the possible establishment of a mechanism that would monitor, encourage respect for, and help prevent violations of a ceasefire.

The council declared that political differences could not be resolved through the use of force. On the humanitarian situation, the secretary general was requested to use all resources to address those affected by the conflict and facilitate the distribution of humanitarian aid. Finally, the secretary general was required to report back to the Security Council within fifteen days of the adoption of the resolution, detailing progress made.

A UN Observer Force was expected to follow this resolution but became irrelevant when North Yemen occupied Aden. The resolution indicated that the United Nations now left foreign mediation and involvement in the war to the GCC/Damascus Declaration states.

The final mediation attempt took place on 4–6 July at a meeting of the Damascus Declaration States—the GCC states plus Egypt and Syria, which signed a security agreement to defend the Gulf states on 6 March 1991, after the second Gulf War when Iraqi invaded Kuwait. They reiterated that unity could not be forced but were unable to do anything to stop the fall of Aden on 7 July 1994.

The North made sure it took part in all peace negotiations and gave the appearance that it was amenable to negotiations. Salih was determined to crush the South, but his pretence to take the negotiations seriously was persuasive.

Pillage and Looting

Human Rights Watch reported that pillage and extensive destruction of property not justified by military necessity occurred during and after the war, primarily in Aden after government forces gained control of that last rebel-held city, but also in many other cities that changed hands during the war.

Looting after the 1994 war President Salih (insert) did little to stop it. Source: Qais Saeed.

Government soldiers and officers in Aden were observed by eyewitnesses in Aden to be engaging in extensive organised looting followed by pillaging; they also failed to stop the civilian looters. It was separatist officials, however, who began the looting of Aden in the final days of the war, no doubt sensing imminent defeat.

When the war was over, many Northern officials, foreigners, and others went or returned to Aden; those who arrived quickly observed looting by civilians and Northern forces. Observers estimated that 25–30 per cent of the looting was well organised and on a large scale; looters arrived in trucks and larger vehicles and loaded up equipment and machinery from the port and elsewhere, using cranes to lift the heavier pieces. Large numbers of vehicles were engaged in this effort even though there was a shortage of vehicles for the water emergency.

The property destruction seemed to target mainly the records, property, and institutions of the former PDRY, now technically the property of the Republic of Yemen. This destruction was tolerated and often authored by government forces.

There was also looting when towns changed hands. At Al-Ataq, centre of Shabwa governorate, for instance, only two hospital mattresses remained by the time civilian government officials arrived. All Lahj hospitals were looted and inoperable halfway through the war. In Mukalla, where there was no battle and no power vacuum, public offices, schools, and buildings were looted. Vacated homes elsewhere, such as in deserted villages and bombed buildings on the outskirts of Aden, were occasionally robbed of small items such as gold rings, but they did not suffer systematic looting. It was not always possible to know who was responsible for each incident, but the frequency of the looting indicated a failure to prevent looting, if not active encouragement of it. Pillage in Aden reached massive proportions in four waves between about 4 July and 14 July. The first stage was carried out by separatist political and military leaders as they prepared to escape the city. Many witnessed looting during the days before Aden fell; a journalist saw Southern soldiers and civilians looting private Northern businesses, including the large, luxury Gold Muhur Hotel, which was later re-looted by Northern forces.

Post-war Human Rights Violations and Arbitrary Arrest of YSP Members

It was claimed by international observers, including the United Nations, that following the defeat of the YSP military forces, hundreds of suspected political opponents were arbitrarily imprisoned by the state political security (Al-Amin Al-Siyasi) in detention centres and other secretive locations round the country. Islah's armed militia in its own capacity detained those whom they regarded as opponents and were accused of ill treatment of detained people. According to evidence available to Amnesty International, the torture and ill treatment of those in detention was widespread, and the authorities were criticised for inhuman treatment of prisoners. A report by Amnesty International stated,

> After the defeat of the Southern forces in early July 1994, hundreds of suspected political opponents, amongst them prisoners of conscience, were arbitrarily arrested and are currently being held in political security detention centres and other locations through out the Republic of Yemen without charge or trial. With very few exceptions they are being held incommunicado, without access to lawyers, family members and independent medical supervision.

The report by Amnesty expressed grave concern about human rights violations in Yemen by Northern forces and went on to say,

> According to information available to Amnesty International, the torture and ill-treatment of those detainees is widespread. In addition, many suspected political opponents, particularly in the Southern and Eastern provinces, have been detained by the armed militia of Islah which has carried out the function which should be exclusively performed by law enforcement officers.

Human rights organisations urged the Yemeni government to establish a commission of inquiry to carry out an independent investigation into all reports of ill treatment of prisoners, but no such commission was ever established. It was also reported that following the war, the regime carried out a campaign of selected political arrests against YSP members and sympathisers from both North and South Yemen. The persecution of the Southerners continued for years after the war and did not stop until the Houthi coup of 2014.

Yasmin Hassan, a woman activist who took part in demonstrations against the war, summed up the feelings and disillusionment of the people when the author spoke to her when writing *The Yemen Civil War 1994*:

> The war in Yemen was about political power, selfish leaders fighting for more power. The leadership were not concerned about the struggles of our people but were worried about their selfish pursuits for more influence. This war was not about us the people, but about them, the leaders. Instead of engaging in constructive discussions they decided to commit a crime against the nation. I am deeply angry and sad that we should allow something as drastic as this to happen to us time and time again.

The war left Yemen isolated from parts of the Arab world, particularly from their close, powerful neighbour Saudi Arabia. In addition it lost the sympathy and understanding of the international community. Salih had much work on his hands to try to heal the country following the bloody war and rebuild Yemen's international reputation. The YSP was almost destroyed, with most of its leaders and senior military officers scattered all over the world. The damage to the structure of the party was irreparable and its future insecure.

Following the 1994 war, the YSP lost much of its own relevance in Yemen and particularly in the South, where the Southern Transitional Council (STC) has, to some extent, absorbed many of its rank and file members. The YSP lost much of its power base as a consequence of losing the 1994 war, and in a sense, their biggest mistake was their own internal fighting throughout the late 1970s and 1980s. The YSP lost many of its own radical supporters into other party structures because they went into an unequal 1990 unification deal without thinking through the consequences of such unification.

The catastrophe of 1986 and the failed unification process, and its outcome in a military defeat, are the narrative of history many people in South Yemen are currently using to describe the YSP. When it comes to its leftist achievements in the South, current political narrative has forgotten the left's golden age that inspired the imagination of Yemeni and Arab intellectuals and was feared by the region and the international community—a golden age that brought in the family law, agricultural reforms, industrialisation, better education, and better healthcare.

The YSP is not remembered for the positive things it achieved in the South but rather for all its negativity and ruthless internal fighting. The YSP today suffers from the reality of the political fragmentation of the past, the cumulative outcome of the many mistakes made by its leadership, the complete ignorance of learning from the past and reorganising itself to meet the political needs of the new circumstances.

It is fair to note that the YSP structures have withered away while other party organs have significantly weakened and fractured, altering their historic place in South Yemen's political life with very low membership and very little influence in the ongoing conflict. Their membership has engaged with other political structures with very little attention to the leftist politics of the past and no clear political or economic direction, and as their political clout continues to decline, their popular base has been left vulnerable to polarisation by more effective and better mobilised and organised local power structures. The future of the YSP is bleak unless it can find new ways to reactivate itself as a party that stands for something in a conflict that is likely to bring about new power brokers.

CHAPTER 8:

Repression and Discrimination (1994–2011)

The military confrontation of 1994 left all Yemenis with the scars of the brutality of war, as well as bitterness, confusion, and frustration. Between 1994 and 2011, a new concept of unification was based on the force of the Northern political class and its dominance. The Northern regime ruled the country as victors of the war; the Southerners had no genuine representation in the power structure. In the South, this rule was seen by many Southerners as characterised by repression and discrimination. Before the 1994 war, Ali Salem Al-Beidh stated categorically that the South would not accept the position of the South being a branch while the North was the stem. But many Southern commentators thought that the 1994 war left a huge vacuum in the power structure and that the Northern regime would now take a tight political and economic grip of the South by filling this vacuum. The Northern leadership in the form of the GPC and Islah were now firmly established in power as the dominant force with no real competitor or partner from the South.

Katherine Zimmerman, in her report for www.criticalthreats.org, "Yemen's Southern Challenge: Background on the Rising Threat of Secessionism", pointed out that the war cost the Southern YSP its parliamentary veto, which allowed the GPC-Islah coalition to retreat on many reforms initiated by the South at unification. The new government amended nearly half of the original articles of the constitution and added twenty-nine new articles, including ones that allowed the president to appoint the prime minister and serve as head of the Supreme Judicial Council. This consolidated power within the Northern-dominated executive office.

The presidential council was abolished to further consolidate power in Salih's hands and to remove Al-Zindani, the guide of Islah, from a position of influence which he enjoyed as member of the council.

After the YSP suffered a humiliating defeat in the war, there were no obstacles to Salih restructuring the state as he wished. In the power-sharing formula, the YRR (Islah) replaced the YSP even though Salih was concerned about the growing power and influence of the Islamists.

Salih was aware that he had to make reconciliation with the Southerners a priority, and he talked big about reconstruction, pledging to remove any impact of the war from Aden by rebuilding, reconstituting the social services, and ordering the withdrawal of all military units from the city, leaving only the Central Security Forces and the police force to regulate daily life. These measures became symbolic gestures not followed by any real economic development in the South. Salih strengthened his link with the loyalists from the Southern region, particularly those who previously supported Ali Nasser in the past, but he did not pursue any genuine reconciliation with the Southerners, especially those he defeated in the war. By cleverly doing this, he created a wedge between those who came from Abyan governorate and those who had defeated them in the catastrophe of 1986.

But despite his sweet words, Salih knew that the YSP as a party was almost finished and, in its current structure, would cause him very few difficulties. It did not take long for the constitutional court to issue a decree calling for the confiscation of all property, equipment, and liquid assets that belonged to the YSP. Islah wanted to go further than Salih and openly believed that the YSP leaders should be tried for treason for initiating the war and threatening unity, but this was a bridge too far even for Salih. In his own cunning way, he asked the YSP to reconstruct itself, elect a new leadership to replace those defeated in the war, and open a dialogue with the GPC. The emasculated YSP agreed. It lost its military and security wing, and it was almost powerless to resist the president's demands. The new leaders condemned the war and the attempt by its former leaders to secede, and a long, hard, not serious dialogue with the GPC began, with the current YSP leaders concerned about their own welfare and demanding the return of seized YSP assets.

It was a sad demise for the YSP, established in 1978 as a single party which survived many upheavals and internal power struggles and strife in Yemen, the bitter and vicious cycles of political violence between its leaders, and conflicts over policy orientation, which significantly weakened its structures. Other issues also led to its collapse, including the demise of the Soviet Union and the negative relationship it had with regional Gulf neighbours. The YSP tried to save itself by pursuing a deadly and futile policy of unification as a way out of its own internal crisis, by being instrumental in achieving Yemeni unity with the establishment of multi-party democracy in the Republic of Yemen in May 1990. However, it did not have an alternative plan in place in case things went wrong, and it was absorbed into the new state as the weaker partner with limited influence.

Following the 1994 civil war, the party's infrastructure and resources were confiscated by the GPC government, and its cadres and members were no longer influential in the new power structure. The military defeat in 1994 was seen by many as the responsibility of the YSP. Following the war, it manoeuvred to boycott the 1997 election and was unable to nominate a candidate for the 1999 election, because any potential candidate required the backing of thirty-one MPs. In 2002, it was one of five parties which formed the Joint Meeting Parties opposition alliance. This further weakened its authority, with the Islah party becoming the dominant player. It returned to contest the election in 2003, received only 3.8 per cent of the popular vote, and won eight seats. The people in the South no longer saw the YSP as their core representative, and the GPC and Islah had established themselves throughout the country. The YSP has lost its influence and power; the emergence of the STC (see chapter 11) has included some of the YSP leaders, but the party itself is almost dead with very little chance for revival.

After the 1994 war, the army was finally merged by a command structure loyal to the president, mainly from those he had personally selected, and Southern military personnel were treated as a spent force. Most of those Southerners holding high ranks were made to retire or dismissed, and soldiers from the South were assigned to different branches of the army. Salih made sure those from the same tribe or province were not in the same brigade. Some fifty thousand Southerners in the army lost their jobs under the pretext that Salih was implementing austerity measures in line with the recommendations of international lending institutions. Sophisticated military equipment was purchased, and particular attention was paid to strengthening the elite Republican Guard later led by his own son, Ahmed Ali Abdulla Salih. President Salih wanted to build a big army of loyalists who could ensure his survival as president and the survival of the regime for many decades to come.

A special meeting was held in Aden on 12 July 1994 devoted to the restructuring of the army. Salih insisted that the army should not be involved in politics and stressed that under no circumstances would the formation of private armies or unofficial militias be allowed. The closure of Islah's training camps was announced. To further curb the influence of Islah, its educational institutions, which were used for teaching political ideology, were merged into the education system as earlier demanded by the YSP. The Political Security Office (PSO), whose raison d'être was to strengthen the position of the president, expanded its activities, which included creating dissention in opposition parties and engaging in dirty tricks such as assassinations, kidnapping, torture, and espionage. It is important to note that while Salih had to some extent completed his mission in the destruction of any Southern opposition, he still kept his eyes firmly open with regards to the Islamists and their future role under his leadership.

On the economic front, the Central Bank in Aden was closed, and the Yemeni dinar, the PDRY's currency, was withdrawn and replaced with the Yemeni riyal. The PDRY's airline, Al-Yamda, was merged with Yemeni airlines, Al-Yemenia. The patronage system of the North quickly crept into the South. Salih gave war rewards to Ali Nasser's followers who had by now built their own relationship with Salih independently from Ali Nasser; they were to be given prominent positions in state organisations. They felt that the shame of the defeat they had endured at the hands of Ismail's wing of the YSP in 1986 was now avenged, and they believed they owed this victory to the leadership of Salih. They did not see themselves as representatives of the South and became very obedient to the president. Salih did not want to see the establishment of an Islamic republic as demanded by Islah, and he used these Southerners who toed his line to counterbalance Islah. The Military Economic Establishment formed in the 1970s to involve the armed forces in development, which had its wings clipped by the YSP, was revived and renamed the Yemeni Economic Institution. It once again dominated state import-export activities and was a main source of revenue for Salih. He was also busy building his relationship with international backers as well as Yemeni local investors.

The Southern tribes were brought under the government's control by incorporation into the tribal-military-commercial complex of the North. Tribal conflicts were fomented, and arbitration under tribal law was encouraged to deplete the tribes' resources and make them dependent on the state for support and mediation.

The state also encouraged the creation of a new tribal leadership which controlled the tribes on behalf of the regime and was incorporated into the state's tribal-military, commercial complex. To further consolidate his power, Salih made sure that all the governors of the Southern governorates were GPC members. The sheikhs always maintained their own power bases, and the governors found themselves managing rather than controlling the sheikhs. Middle ranking, relatively honest sheikhs well connected to the people were vital to both the government and the top sheikhs for the implementation of government policies. But their power was curbed because they were not permitted to accumulate wealth and establish their own power bases. In some cases, tribal parochialism was replaced by nepotism and corruption. Key government posts were given to the president's relatives or persons loyal to him, mostly from the Sanhan and Hamdan tribes, which are part of the Hashid tribal confederation. Endless bargains were made between the regime and the leaders of individual groups; this prevented the emergence of strong interest group coalitions and a united opposition. Salih also made sure that Northern governors were appointed in the South, and some Southern governors were appointed in the North, a move that would strengthen unity under his command.

To give Salih's regime a veneer of democracy, the National Council for Opposition was formed. It was made up of seven opposition parties which dissented from their mother parties and replaced the genuine Supreme Coordination Council for the Opposition. The regime used this council to help secure foreign loans.

Ahmed Abdel-Karim Saif concluded in his thesis, "The GPC was established in the North at the beginning of the 1980s as an alternative to party politics. It was intended that local communities should elect regional committees and the whole would culminate in a national committee structure, which would reflect the will of the people. Very rapidly however, the system came to work from the top-down, through an elaborate system of patronage, opposite to the intended direction. The state became corrupt, turning into a family business. Power centres developed around the military family, which were strongly linked to the centre by interdependent interests."[19]

The state was effective in consolidating its political, military, and security control but was weak in providing services such as healthcare, education, social security, and so on. The rentier economy continued, with a large share of government revenues going to the army and security forces. The president engaged in excessive spending vital to the survival of the regime. Development targets were not met owing to a shortage of funds. A huge proportion of the Yemen state budget was spent on the military and security apparatus of the state, depriving the economy of vital income from oil to develop economic projects in the interest of the wider population. Salih saw the military as the critical factor in his own political survival.

The cost of the war

Robin Allen, writing in the *Financial Times* in April 1995, summarised the political post-war reality: "Hopes that national reconciliation after a bitter civil war might lead to economic and political stability are evaporating. Yemen may have a parliament, even a cabinet and ministers. But power is in the hands of the president and his family."

It appeared that by bombing Aden with great intensity, Salih expected to transform its people into loyal citizens. This never happened, and as the repression by the Northern regime escalated, the people turned against the government and frequently demonstrated against human rights violations, media censorship, and discriminatory employment policies which gave the top managerial posts to Northerners who also sequestered prime real estate on the coast.

As Brian Whitaker pointed out in *The Birth of Modern Yemen*,[20] there were wildly conflicting claims of the war's cost in human life. Soon after the war ended, Salih announced that 931 soldiers and civilians had been killed—a surprisingly low figure. A year later, however, he conferred posthumous medals on three thousand military "martyrs". If that was a more accurate reflection of casualties amongst troops on the victorious Northern side, an overall death toll in the region of eight to ten thousand sounds plausible, taking into account civilians killed by shelling or bombing. There are no authoritative figures, however, and several years after the conflict, a senior Northern politician continued to maintain that casualties had been remarkably low.

The financial cost of the war was officially estimated at over $10 billion. This was a very serious blow to an already hopeless economic situation. Those responsible for the bombing of Aden gave little thought, if any, to the economic consequences of rebuilding it. Aden never received the massive state cash injection Salih promised to heal the wounds of war. Today, the battle-hardened city bears the scars of numerous conflicts whose marks are etched on the walls of many buildings and in the hearts of its disheartened citizens. The Seera brewery, one of the few profitable industries in the city, was the only legal producer of alcohol in the entire Arabian peninsula. It became an obvious target for the Islamists

---

[19] Ahmed Abdel-Karim Saif, "The Politics of Survival and the Structure of Control in the Unified Yemen 1990–9", MA dissertation, Department of Politics, University of Exeter, September 1997.
[20] Whitaker, *Birth of Modern Yemen*, 207.

who eventually destroyed it despite plans put forward to convert into a soft drinks or vinegar plant or, if it remained a brewery, to close it each year during the month of Ramadan.

Human Rights Watch reported that the damage in Aden was estimated initially by the United Nations at US$100–200 million, according to Yemeni officials. Specific sites and property looted included the UNDP, UNHCR, and Ministry of Health/WHO offices; the Ministry of Justice; the public textile factory; the cigarette factory (80 per cent privately owned); the Seera brewery; the British, German, Italian, and Russian consulates; the offices of Elf Aquitaine and Canadian Occidental; the Chamber of Commerce; the offices of the Organisation for the Defence of Democratic Rights and Liberties (a nongovernmental human rights group); Mansoura Prison (including the carpentry workshop); the administrative offices and many large warehouses of the Domestic Trade Corporation (a large, state-owned trading company); all YSP and independent newspaper offices; the YSP headquarters; the Aden Movenpik Hotel; the Gold Muhur and other private and public sector hotels; all of Aden's museums; the city's sanitation trucks; vehicles from Yemeni and international institutions; and all the docking facilities and warehouses at the port. The hospitals where ICRC delegates were stationed throughout the conflict were not looted on the inside, but all ambulances and other objects in the hospital courtyards were taken.

Most of the smashing by Islamists of an estimated $7 million store of hard liquor taken from a government warehouse, and other liquor seized from private homes took place in front of news cameras near the Gold Muhur Hotel. The looting of the Aden Movenpik Hotel was far less thorough than of the Trade Corporation or Justice Ministry.

In addition to the looting, some of Ali Nasser's supporters on their own initiative reoccupied forty to sixty villas in which they had formerly resided, including luxury villas already rented to international organisations like Swedish Save the Children and foreign oil companies. Three judges were assigned to give priority to the property issues raised by these cases. Typical of the confusion in post-war Aden were official statements on the problem, each varying widely from the next: the minister of the interior claimed the police had the authority to evict the "Ali Nasser squatters" without a court order. Because of looting and destruction of Ministry of Justice property, the courts had not reopened. A foreign national employed by an oil company complained to the police that he had an order awarding the company possession of a villa for which it had paid rent, but the colonel occupying it since Aden had fallen would not move out, and no police or army official had the nerve to dislodge him. There was no evidence in late July 1994 of efforts to bring looters to justice as a means of complying with the duty to prevent and stop pillage.

After the war, Al-Beidh and the other leaders of the DRY fled to Oman. Salih charged them with various crimes, but he was eager to bring about reconciliation with the Southerners, and a general amnesty was soon declared for all sixteen DRY government members with the exception of Al-Beidh, Al-Attas, and Al-Jiffri. What remained of the PDRY regime had been destroyed, and Salih was keen to entice its former leaders back to Yemen, offer them government positions, and allow them to represent parts of the South as long as they did not challenge his leadership or idea of unity. He adapted his divide and rule tactics to the situation in the South with a great deal of success. Al-Beidh stayed in Oman until 2014, when his citizenship was revoked as he started engaging in political activities and called for the independence of the South. Now aged eighty-two, he is in Beirut, where he runs a television station allegedly financed by the Iranians.

The aftermath of the war witnessed the formation of a new government and presidential council. The YSP was allowed to operate under strict conditions as an opposition party, despite its official support for the president. Relations between the YSP and those in power were tenuous. Its members were frequently harassed, and its policies were closely monitored and scrutinised. The absence of many of its leading members damaged the party.

Continuing Human Rights Violations

In its report "Human Rights in Yemen During and After the 1994 War", Human Rights Watch stated that although a state of emergency was declared on 5 May 1994, the government's obligations under the International Covenant on Civil and Political Rights (ICCPR) were not suspended because the government failed to take the proper steps under the ICCPR.

Yemen violated the civil and political rights of its citizens during the conflict; in particular, it detained persons without charge and denied them access to legal counsel and families. After the conflict was over and the state of emergency was lifted on 27 July 1994, the government continued to detain several hundred people despite a general amnesty applicable to them. Furthermore, it carried out the death penalty on five common criminals and confirmed that penalty for nine others. Participants in a journalists' seminar after the war ended were arrested, beaten, and then released. Presses were vandalised during the conflict, making it difficult for the vibrant press to re-establish itself after the war; by October, even the functioning presses were warned by the government not to publish non-government newspapers.

After the war, the regime severely curtailed freedom of expression. Editors, including those of the YSP, were arrested. Some opposition newspapers had to close down. Human Rights Watch wrote,

> During the war most of the dozen Arabic newspapers regularly on the news stands closed down. Some were published on private printing presses such as the YSP press, which were looted or destroyed early in the conflict. After the war was over, several of the newspapers that were not aligned with the governing General People's Congress or its ally the Islah party opened up under new government-appointed editors who were stalwarts of the GPC or Islah.

Amnesty International reported that the authorities detained people solely on the basis of their region of origin or because of their perceived association with the YSP and its leadership. The propaganda campaign and attacks on the YSP and its exiled leaders was relentless. Anyone who attempted to argue reasonably was accused of being a secessionist (*infisali*). The victors used this kind of language of provocation to convince the population of their strength and their contempt for the losers, but more important, this was an attempt to make them the single legitimate source of authority.

The then minister of information, Mohamed Salem Ba-Sandwa, in an interview on 7 January 1995, claimed that it was unthinkable to allow individuals who fought with the *infisalis* or showed enthusiasm for secession to remain in their jobs. On 15 August 1994, Salih told *Al-Hayat* newspaper that socialists inside Yemen would be watched to ensure they were loyal to Yemen's unity.

In her presentation to an international Zoom conference organised by Friends of South Yemen (FOSY) in July 2020, lawyer, political activist, and journalist Linda Mohamed Ali Hussain said that the 1994 war led to the destruction of the South as a national and social entity. Its state, system, services, culture, identity, and history ceased to exist. Hussain summarised the destruction that took place:

1. The public health system and its free services provided to all Southern citizens were destroyed.
2. The free compulsory education system was destroyed, and widespread illiteracy ensued.
3. All institutional life was destroyed through the abolition of the administrative, judicial, and public prosecution system, which was replaced with the traditional tribal system based on sheikhs and families.
4. More than 150 government institutions, factories, services, and companies were destroyed,

and their assets were distributed amongst the Northern regime's leaders and supporters.

5. The Southern fisheries were destroyed through the distribution of the fishing grounds between the Northern tribal leaders (sheikhs) and the leaders of the Northern regime. Southern public companies were leased to foreign companies that engaged in illegal and unregulated fishing in violation of environmental laws and regulations. This led to the extinction of rare fish species.

6. The seizure of more than eighty agricultural and service cooperatives and state farms by the leaders of the regime and their supporters resulted in the unemployment of thousands of peasants and agricultural workers. A number of factories were also closed.

Tragic consequences for Southern citizens resulted due to the actions of the Northerners. Further repressive measures followed, namely:

1. The dismissal of more than two hundred thousand soldiers and officers from the army and security forces, including professionals such as pilots, engineers, doctors, and lawyers, who became unemployed. Many of them were nowhere near retirement age.

2. Compulsory layoffs of more than 170,000 administrative employees and skilled workers in ministries, departments, factories, companies, economic institutions, and judicial and representative agencies after their closure, as well as the acquisition of all the South's resources and assets by the Northern regime.

3. Replacing skilled Southern workers with Northern workers.

4. Prosecuting and abusing Southern merchants and agents and forcing them to surrender commercial enterprises to the Northern agencies, with the collusion of some influential politicians.

5. Enactment of discriminatory laws and regulations against Southerners which prevented them from taking advantage of educational opportunities in Yemeni universities, foreign scholarships, and military, security, and judicial colleges. Students in the North were favoured while Southerners were denied educational opportunities. Single-sex rather than co-ed schools were encouraged.

6. The destruction of all cultural monuments and the closing of theatres, cinemas, public libraries, museums, musical bands, theatre groups, and all forms of art, literature, music, and other creative endeavours. This was done mainly by the Afghan Arabs and Islah.

7. Ensuring the spreading of tribal culture and nurturing tribal wars and the culture of revenge in the South, in conjunction with the spread of arms and ammunition. Arms trading was under the control of influential Northern arms dealers in the military and security institutions. The creation of YSP party cells throughout the country had to some extent broken the bonds of a tribal structure. During the war, Al-Beidh appealed to tribal loyalties in his constituency to rescue him from the mess he was in, but this proved ineffective. Before him, other Southern leaders like Rubayi and Ali Nasser appealed to the tribes for help but were also unsuccessful. Salih was in the opposite position, and his appeal during the war led to unquestionable support from his tribe. The Yemeni state was often held hostage by the immense power of the tribes. The hijacking of Western oil workers, the inter-tribal fighting, and the illegal sale of military weapons bore witness to this power. Some political observers commented that the Yemeni state existed only in Sanaa and Aden while the tribes controlled their own areas.

8. Ali Abdullah Salih appointed his right-hand man, General Ali Mohsen Al-Ahmar, the current vice president, to organise and facilitate the entry of terrorist groups coming from Afghanistan. Their commanders were given high military ranks in the Yemeni army, and they were allowed to establish terrorist training camps in Abyan province with the aim of threatening the international community. These groups were used to carry out terrorist operations against Southern cadres and against influential Southern leaders and individuals. This clearly illustrates that the Northerners

did not see the South as part of their homeland but rather as a booty of war that they used for immoral and illegal purposes.

The Southern Opposition Movement

The departure of the YSP leadership and other political personalities from Yemen left a political vacuum at all levels of the state and army. This vacuum was quickly filled by forces loyal to Salih during the war. The YSP as a party was allowed to remain as an opposition party that was weak, demoralised, and lacking in confidence. YSP leaders within Yemen reorganised and elected a new politburo in July 1994. However, much of its influence had been destroyed in the war. Salih was elected by parliament on 1 October 1994 for a five-year term. However, he remained in office until 2012.

After the war, grievances remained high amongst the residents of the South. Accusations of corruption, nepotism, and electoral fraud were levelled against the new ruling party based in Sanaa, as well as a mishandling of the power-sharing arrangement agreed to by both parties in the 1990 unity deal.

Many in the South also felt that their land, home to much of the country's oil reserves and resources, was being exploited after the unity deal. Privately owned land was seized and distributed amongst people affiliated with the Sanaa government. Several hundred thousand military personnel and civil employees from the South were forced into early retirement and compensated with pensions below subsistence level. Although equally low living standards were prevalent throughout the whole of Yemen, many in the South felt that they were being intentionally targeted and dismissed from important posts, and they were being replaced with Northern officials affiliated with the new government. Aden also witnessed neglect both socially and economically, whilst new investments appeared to be focused instead on Sanaa.

Beyond the economic grievances, there were also cultural and social grievances. Many in the South long believed their history was distinct from that of their Northern neighbours. This became more evident after the 1990 unity. After 128 years of British rule, South Yemen was an independent state for 23 years. Despite the economic difficulty in its later years with the collapse of its main backer the Soviet Union, the socialist state prided itself on its free healthcare, education, and welfare system.

Many in Aden spoke foreign languages and had technical skills as a result of their state-sponsored education abroad enjoyed in the days of pre-unity South Yemen. Unlike the North, tribalism was looked upon with disdain and generally stamped out of everyday life in the South, which instead preferred the law and order of civil society passed on to them from British rule.

Post-1994 unity saw a gradual return of tribalism into Southern society. It was not uncommon for residents of the South to even refer to those from the North as *mutikhalifeen* (backward).

In May 2007, grieving pensioners who had not been paid for years began to organise small demonstrations and demand better rights and an end to the economic and political marginalisation of the South. As the protests spread throughout Aden and grew more popular, so too did the demands of those protesting. Eventually, calls were being made once again for the secession of the South and the re-establishment of South Yemen as an independent state. The government's response to these peaceful protests was heavy-handed, labelling the protestors as "apostates of the state" and using live ammunition to disperse the crowds.

The protest movement eventually gave birth to the Yemen's Southern Movement, or Al-Harakat Al-Janubiyya, an umbrella group for various Southern anti-government factions that traced their origins back to the 1994 civil war. The Southern Movement grew to consist of a loose coalition of groups seeking complete secession from the North. Their presence in the South was restricted, and their actions were limited to the organising of protests and marches across the South which were often met with deadly violence. To raise the former flag of South Yemen was considered a crime in Aden, although it was a common practice outside of the city, where government control was limited. From 2007, the Southern Movement's calls for the secession of the South and the re-establishment of an independent Southern state grew in strength across many parts of South Yemen, leading to an increase in tensions and often violent clashes.

In his thesis "Successful Separationists in a Unity Fan Society: Al-Hirak Al-Janubi Social Movement in the Republic of Yemen", Mohammed Garallah described Al-Harakat as having a mixed structure and organisation. "It has a charismatic centralized leadership and works in factions at the same time. It is called Al-Hirak (the moving*),* not Harakah (movement), which explains the kind of structure it contains. The Hirak is a loosely organised popular movement, internally diverse and fluid, that houses a number of important historical, regional and ideological trends. It consists of "various locally and regionally organised groups that loosely coordinate their activities, but often act independently. Therefore, it has many factions. Some factions agree on the end state and disagree on the means, other factions agree on the means but disagree on the end state, and some disagree on both the means and the end state."

Garallah went on to say, "Al-Hirak Al-Janubi is a set of individuals who lead and represent their tribal clans, previous political affiliation, and military position. It is divided between radicals who want separation and accept dialogue only under international supervision to reach an agreement with the government, and moderates who seek solutions to their people's grievances under the unity umbrella. In turn, the radicals are divided between extreme radicals who call for armed resistance, and others who call for peaceful resistance like demonstrations and civil disobedience. The most extreme and strongest faction is led by retired military officers who know nothing but fighting and are supported by Ali Salem Al-Beidh. Other factions that ask for civil disobedience are led by Abu Baker Al Attas, Ali Naser Mohammed, Hassan Baum, and Mohammed Ali Ahmed. The current leadership of the YSP is less extreme and demands solutions to the Southern people's grievances under a united government."

Al-Hirak factions vertically and horizontally intersect with each other on their goals, leaders, and active members. They move like thick water from side-to-side, joining one another at times, and leaving one faction to join another at other times, according to situations, resources, and leadership." Garallah identified the following groups in Al-Hirak's network structure:

1. *The Supreme Council of the Peaceful Movement for the Liberation of the South (Al-Majlis Al-A'La Lilhirak Al-Selmi Letahrir Al-Janub)*
The Supreme Council of the Peaceful Movement for the Liberation of the South (Al-Majlis Al-a'la Lilhirak Al-Selmi Letahrir Al-Janub) is the largest component of Al-Hirak and was established in May 2009. It is very popular in all the provinces of the South, and its leaders have political and social weight in the South, as well as at home and abroad. It depends on businessmen from Gulf countries and some expatriates for financial support, as well as international funding indirectly and non-exposed. It is predominantly led by Ali Salem Al-Beidh from exile, and Hassan Baum in Yemen, and relies upon other sub-leaders like Salah Alshunfura, Abdullah Mahdi, Ali al-Saadi, Qasim Aldaara, Saleh Abdel Haq, Ali Al-Bishi, and Nasser Al-Tawil. This faction has variations, significantly between those who embrace independence and separation as well as disengagement from the North and who consider the South an occupied territory. The most prominent leader of this trend, Hassan Baum, is also the most popular and most influential. Others are calling for the federal system (two regions within the framework of the federal state) for the people of the South with the option of a referendum for free self-determination. Among those who embrace the federal system are the first unity government prime minister Haidar Abu Bakr Al-Attas and the former President of the South, Ali Nasser Mohammed. However, both seem to be more independent in their actions from this faction, and also have independent supporters.

2. *National Council of Al-Hirak: The National Council to Return the National Nation (Al-Majlis Al-Watani listi'Adat Dawlat Al-Janub)*

The National Council to Return the National Nation, led by Abdul Hamid Shukri and Amin Saleh, was strong at the grassroots level. However, currently most of its leaders have joined Ali Salem Al-Beidh's faction, which has weakened it significantly.

3. *The National Commission for the Southern Movement and the Retired Military Officers Committee (Almajlis Alwatni Lelhirak Al- Janubi and Jamiat al-Mutaga'Idin al-Janubiien)*

Although Brigadier Nasser Al-Nuba and Brigadier General (retired) Nasser Al-Tawil established (within the Retired Military Officers Committee) the roots of Al-Hirak, this faction has become one of the weakest components, as it is confined to some events in the province of Shabwa and Ad Dali', with some activities in the governorates of Abyan and Hadhramaut.

4. *Youth and Student Movement (Harakat Al-Shabab Waltullab Al-Janubiin)*

The Youth and Student Movement exists mainly in the province of Aden, but is also present in almost all Southern governorates. It is led by Fadi Hassan Baum, Ali Abdulrab, and Abdel Fattah al-Rubaie. This movement was intended to contain youth anger through some activities, media presence, and good communication via social networking sites.

5. *South Youth Federation (Ittihad Shabab Al-Janub)*

The South Youth Federation is one of Al-Hirak Al-Janubi's weakest factions. Its leaders, Ali Al-Saiia, Wajdi Shu'Aybi and Anwar Ismail, broke away from the Al-Beidh movement. It is characterised by its adoption of the establishment of the so-called State of South Arabia.

6. *The Movement of the People of the South (Southern Democratic Congress Tajj) (Harakat Tajj)*

Tajj was established and officially announced in July 2004. Jalab 'Ubadi was the exiled leader of the Tajj, and Saleh Al-Yafi' was his deputy and local leader. So far this faction exists only in the media, and does not have a presence in the field. This movement had strong ties with the Supreme Council of the Peaceful Movement for the Liberation of the South; however, in the first week of May 2013, the Tajj leadership met in Cairo to discuss changing its activities, according to the new leadership's affiliation and situations on the ground.

7. *The Movement for Self-Determination HATAM (Haraka Taqreer Al-Maseer)*

HATAM is one of the oldest faction of the Southern Movement, beginning in 1994 as a result of the civil war. It targets security checkpoints, some security institutions, and assassinations of military officers. Ali Salem Al-Beidh adopted the movement recently, along with its leaders Shaikh Hassan Banan, and Abdulfattah Al-Rubai'i, who are affiliated with the Supreme Council and Ali Salem. HATAM is considered to be the symbol of the Southern revolution against what is called the Yemeni occupation. It is adamant the northern occupiers must be kicked out of the south.

Zimmerman wrote that at its inception in 2007, the Southern Movement lacked clear leadership or organisation, instead drawing guidance from local elites. After it gained momentum, two voices—those of Al-Beidh and Tariq al Fadhli—have dominated the organisation. Al-Beidh lived in exile, first in Oman, then in Germany, and later in Lebanon, having fled Yemen after leading the 1994 secession efforts. He and Haider Abu Bakr Al Attas (prime minister, 1990–94) voiced support for the movement from their respective homes in exile. Yemen's extradition requests for the two showed the threat the pair posed to the regime; Yemen had security and cooperation treaties with both Oman and Saudi Arabia. On 21 May 2009, the eve of the anniversary of the unification of Yemen, Al-Beidh declared himself the leader of the separatists in the South. He has since continued to issue statements of support for the Southern Movement from exile as well as regularly addressing crowds in the South via telephone. Al-Beidh, following his two critical mistakes—in the formation of a failed unity experiment in 1990 and later in his failure to win the war—made him politically redundant, and others are now preparing to lead the South into a new path. Some in the South actually blame him for all the difficulties faced by the South and demand that he apologise for his role in undermining the Southern state

While Al-Beidh dominated the international voice of the Southern Movement and served as its nominal leader throughout the 1990s, Tariq Al-Fadhli, an Islamist and a former *mujahideen* soldier, emerged as one of the dominant leaders inside Yemen. A veteran *mujahid* who had fought in Afghanistan against the Soviets, he was a controversial leader for the more secular South because of his former ties to Osama bin Laden; he had a degree of local credibility, however, because his father was a former sultan in the Southern Abyan province. Al-Fadhli's family lost most of its land to PDRY nationalisation prior to the 1990 unification, much of which he recovered by supporting Salih during the 1994 civil war. He defected from the government in early spring 2009 and openly called for separation from the North during a 27 April rally in Abyan province. Al-Fadhli controlled militia forces in Abyan province, and officials noted that many of those participating in violent attacks against government troops were affiliated with him.

The government accused Al-Fadhli of supporting an assassination attempt on Nasir Mansour Hadi, the head of Yemen's political security body and the brother of the vice president. Al-Fadhli's position as a leader and his command over one militant faction of the Southern Movement led the government to ask the former Salih ally to surrender or leave the country. Some commentators claim that his relationship with Ali Mohsin was strong and cemented by the former's marriage to his sister, therefore forming a family alliance. Al-Fadhli was a politically ambitious man but lacked the credibility to gain any support from the wider Southern population. He quickly withered away and became an irrelevant political factor in wider Yemeni politics.

During 2009, the Hirak movement demanded more attention from Sanaa as anti-government demonstrations became a regular occurrence and factions within the movement became more militant. The secession issue resurfaced in 2007 when retired former Southern military officers demanded the reinstatement of their pensions and other Southerners began to voice concerns over political and economic exclusion. Salih was advised by those close to him to deal with these simple grievances made by the retired officers, but he continued to ignore them with the view that they would simply disappear into thin air and that his own strategy would eventually work. Salih disliked any opposition that targeted him personally, and because of those loyal supporters around him, who continued to say "Yes, Fendum (Sir)" to everything he wanted, he believed that he was a supreme leader who could do no wrong. This emboldened his dictatorship. The Hirak movement continued to grow. March and April 2008 witnessed multiple riots in Dhale and Radfan provinces in the South, during which tens of thousands of protestors demonstrated and set fire to police stations and army property. Prior to this, violent demonstrations were anomalies—the Southern Movement had used peaceful means to protest against the regime, and only after the regime used increasingly repressive tactics did supporters call for an armed revolution. The government further added to the secessionists' anger when, in April 2009, it instituted new security checkpoints in problem areas in preparation for a secessionist rally commemorating the fifteenth anniversary of the start of the civil war.

Tensions escalated over the summer as the government established a special court to prosecute members of the press for inciting sedition, arrested over five hundred Southern elite people, and continued to clash with protestors. A major rally held on 23 July 2009 in Zinjibar, the capital of Abyan province, resulted in the death of at least sixteen people after security forces tried to disperse the angry crowd. Additional fighting occurred along the roads into Zinjibar when security forces tried to prevent armed men from the village of Yafaa from joining the demonstration. Separatists still managed to shell local police headquarters and other government buildings despite the increased security in the area. In addition to mass demonstrations, the separatists carried out attacks on government targets, killing four soldiers in an ambush in Abyan province five days after the Zinjibar rally and bombing the GPC's office building in Zinjibar.

The key figures in the Southern movement's leadership became clearer in the early 2000s owing to two important events. In December 2001, a group of Southern political, economic, and tribal leaders chaired by Ali Al-Qufaish sent a letter to Salih detailing a list of region-specific grievances under the name of the Public Forum for the Sons of the Southern and Eastern Provinces.

When Salih failed to respond, the group published the letter publicly, triggering a series of campaigns against Salih, who demonstrated to Southern Yemenis his unwillingness to seriously respond to Southern complaints. In May 2007, a group of Southern military officers began holding weekly protests in the cities and towns of the South, demanding better compensation for their forced retirements after the 1994 civil war; amongst them was Nasir Ali Al-Nuba, leader of the Coordinating Committee for Southern Military Retirees. Nuba was one of a far larger group of former PDRY officials and military officers who, when disenfranchised after the 1994 civil war and the following efforts by former North Yemen to dominate and marginalise the South, formed the base of the Southern Hirak movement and, later, the Southern Transition Council (STC) itself, which was set up in 2017 (see chapter 11).

Another opposition party was the National Opposition Front (Mowj). Within three months after the end of the war, the defeated Southern leaders appeared to be retreating from separatism and threats of imminent guerrilla war and pledged to continue their struggle against Northern domination. This was a project set up and established in London in the late 1990s, and it was extremely effective in getting a number of motions from the UK parliament and later a resolution from the European Union. After lobbying by Mowj, Jeremy Corbyn tabled the following Early Day Motion on 13 November 1997 as recorded by Hansard

> That this House expresses concern at the increasing number of human rights violations in the Republic of Yemen despite the recent extensive reports calling for an end to human rights abuses in that country by Amnesty International, the United States State Department, Human Rights Watch and other non-governmental organisations; notes with concern that the recent wave of arrests of activists from opposition parties, including doctors, lawyers, poets and others, is continuing despite international condemnation; regrets that these arrests were in violation of the law of the land and the Yemeni constitution; is gravely alarmed at reports that some detainees have been tortured; deplores the Yemeni authorities' attempts to suppress press freedom by banning the publication of the newspaper *al-Haqiqa*; and urges the Government to exert pressure on the Yemeni authorities to abide by United Nations Resolutions 924 and 931, the recent European Parliament Resolution on Yemen and the undertaking given by the government of Yemen to the Security General of the United Nations on 7 July 1994 to safeguard fundamental human rights and seek national reconciliation, with particular reference to the Yemeni Civil War of 1994.

Corbyn tabled another motion on 16 June 1998 as documented by Hansard:

> That this House is deeply concerned about increasing violence in the Republic of Yemen, particularly recent incidents in the provinces of Dhala, Mukalla, Abyan and other places; notes that violence, hostage taking, bombings and increasing poverty will only bring further instability and deteriorating economic conditions to the country; appeals to the President to initiate a process for political dialogue with peaceful, popular and democratic opposition groups in order that a comprehensive national reconciliation can be achieved; urges him to set up a balanced political structure which includes systems of local government and an independent judiciary; and further urges him to recognise that only through these measures will peace, stability and national unity in the Republic of Yemen be attained.

Veteran Labour MP Stan Newens, who was also a member of the European Parliament from 1984 to 1999, was instrumental in parliament passing a number of resolutions on Yemen.

Because of its successful lobbying, the office of Mowj in London was seen by Salih and Ali Mohsin as a danger to the regime's relations with the international community. Seven of the former leaders of the South, led by Abd Al-Rahman Al-Jiffri, moved to London, where they set up Mowj, whose declared aim was confronting "the forces of hegemony, tyranny and authoritarianism in Sanaa". Mowj issued a 1,200-word document which did not talk about a separate state. It pledged to work for national unity based on the Document of Pledge and Accord. Jiffri did not totally rule out an armed struggle but said Mowj would seek to achieve its aims through dialogue. He was convinced that Yemen's growing economic and social problems and pressure from foreign governments would eventually force Salih to talk to Mowj. This never happened. The Southerners appeared to have little faith in pre-war leaders who did not have the political skills, cunning, and negotiation skills of their Northern counterparts. Without an army, there was little prospect of the emergence of an independent Southern state once again.

Mowj made effective gains in the international sphere, but Jifri was very careful not to upset the Saudis through his publications, which included the English-language monthly newspaper *The Yemen Observer*. The Yemeni government became concerned by Mowj's professionally produced publications and press statements, and a deal was made by Salih with the Saudis to wind up the movement. The Saudis stopped paying the salaries of large numbers of Southerners who supported Jiffri, and his confiscated properties and land were given back to him. Mowj suddenly ceased all its activities in 2000 in the wake of the Saudi-Yemeni border agreement (which included a clause prohibiting interference in each other's internal affairs). A statement on the group's website praised President Salih for "his ability and political will to address the urgent internal issues" and announced the suspension of opposition activity "so that we can all effectively contribute to national and regional stability and cement by our combined efforts the principle of regional partnership laid down in the Jeddah border agreement between the Republic of Yemen and the Kingdom of Saudi Arabia".

Repression of the Southern Movement

When Aden fell in 1994, the war against the South began. In the seventy-three-page report "In the Name of Unity: The Yemeni Government's Brutal Response to Southern Movement Protests", Human Rights Watch documented attacks by security forces on supporters of the Southern Movement as well as on journalists, academics, and other opinion-makers. Based on over eighty interviews with victims in Aden and Mukalla, the report found that security forces used lethal force against unarmed demonstrators on at least six occasions. Throughout 2009, the authorities arbitrarily arrested thousands of people for exercising their right to peaceful assembly, suspended independent media critical of government policies, and detained journalists and writers on spurious charges. "Yemeni authorities are violating basic rights in the name of maintaining national unity," said Joe Stork, deputy director of Human Rights Watch's Middle East division. "Southern Yemenis should have the right to peacefully assemble and express their opinions, even on critical issues like secession."

Protests in 2007, initially led by retired military officers calling for increased pensions or reinstatement, quickly grew to encompass demands for more jobs, less corruption, and a greater share of oil revenues. Subsequently, the protests were led by the Southern Movement, whose demands escalated to include secession and formation of an independent state. On six occasions during 2008 and 2009, Human Rights Watch found in its investigation, security forces opened fire on unarmed protestors, often without warning, aiming at them from short range. At least eleven people were killed, and dozens were wounded.

The Southern Movement was avowedly peaceful, though many civilians in the South had weapons. From July 2009 there were more reports of protesters bringing weapons to demonstrations. Following a Southern Movement protest on 23 July in Zinjibar, Abyan province, armed guards of Shaikh Al-Fadhli fought a pitched gun battle with security forces some distance from the protest site, in which at least twelve died and eighteen were wounded.

The Southern protests were often planned on days of historical significance, such as the anniversary of independence from Britain in 1967. In its report, Human Rights Watch documented arbitrary arrests of scores of people, including children, before or during the protests. Some of those arrested were peaceful participants, whereas others were simply passers-by. Although the authorities released most within a matter of days, suspected protest leaders were held for longer periods, resulting in subsequent demonstrations demanding their release, which led to fresh police violence.

Demonstrators holding pictures of Ali Salem Al-Beidh call for secession. Source: Qais Saeed.

In a campaign that appeared to escalate in May 2009, Yemeni authorities suspended newspapers, attacked media offices, and arrested (and in some cases charged and tried) journalists, apparently for expressing their views peacefully.

The information minister, Hasan Al-Luzi, suspended distribution of eight newspapers in May. By July some, but not all, were allowed to resume publication. On 12 May, security forces fought an hour-long gun battle with guards at the Aden compound of *Al-Ayyam*, Yemen's oldest and largest-circulation independent newspaper, killing one bystander and severely wounding another.

Gha'id Nasr Ali, the Radfan correspondent for *Al-Shari'* and *Al-Thawri* newspapers, was arrested in April 2008 and again in January 2009 over coverage of protests. In May and again in July, security forces prevented Al Jazeera satellite television station correspondents in Aden from leaving their hotel rooms to cover protests. The authorities also arrested website editors and writers covering protests.

Trials began in 2009 against a few dissidents and opinion-makers, based on charges that criminalised free expression. Qasim 'Askar, a former ambassador of the South Yemeni state, was put on trial for "threatening national unity", as was Husain 'Aqil, an Aden university professor and Southern Movement spokesperson. Salah al-Saqladi, a website editor, went on trial in mid-November on charges of "insulting the president", "stirring up strife and inciting against unity", "being in contact with secessionists abroad", and "incitement of violence". In July, a court of first instance in Qubaita, Lahj province, sentenced the local *Al-Ayyam* correspondent, Anis Mansur, to fourteen months in prison for his coverage of Southern protests.

"Yemen's reputation as a country where one can freely speak one's mind is being badly damaged," said Stork. "The government's attacks on the media and journalists are unprecedented and herald a dark chapter of state repression if they continue."

A grave human rights crisis was unfolding in Southern Yemen. The protests escalated, and by 2008 many Southern Yemenis were demanding secession and the restoration of an independent Southern Yemeni state.

The security forces, and central security in particular, carried out widespread abuses in the South—unlawful killings, arbitrary detentions, beatings, crackdowns on freedom of assembly and speech, arrests of journalists, and more. These abuses created a climate of fear but also increased bitterness and alienation amongst Southerners, who said the North economically exploited and politically marginalized them. The security forces enjoyed impunity for unlawful attacks against Southerners, increasing pro-secessionist sentiments which plunged the country into an escalating spiral of repression, protests, and more repression.

While the government publicly claimed to be willing to listen to Southern grievances, its security forces responded to protests by using lethal force against largely peaceful protestors without cause or warning, in violation of international standards on the use of lethal force. Protestors occasionally behaved violently, burning cars or throwing rocks, usually in response to police violence.

At the six protests investigated in depth by Human Rights Watch, Yemeni security forces violated almost every aspect of international standards. During a 15 April protest in Habilain, Central Security riot police, without warning or provocation, fired automatic weapons directly at protestors, wounding one man in the foot. During a 21 May protest in Aden, security forces on several different occasions opened fire without warning or provocation, wounding twenty-three protestors including Nasr Hamuzaiba, a former army officer and Southern Movement activist. Protestors responded by throwing rocks at the security forces, who again responded with deadly force.

The security forces made it increasingly difficult for wounded persons to obtain medical care by ordering public hospitals not to treat persons wounded at protests, stationing officers from the Political Security Organisation (PSO) and other security agencies at hospitals, and even carrying out attacks inside hospitals or seizing wounded patients from their beds. Such actions gravely endangered the lives of wounded persons, many of them unlawfully shot by the security services. Two days after he had been hospitalised, security officials arrested a fifteen-year-old student, who was shot through the ankle with a live bullet during the 21 May 2009 protests, from his hospital bed. Guards at the Shu'aibi public hospital in al-Dhali' governorate refused to let protestors wounded at the 4 July 2008 protest enter the hospital, forcing them to seek out private treatment.

There were also at least two incidents involving clashes between groups of armed men and the security forces, following which the Yemeni authorities accused the Southern Movement of harbouring terrorists. Armed clashes in the Ahmarain mountains around Habilain some one hundred kilometres north-east of Aden in late April and early May 2009 left several soldiers dead and civilians wounded. In July 2009, a clash between followers of Al-Fadhli and security forces in Zinjibar, the capital of Abyan province, left at least twelve persons dead in the wake of a "festival" promoting Southern demands.

Furthermore, on two occasions in July, Southerners attacked Northern shopkeepers living in Southern Yemen. In the worst such attack, three Northern shopkeepers were abducted, and two of them were killed in Radfan district in July 2009. Vigilante violence by supporters of a united Yemen also appeared to be increasing: the central government helped establish Committees to Protect Unity. Groups of pro-unity supporters, some of them armed, carried out armed attacks on suspected Southern activists.

Although still exceptional—and contrary to the stated peaceful orientation and conduct of the bulk of the Southern Movement—these attacks by Southerners underlined the combustible nature of the situation. The armed clashes showed the potential for armed conflict throughout the South and appeared to be indicative of elements that sympathised with the goals of the Southern Movement but were also prepared to pursue them by violent means.

Yemeni prosecutors have charged only a few detained leaders and put them on trial. In April 2008, security forces arrested twelve leaders of the Southern Movement and detained them until President Salih amnestied them in September. The leaders included Ahmad bin Farid, Ali al-Gharib, Yahya Ghalib al-Shu'aibi, Hasan Ba'um, and Ali Munassar, amongst others. They spent six months at the Political Security Organisation's (PSO) prison in underground cells and were later prosecuted on vague and politicised charges of "acting against national unity", "fomenting secession" or incitement. Many Southern Movement leaders hid in the mountains to escape arbitrary detention and political charges.

In 2009, the authorities continued to rely on specious politicised charges against Southern Movement leaders. In April, they arrested Qasim al-Askar Jubran, former ambassador of the PDRY to Mauritania, charging him with "threatening national unity and inciting a fight against the authorities". Jubran was transferred to Sanaa's PSO prison and put on trial based on evidence of "speeches, documents, a handout titled 'Project on the Vision of Peaceful Struggle Movement for the Southern Issue & Future of South Yemen's People', and a document of affiliation with the Supreme National Council for Liberating and Restoring State of South Yemen."

The government imposed unwritten "red lines" in an effort to ensure that the media exercised self-censorship. These were generally understood by journalists to include a ban on publishing interviews with exiled Southern politicians or Southern Movement leaders, publishing pictures of the violence committed by the security agencies against demonstrators, or even mentioning the formal names of the organisations behind the protests.

Yemeni authorities arrested popular bloggers Salah al-Saqladi and Fu'ad Rashid. Saudi secret police arrested Yemenis blogging from Jeddah for websites featuring news about the Southern Movement, and secretly rendered Ali Shayif to Yemen in May or June 2009. Academics were also not free to express their opinion. Security forces arrested Professor Husain 'Aqil after he wrote in the press and lectured about economic injustices faced by the South; 'Aqil was a professor of economic geography at Aden's university. Human Rights Watch also detailed four other cases of harassment and detention of academics who spoke out against what they perceived as repression by the Northern central government.

Despite the host of repressive measures and their wide application, calls by Southerners for their reinstatement into the army and civil service, higher pensions, an end to corruption, and a fairer share of Yemen's national wealth—especially oil revenues—continued unabated.

Human Rights Watch noted that international attention on Yemen, one of the poorest Arab states, was more focused on two other challenges. In August 2009, the five-year-old episodic war with rebels from the Houthi movement in the North flared again, leading to more deaths and displacement, and 2009 also saw increased activity by Al Qaeda in Yemen. The human rights crisis in the South was largely ignored.

On 10 January 2010, a general strike organised by the Hirak movement paralysed the Southern provinces of Dhale, Lahaj, Shabwa, and Abyan. The Southerners came out in the streets calling for independence and waving the South Yemen flag. The strike was called by the Southern Movement as another protest against the Northern regime's domination of the South. Salih was concerned about the level of opposition activity in the South but remained confident that it could be crushed by his military and security forces.

The deteriorating situation described in great detail by Human Rights Watch continued until the Houthi coup of 2014. The Southern Movement continued to enjoy popular support and hosted regular anti-government demonstrations, but its voice was not heeded by the Yemeni government, regional powers, or the international community.

Politics, Economics, and Elections

After the 1994 war, Salih had to form a government which had to be seen to represent the whole of Yemen. The socialists who dominated the South were replaced with ex-YSP members, many of them supporters of Nasser. Four of them were given ministerial posts as members of the GPC, which they joined after leaving the YSP. Abdroba Mansur Hadi was appointed vice president. Despite its support from Salih, Islah got only three extra cabinet places and the education portfolio, which was very important to them. Salih hoped that involving Islah in government would encourage the party to moderate its policies. If they were excluded, they would undoubtedly become more extreme.

Salih made an attempt to combat terrorism by adopting tough law-and-order measures. This was done partly to appease and enhance relations with other Arab countries such as Egypt that were affected by Islamist violence. Johannes Weinrich, allegedly an associate of Carlos the Jackal, was extradited to Germany.

Salih also tried to combat institutionalised corruption, but his efforts were not very successful. He used to drive incognito along the Aden-Sanaa road to see for himself how bribes were taken at roadside checkpoints. He also visited government offices to check on absenteeism and would lock empty rooms and take away the key. A number of civil servants were suspended, and some military officers were demoted, but these widely publicised gestures did little to change the culture of corruption which continues to plague Yemen and hinder its development. The duplication of civil service jobs was brought to an end with massive redundancies, mostly in the South.

Before the 1997 elections, the Law on Political Parties was implemented. Members of the armed forces were banned from party membership, and army officers were shown on television handing over their party membership cards to Salih. With the demise of the YSP, Salih felt he was able to implement the bill for democratic local government published in 1996. He no longer feared the YSP could use it to bring about secession through the back door.

In *The Birth of Modern Yemen*, Brian Whitaker writes,

> The 1997 parliamentary election, which produced an overwhelming majority for the GPC, took place on schedule—four years to the day since Yemen's first multi-party election. Despite a number of violent incidents, this time the election was better prepared and organised. Voting procedures were much improved, especially in the use of party symbols to help illiterate voters. The process was closely watched by international monitors, candidates' representatives and thousands of trained Yemeni observers. After the controversy surrounding Yemeni observers in 1993, this time they carried out their tasks with government blessing. Perhaps because of the larger number of observers, many irregularities were reported on election day, though most were relatively minor—the result of administrative errors rather than conspiracies.[21]

The Washington-based National Democratic Institute described them as "a positive step in the democratic development of Yemen" but said the validity or otherwise of the results was a matter for Yemenis themselves.

---

[21] Mohammed Garallah, "Successful Separationists in a Unity Fan Society: Al-Hirak Al-Janubi Social Movement in the Republic of Yemen", Thesis, Naval Postgraduate School, Monterey, California, 2013, 37–45.

The GPC won 187 of the 301 seats (64 more than in 1993). Its only significant rival, Islah, won fifty-three; five seats went to Nasserist (supporters of Jamal Abdul Nasser's concept of Arab unity) and Ba'athist parties, and fifty-four went to candidates described as independent. The GPC's margin of victory was greater than it at first appeared because thirty-nine "independents" later declared their support for the party (as well as six for Islah).

The main opposition parties—the YSP, the Yemeni Unionist Aggregation, the Union of Popular Forces, and the Sons of Yemen League—boycotted the elections, citing irregularities. With a comfortable majority, Salih ended his coalition with Islah. Sheikh Al-Ahmar, who was close to the Saudis, did well and this paved the way for a rapprochement with the kingdom. Salih was keen to see Yemeni workers return to Saudi Arabia after they were expelled for Yemen's support of Iraq during the invasion of Kuwait in 1990–91. He also wanted to secure Saudi financial assistance for Yemen and resolve the long-standing border dispute.

Faraj Ben-Ghanim, an economist and professional technocrat, was asked to form the new government. Islah's power was curbed by the appointment of the secretary general of Al-Haq as minister of Awqaf (religious endowments). The Al-Haq party is a supporter of the Zaidi tendency, an offshoot of Shia Islam, whereas Islah is a fundamentalist Sunni party.

Ben-Ghanim needed all his skills as an economist to tackle the country's problems, characterised by a chronic deficit in the balance of payments, a continuing deficit in government spending, and a mounting foreign debt. By the end of 1995, the official foreign debt was around $10 billion, including debts of $3–4 billion owed to the former Eastern bloc. Foreign aid was resumed, but not at the high level that prevailed in the 1980s. Unemployment was also a major problem with between 40 and 50 per cent of the labour force either unemployed or underemployed.

After the 1997 elections, Salih began the creation of an upper house of parliament and appointed fifty-nine members to the new Consultative Council, a body intended, according to the constitution, to "broaden the base of participation". In an attempt to make peace with the press, Abd al-Aziz al-Saqqaf, publisher of the *Yemen Times*, who had been arrested several times since the war for his journalistic activities, was appointed. Sheikh Tariq Al-Fadli from Abyan, who had been suspected of organising the "Afghan" guerrillas responsible for the 1992 Aden hotel bombings and attacks on the YSP, was also included in a move calculated to pacify him and keep him on the side of the establishment.

The first direct presidential election, held in September 1999, was a farcical affair in which President Salih's only challenger was an obscure member of his own party, Najib Qahtan Al-Shabbi, standing as an "independent". Al-Shabbi was the eldest son of a former president of South Yemen who had joined the GPC after unification and became a member of parliament.

Yemeni democracy was not without its problems. There was little understanding of the nature of the opposition which was often equated with rejectionism—boycotting elections and trying to destabilise the government. The National Democratic Institute noted in its report,

> At the same time, many opposition parties seem unwilling or unable to establish themselves as an effective opposition and present clear alternatives to the government in a consistent way. The delegation observed that many parties were more content to complain about their current predicament, and to insist on external conditions for their participation, than to organise themselves to expand their membership and influence. Each party needs to assume responsibility for its own situation and to consider the future of a united Yemen instead of nurturing historical grievances. We are also concerned that many opposition parties are actually weakening themselves over the long term by focusing their energies on negotiating safe passage to parliament for a small number of their leaders rather than on expanding their outreach to voters, developing and articulating a persuasive message, and strengthening

their internal democratic organisation. This approach may have been a good tactic in the early days of Yemen's multiparty era, but if opposition parties remain focused on negotiating a comfortable arrangement with the GPC, they will not present themselves as viable democratic alternatives. Until they are able to establish a genuine base of support among voters, these parties are unlikely to earn a permanent place in Yemen's political arena.

Local government elections held in February 2001 were a chaotic and violent affair in which a number of winning candidates were killed. As 26,000 candidates vied for 7,000 seats, more than a hundred violent incidents were reported across the country.

A referendum was held on the same day as the elections. It reportedly gave a 7 per cent approval to constitutional changes accepted by parliament, which extended the president's term from five years to seven, and that of parliament from four years to six. This consolidated the GPC's monopoly on power.

The next parliamentary elections were held in April 2003. A total of 1,396 candidates from 22 parties, plus independents, contested the 301 parliamentary seats. Eleven female candidates contested the election, and one was elected. The proportion of women registered to vote (about 40 per cent of the total) was amongst the highest in the Middle East, suggesting Yemen was moving away from a traditional view of the role of women in society.

Once again the result was an overwhelming win for the GPC, with 58 per cent of the vote and almost 80 per cent of the parliamentary seats. The socialists took part in the elections with 109 candidates and reached an agreement with Islah not to split the anti-government vote.

In a broadcast marking the thirteenth anniversary of Yemeni unification, Salih formally pardoned the exiled separatist leaders and urged them "to take part in building the country which has enough room for everyone". A few days later, he met Ali Salim Al-Beidh face-to-face in Abu Dhabi for the first time since the war. It was a magnanimous if belated gesture, which Salih could well afford to make: in the elections, the rump of the YSP had fared worse than ever, winning only seven seats out of 301.

In July 2005, Salih said he would resign: "I hope that all political parties find young leaders to compete in the elections because we have to train ourselves in the practice of peaceful succession. Our country is rich with young blood who can lead the country … let's transfer power peacefully among ourselves, people are fed up with us, and we are fed up with power." When he made the announcement, people begged him to stay, and he contested the next elections and was re-elected once again with a huge majority.

Commenting on Yemeni democracy, Brian Whitaker wrote, "The maturing of Yemeni democracy cannot be said to have progressed very far and in some respects it has moved backwards, as illustrated by the fate of the press which, since the heady days of 1990, has become more constrained over the years. Hopes that electoral politics might lead to a peaceful alternation of power seem as remote as ever." In a nutshell, Yemen was nominally a multi-party democracy, but in practice it was a presidential autocracy where the ruling party maintained hegemony through co-option, corruption, and commandeering of state resources. Salih hosted two international conferences promoting democracy, but although he talked the talk, he did not walk the walk in his own country.

A Chatham House briefing paper published in 2008 stated, "Yemen remains an incomplete state where the majority of the population live without reference to laws made in Sanaa. A corrupt, self-interested government that fails to provide the bare minimum of social services has little relevance and legitimacy outside, and even inside, the major urban areas." In the same year as the paper was published, Yemen ranked twenty-first in the Carnegie Endowment's Failed States Index, which is based on twelve "indicators of instability"—an improvement on 2005, when it was in eighth place.

Salih was reasonably successful in keeping Al Qaeda at bay, but problems with the Houthis started in 2004 when their rebellion began in Saada in the far north of the country on the border with Saudi Arabia. The Houthi family leading the rebellion are members of the Zaidi sect, prevalent in North Yemen. A movement of the Believing Youth (al-Shabab al-Mu'min) caused disruption at mosques with their chants of "Death to America, Death to Israel" after Friday prayers.

The movement was led by Hussein al-Houthi. He was killed when the rebellion first started, but opposition to the government continued as the area inhabited by the Houthis was one of the most marginalised and economically deprived in Yemen, with scant electricity and services. One journalist who visited the region in 2000 described it like returning to the time of the Bible, with donkeys being the only means of transport.

In the South, dissatisfaction was growing as the people felt marginalised and excluded from the regime's business, political, and patronage networks in the North. A festering issue was the arrangements for some one hundred thousand state employees (military and civilian) who had lost their jobs in the wake of unification and the 1994 war; this issue was never satisfactorily resolved and continues to be a cause for protests. Since 1994, Salih's regime always dealt with protests in the South with a heavy hand and violence. (See the subsection Repression of the Southern Movement Chapter 8.)

As the International Crisis Group's report put it in 2009, "Yemen currently confronts simultaneous political and social crises made all the more serious by the global financial meltdown. Increasing domestic repression under cover of an anti-terrorism campaign reflects growing state insecurity; meanwhile, massive protests are occurring in what once was South Yemen, where secessionist sentiment is on the rise. Finally, there is the Saada [Houthi] conflict, which the government has been singularly unable to end. Each of these developments is a reason for worry in a country that, a mere decade ago, was engaged in a promising and remarkable democratization process."

These problems heralded an Arab Spring in Yemen in 2011, and it looked as if the country was finally on the road to a genuine democracy.

(4) Whitaker, *Birth of Modern Yemen* page 213.

PART THREE
Disintegration and Re-emergence

CHAPTER 9

The Arab Spring, the National Dialogue Conference, and the Houthi Coup (2011–15)

An ancient Yemeni poet said, "The unluckiest man in the world is he who rides the lion or rules Yemen." This is as true today as it was centuries ago. As always, Yemeni politics today is complex: many lines become crossed, and contradictions coexist where ideology goes hand in hand with patronage and nepotism with discipline. In the words of Ali Abdullah Salih, "Ruling Yemen is like dancing on the heads of snakes."

Change Squares
Helen Lackner, writing in the *Jacobin*,[22] described how in early 2011, hundreds of thousands of Yemenis created "change squares" throughout the country, demanding political, economic, and social transformations of their country. They wanted the removal of Yemen's long-serving leader, Ali Abdullah Salih, and the system he had managed for decades.

Anti-government protests in Sanaa. Source: Wikipedia.

The slogans that Yemen shared with many other Arab countries at the time were first and foremost *Irhal* (Get out) and *Yaskut al Nidham* (Down with the system). Salih had been in power for almost thirty-three years, first running the Northern Yemen Arab Republic and then the Republic of Yemen, after its unification with the Southern People's Democratic Republic of Yemen in 1990. His government was now basically collapsing under the strain of multiple issues. Senior officers in the president's camp began to

---

[22] Helen Lackner, "How Yemen's Old Order Snuffed out the Country's Hope for a New Dawn", *Jacobin*, 18 March 2021.

realise that things were slipping from Salih's hands, and one in particular told the author that for the first time in a very long time, the international community was looking the other way: " The big ones are not on our side any more, and the Arab Spring has convinced them that change is required," he said.

People held Salih personally responsible for high levels of corruption and the increasing poverty of the majority of Yemenis, which to some extent is the same complaint that was made against other leaders in the Arab world during this period. They railed against the lack of economic opportunities and high youth unemployment, not to mention the military conflict in the far north against the Houthi movement. The South was calling for independence, and opposition of the Southern Movement to Salih's rule grew. The Arab Spring in Yemen brought together the collective grievances against Salih's regime with a demand for him to step down with his regime. Regrettably, the various factions engaged in the Arab Spring in Yemen had no collective understanding of a way forward that could help the country build a new system of government.

Sit-ins and demonstrations had started in Sanaa many months before the trigger events which led to the Arab Spring in Tunisia and Egypt. However, the successful ousting of the rulers in those countries proved to be a great boost to the Yemeni movement, expanding its scope and levels of participation. After decades of stasis, the fact that people had removed their leaders elsewhere gave hope to millions that change was now possible.

Speaking to *Al-Jazeera* ten years after the start of Yemen's Arab Spring, a young man called Taha recalled that Change Square in Sanaa had become a sea of colourful banners and flags as more and more people gathered to protest peacefully every day. Some of them pitched tents, organised the distribution of food, and shouted chants and slogans. "The presence of more and more women—determined, courageous— day by day was extraordinary," said Taha. "It made the square safer, kinder and more peaceful. People were sure that protesting was the right thing to do and they would succeed in their intent, because change was being demanded by all the Arab people at that time.

"The verse of the prayer of the protesters, 'There is no God but God,' was impressed in my mind. I can't forget the sense of brotherhood, belonging—the belief that together, in one body, we would be able to recompose a country and free it from the dictator."

The first months of the protests were mostly peaceful. "The more I went to the square, the more I saw the crowd grow. There were so many people. I was so excited to realise that it wasn't just me who wanted change. There were also shows: it was like a carnival," Taha said, his eyes shining at the memory.

"We would also pray in the midst of the protests but there was no water. I remember that among the protesters was a plumber, who managed to build mobile toilets so we could wash ourselves before the collective prayer."

"Change squares" where people spent their entire time spread from the main cities of Sanaa and Taiz to the capitals of all the governorates, including some that were barely more than villages, such as Mahweet, Zinjibar, and Al Jabeen. By late January and early February 2011, thousands of people had joined the movement from all over the country.

The Youth 16 February (Shabab 16 Febrair) was one of the Arab Spring creations and had a known leader, Hasan ben Shu'aib. It started as a movement to change the regime in Sanaa under the same slogan: *"Al-sha'ab yurid isqad al-nitham."* However, it deviated to become one of the separatist factions. What is significant about the group is its use of religions leaders to justify violent actions against what is called the Northern occupation. It participated in blocking streets and damaging some interests of Northern businessmen in Aden. This faction tended not to reveal its leaders and members. It seemed to be a shadow for other bigger factions in the Al-Hirak movement. It later disappeared into thin air, and although the Hirak Movement was divided into too many factions, they were all able to work towards a common goal.

During these early weeks, the dominant discourse was that put forward by independent revolutionaries. The established opposition parties—particularly their younger members—were present, but they were there as individuals. Their organisational affiliations did not prevent them from taking positions and supporting aims that were not part of their parties' programmes.

The Change Square routines took the form of daily meetings in different tents, along with speeches and other performances on the main stage just outside the gates of the new university—the main site of the Sanaa revolutionary movement. Friday prayers were said on the sixty-metre ring road, followed by marches with different slogans and destinations.

Every Friday of action received its own name to mark a specific demand or event. Men and women both took part. Although the latter participated in much smaller numbers, this was still highly significant in a country where gender segregation is the norm.

The events of 18 March fundamentally altered the dominance of independent political thinkers expressing a range of demands. Although there had been clashes in previous weeks between the revolutionaries and Salih's forces, including groups of thugs employed as provocateurs, the movement had ensured that its "peaceful" slogan was respected—by its own side, at any rate. But there were hospitals and medical posts in the square ready to deal with injuries.

That Friday, Salih's snipers settled on the roof of a nearby building and shot at the crowd after prayers. They killed fifty-two demonstrators and wounded hundreds more. The day became known as the Friday of Dignity. It was a crucial turning point that transformed the movement and the whole political situation. In its immediate aftermath, the party-political opposition—known as the Joint Meeting Parties (JMP) and led by the Islamist/tribal Islah party—formally joined the revolution. Ali Mohsen al Ahmar, who had been the senior military commander in Salih's war against the Houthi movement, deserted the president and now expressed his determination to "protect" the revolution with his powerful First Armoured Brigade.

A number of ministers, parliamentarians, and ambassadors from Salih's General People's Congress (GPC) also quit, some of them later forming the new Justice and Construction Party. This split the government's military and political forces, with the military element being the most significant.

The Change Squares remained active centres of debate well into 2013, in Sanaa in particular, although the composition of the participants changed over time. In Sanaa and some of the other main cities that had a mixed population, the squares provided the first-ever opportunity for Yemenis from different regions and social status groups to meet and discover that they shared many ambitions and concerns.

This helped overcome deep-rooted beliefs that there were permanent, insurmountable barriers between tribespeople from different areas, or between members of different social strata. In the process, the elements of a new social consciousness, more aligned with shared class interests, began to emerge based on similar experiences of authority and economic deprivation. This embryonic transformation was one of the features of the Yemeni revolution that changed popular perceptions. It may, in the future, help heal the fragmentation precipitated by the civil war which followed the Arab Spring.

A factor that was probably more significant in Yemen than elsewhere was the close link between rural and urban areas. Yemen is still predominantly rural, with more than 70 per cent of the country's population based in thousands of villages and dispersed settlements. However, by the first decade of the century, the people of these areas were no longer isolated thanks to the rapid spread of mobile telephones and satellite television channels, as well as the increased mobility of the male population.

The "change squares" provided the first-ever opportunity for Yemenis from different regions and social status groups to meet and discover that they shared many ambitions and concerns.

Agriculture was no longer the main source of income for the majority of rural households. Men—mostly younger ones—worked in Yemeni towns and cities, because the opportunities for international labour migration had shrunk dramatically. Many young people also studied in the cities, and while most of them were male, there were female students as well. Information on national developments and news from local participants in the squares spread to the most remote communities, helping the movement gain broad support.

The role of tribal elements was another specific feature of the Yemeni movement. Observers had formerly predicted that any popular movement in Yemen would give rise to heavy fighting within days, citing the widely held prejudice that tribesmen resort to arms at the first opportunity. The Yemeni uprising disproved this stereotype by remaining true to its "peaceful" slogan while gaining massive support from tribesmen everywhere in the country.

Religion did play a role in the uprising, but in a unifying rather than divisive and sectarian sense. Although Yemen has a large Zaydi minority and a Shafi'i majority, both groups often pray together, and there are few doctrinal differences between them. Friday prayers were the focus of weekly events, and the discourse of the period was focused on political and social change.

There is no doubt that many of the thousands who took part in the movement were genuine revolutionaries, struggling to establish a new regime that would uphold basic elements of what could be considered socialism in its broadest sense: equality of rights and duties amongst citizens, universal access to social services, equitable economic development, better living conditions for all, and other universal human rights. However, few claimed fidelity to specific ideologies, and there was a wide range of views and allegiances in evidence at different times. The Southerners played an important part in bringing the regime down, but their main interest was to have their own state in the South—something that wasn't shared by the majority in the North.

The absence of concrete policies to address the economic crisis was a major weakness. There may have been talk of a "national economy", but no proposals set out detailed mechanisms for how it should be established or what its characteristics might be. Indeed, there was no direct challenge to the neoliberal agenda of the Bretton Woods institutions.

Many revolutionaries thought that ending corruption would in itself ensure equal economic opportunities. They believed that the private sector was better than the public, while at the same time everyone wanted secure public-sector jobs for themselves. They did not recognise that the Salih regime and institutions like the International Monetary Fund and World Bank had a shared vision that strengthened the rich at the expense of the poor, favouring policies of privatisation over the needs of the majority.

Politically, the independent elements of the movement rejected the existing political parties. This was understandable, given the track record of those parties and their patent failure to address the social and economic issues facing the nation—not to mention the fact that Salih's patronage system had largely integrated them into its workings. But the activists proposed no alternative ideology.

Its rejection of political parties meant that the movement lacked organisational structure and leadership. Although a structure would certainly have been in direct competition with the existing parties of the JMP, its absence prevented the movement from developing a coherent strategy and programme. Such an organisation would have been able to mobilise supporters and propose alternatives to the established parties and institutions.

The GCC Agreement—Salih Steps Down

The split in the government led to the intensification of military clashes between forces loyal to Salih and those opposed to his continued rule. Leading Yemeni politicians got involved in seeking a way out of the crisis through some form of compromise, given the effective stalemate between Salih supporters and the broad opposition.

In 2011, Yemen stood on the brink of civil war, and the Yemeni people were demanding change and a better future, which was common with millions across the Middle East. The failed plot by the Yemen-based Al Qaeda in the Arabian Peninsula (AQAP) to blow up an airliner over Detroit in December 2009 acted as a catalyst in crystallising growing concerns in the international community about Yemen's prospects and its impact on security in the region.

The Friends of Yemen was established in January 2010 at a meeting of ministers in London to help bolster international political support for Yemen and assist Yemeni-led efforts to tackle the underlying causes of instability. Thirty-nine countries and international organisations became members of the Friends of Yemen.

A Gulf Cooperation Council initiative formalised this intervention, which led to the GCC Agreement that Salih signed in November 2011, agreeing to give up power after thirty-two years, relinquish the presidency by February 2012, and hand over power to Abdroba Mansur Hadi. The primary aim of international involvement was to remove Salih from power without disrupting the neoliberal regional order or encouraging others in an Arabian Peninsula dominated by hereditary rulers to seek democratic change.

Along with his control of the military/security apparatus, Salih enjoyed a surprising residual popularity that was rooted in widespread popular perceptions of him as a nationalist leader who had achieved Yemeni unity. Many people had also appreciated the material support that his patronage system provided in various places, whether this took the form of roads, schools, or other projects. Salih's military and political strength prevented his removal from the political scene.

The GCC Agreement demonstrated the extent of Salih's remaining influence. Not only did he remain head of the GPC, but also the pact formally guaranteed his immunity from prosecution, to the fury of many thousands of demonstrators. The GPC received half the ministries in the government of national unity established for the two-year transitional period imposed by the agreement. The opposition took the rest. This included the formal JMP and the new forces emerging from the street revolutions: women, youth, and civil society.

The transitional government allowed Salih's ministers to continue using the institutions they controlled to consolidate their support. The Islah party dominated the other half of the coalition and did just the same, while the minor parties (Socialist, Baath) and the new revolutionary forces had little influence. As a result, the government was both ineffective and corrupt.

The National Dialogue Conference (NDC)

A key part of the GCC-brokered agreement was the National Dialogue Conference, a ten-month process that began in March 2013 and was intended to result in a new functional, representative, and inclusive government. The NDC was supposed to represent the whole population, giving voice to the new forces in particular. In practice, however, the traditional ruling elite dominated this space. The people at large and the majority of revolutionaries had vacated the squares. They continued to debate, and some took part in the NDC, but most felt that the course of events constituted a betrayal of the revolution because they saw no improvements in their lives. Two Houthi representatives were shot dead in Sanaa as the talks were in progress.

Writing in the *Journal of Intervention and State Building*,[23] Moosa Elayah, Luuk van Kempen, and Lau Schulpen described the NDC as the most important element in the Gulf Cooperation Council (GCC) Initiative. Signed in November 2011 by the European Union, Saudi Arabia, the Gulf countries, and the United States, this initiative aimed to persuade the conflicting Yemeni parties to enter peace talks, following international concern that growing instability would leave Yemen exposed to Al-Qaeda and other extremist organisations. The NDC, held in a heavily fortified five-star hotel in Sanaa, ran for a two-year period of political transition after President Salih "agreed" to step down after thirty-three years, and Hadi was installed as interim president. Backed up by UN Security Council Resolution 2051, the NDC finally took off in early 2013 with high hopes from both the international community and ordinary Yemeni citizens.

موتمر الحوار الوطني الشامل
National Dialogue Conference
— بالحوار نصنع المستقبل —

President Hadi smiles at the end of the National Dialogue Conference when a final paper is produced. Source: Wikipedia.

The conference was headed by a nine-member presidency including Abdroba Mansur Hadi (NDC Chairman), Abdul-Kareem Al-Eryani (General People's Congress), Yassen Saeed Numan (Yemeni Socialist Party), Sultan Al-Atwani (Nasserite Unionist Party), Yassin Makkawi (Peaceful Southern Movement), Saleh bin Habra (Houthis), Abdul-Wahab Al-Ansi (Islah Party), Nadia Al-Saqqaf (a journalist), and Abdullah Lamlas (a South Yemeni politician). The conference was overseen by Jamal Benomar, a representative of the United Nations.

There were 565 delegates. The selection of the delegates showed that the Southern issue was given considerable attention as 50 per cent of the delegates were of Southern origin; 20 per cent were "youths" (under forty years of age), and 30 per cent were women.

The conference was divided into separate working groups, each with their own members:

---

[23] Moosa Elayah, Luuk van Kempen, and Lau Schulpen, "Adding to the Controversy? Civil Society's Evaluation of the National Conference Dialogue in Yemen", *Journal of Intervention and State Building* 14, no. 3 (2020).

The Southern Issue Working Group

The Sa'ada Issue Working Group, the National Issues Working Group

The National Reconciliation and Transitional Justice Working Group, the State-Building Working Group

The Good Governance Working Group

The Foundations for Building and the Role of the Armed and Security Forces Working Group

The Independence of Special Entities Working Group

The Rights and Freedoms Working Group

The Development Working Group

The Special Social and Environmental Issues Working Group

The Formation of the Committee to Draft the Constitution Working Group

The Assurance of Successful Implementation and Conference Outcomes Working Group

At first the high hopes for the conference seemed to come true. The nine working groups under the NDC covered both thorny political dilemmas, such as the highly contentious "Southern" issue and the Sa'ada (Houthi) issue, and more developmental goals. And after a four-month overrun on the original timetable, an outcomes document was signed on January 25, 2014. It contained a roadmap towards a new territorial division and the set-up of more inclusive institutions. Although the political issues on the table were not fully resolved, the initial reaction to the agreement was positive, and the NCD was heralded as a success by most national and international stakeholders. It is important to note that elements of the Hirak movement led by Hadi supporters did engage in the conference, but most of the Southern Hirak movement did not engage because they believed that their struggle and agenda were not included.

The outcomes document agreed to extend Hadi's presidency for another year so he could carry out certain reforms and continue overseeing the transition process. It also called for the restructuring of parliament and the Shura Council, which would be composed of 50 per cent Northerners and 50 per cent Southerners. On the Southern issue, after thirty meetings during the course of the conference, the Southern Issue Working Group was unable to come up with a plan for a new political system that would fairly represent the South. On the Sa'ada issue, an attempt was made to defuse sources of tension in Sa'ada Governorate. The document guaranteed freedom of religion, made stipulations on the non-sectarian nature of the government, outlawed illegal financial or arms support from foreign powers, called for a return of stolen government weapons, prohibited the possession of medium to heavy arms, and called for addressing the feuds that contributed to conflict. These outcomes were enshrined in the forthcoming constitution.

Conference members also agreed that Yemen would be transformed into a six-region federal system. The regions would be Azal, Saba, Janad, Tihama, Aden, and Hadhramaut. Sanaa would have a special status and would not be part of any region. Aden, the former Southern capital, would also have a special status. Azal, Saba, Janad, and Tihama would be Northern provinces, and Aden and Hadhramaut would be Southern. The federal system was rejected by Southern leaders including Mohammad Ali Ahmed, a member of the NDC who resigned after expressing frustration with the transitional process.

The Southerners were not happy with the way their issue was dealt with by the NDC. Charles Schmitz[24] described their reservations in detail in a paper published by the Washington based Middle East Institute.

Indeed, when the issue of the Southern Movement's representation in the National Dialogue arose, many Southern factions rejected any participation. Southern society seemed disinclined to trust a settlement arranged by Sanaa's elite. Yet for the Northern elite and the international overseers of the Gulf

---

[24] Charles Schmitz, "Yemen's National Dialogue", MEI Policy Paper, February 2014.

initiative, Southern secession was not an option. Seeing the call for secession as destabilising, the United Nations, the United States, and Saudi Arabia rejected calls for a separate Southern state and insisted that the National Dialogue was the only means to resolve the Southern issue. As a result, the representation of the Southerners became the most problematic issue to arise in the preparation for the dialogue. No clear voice emerged to speak for the South. When it seemed that the issue of Southern representation would derail the dialogue before it even began, Hadi resolved the issue by appointing members of his faction in the South. This solved the immediate problem of Southern representation, but it set the stage for even more serious issues because the Southern representatives lacked the legitimacy needed to speak and negotiate for the South.

The selection of the Southern representatives was only the beginning of the controversies. Outside of the subcommittee looking directly at the Southern issue, the subcommittee investigating the structure of the state became the arena of disputes related to the Southern issue. The Southerners from the Hirak participating in the NDC insisted that the state must be a federal one composed of two states formed from the territories of the former Yemen Arab Republic in the North and the former People's Democratic Republic of Yemen in the south. The former territory of the PDRY would be divided into two areas, one composed of the western portions of the South and the other made up of the eastern portions. The Hadhrami elite in the east liked this solution because it gave Hadhramis some independence from the mostly former socialist constituencies of the western portions of the South. The Hadhrami business elite and tribal leaders suffered greatly under socialist rule and were disinclined to allow people associated with the socialist regime in Aden back into power. Northerners, the Group of Ten, and some Southerners outside the Hirak rejected the return of the two states. They proposed an alternative of five or six states that would prevent the former South from reconstituting itself. Hadi's committee appointed to resolve the issue decided upon the six-region solution.

Demonstrations in the South renouncing the dialogue and calling for secession drew large crowds. The UN and the Group of Ten tried hard to build support in the South for the dialogue. For instance, a committee was formed to address the pensions and employment of those in the Southern bureaucracy and military who were dismissed after the 1994 war, and another committee was charged with resolving the issue of land and property in the South. In addition, Hadi announced the creation of a trust to fund efforts to resolve issues and compensate those hurt in the South during the last two decades of Salih's rule. Qatar donated $350 million to the fund.

As the stubbornness of the Southern issues stalled negotiations, a special high-level committee within the NDF was created to negotiate the issues of the South outside of the framework of the Southern issue subcommittee. This special committee was called the "committee of sixteen" because it was composed of eight representatives from the South and Eight from the North.

The South was unimpressed by these measures. When the Security Council looked into Jamal Benomar's latest report at the end of November 2013, demonstrators outside the United Nations in New York and in Aden continued to demand that the United Nations recognise the right of the South to self-determination. As before, the United Nations' and the Group of Ten's responses to the Southerners have been to reject calls for secession and to insist in no uncertain terms that resolution of the Yemeni crisis will be in the context of a single, united Yemen.

The United Nations and the Group of Ten have tried ostracising those who call for secession by linking them to Iranian aspirations in Yemen or by painting them as self-interested individuals who would sacrifice the country for personal political gain. These accusations have mostly been levelled at Ali Salem Al-Beidh, the former president of the PDRY before 1990, but in his UN report, Benomar accused

Mohammed Ali Ahmad—the most prominent Southern leader participating on and off in the NDF, and a close associate of Hadi—of delaying the process. Accusing Ali Ahmad of delaying the dialogue was tantamount to labelling the dialogue's efforts on the Southern issue a failure, because Ali Ahmad was amongst the few in the Southern Movement who was willing to participate in the NDC.

The Southern Nation National Congress (Almutamar Al-Wattani Lisha'B Aljanub) represented the people who accepted and participated in the NDC. Its leaders, Ahmed Al-Surimah, Mohammed Ali Ahmed, and Yasin Umar Makkawi, represented Al-Hirak on the NDC in Sanaa. However, Ahmed Al-Suraimah withdrew from the NDC on 1 May 2013 and described those who stayed as traitors. Mohammed Ali Ahmed was now the leader, along with Yasin Umar Makkawi, who was nominated as the NDC president's deputy by the president of Yemen. It was recognised that these individuals did not have the authority to speak on behalf of all Southerners, but their presence was an attempt to convince the international community that there was Southern representation in the dialogue conference.

As the National Dialogue Conference was coming to an end, it became increasingly clear that its aims were not being realised, owing to a number of serious shortcomings. The economic problems which sparked off the Arab Spring protests were not being dealt with. The grievances of the Southerners were not being adequately addressed, and they still felt discriminated against and marginalised. The grievances of the Houthi movement and those of the North Yemenis, including the Sunnis, were not adequately addressed either. The issues were clearly identified and described by the NDC, but the political will needed to implement reforms was lacking because the political elite played a main role in the conference, even though all areas of society were represented. It was now becoming clear that those in the political elite within Saleh's regime were playing the dominant role in proceedings. The Southerners made a mistake not engaging with the conference. This was a big opportunity, with the presence of the regional and international powers, to advance the case for Southern statehood. The main reason for their absence was the inability of the various factions within the Hirak movement to come up with a united voice. This was a missed opportunity to advance their case and put forward a unified Southern agenda in the conference. It is important to note that their absence allowed different political factions to exploit that gap.

The Houthi Coup
Living conditions for ordinary Yemenis continued to deteriorate, and the provision of services became even scantier than before. In 2012, the international community had committed itself to support the transition with $7.9 billion to finance development investments. However, these pledges did not materialise, owing to the lengthy negotiations between the funders and the Yemeni government on the practicalities of implementation.

While the transition was unfolding, as Salih's influence waned, he began to cooperate with his previous arch-enemies, the Houthis, in opposition to the transitional regime. Away from the cities, the Houthi movement widened its area of influence and power. In the South, the calls for independence increased while frustration increased everywhere in Yemen.

By mid-2014, when the Houthi-Salih partnership encouraged uprisings against the removal of fuel subsidies, it had the support of thousands who should have demonstrated against the alliance. The government had lost any credibility as an administration representing a shift away from cronyism and corruption. This allowed the Houthi movement to take over the capital bloodlessly in September and, soon thereafter, control about one-third of the country's land.

The Houthis had fought six wars against the government of Ali Abdullah Salih, and their takeover of Sanaa was a continuation of this conflict in which the Houthis ousted the Salafis from Sadah on the pretext that their seminaries were training camps for Al-Qaeda. Mosques and houses were blown up. After taking over Amran, a small city in western Yemen, on the pretext of fighting corruption, the Houthis took their fight to Sanaa under the same pretext.

When they reached Sanaa, the Houthis called for protests against the decrease in fuel subsidies, but unlike other protests, these were armed. The capital was stormed by armed protestors, Houthi fighters, and renegade Yemeni soldiers from Salih's forces. President Abdroba Mansur Hadi, along with Yemen's political parties, agreed to the Houthis' demands, but the rebels continued their coup, kidnapping Hadi's chief adviser, Ahmed ben Mubarek; attacking and looting state institutions as well as Hadi's residence; and placing the president himself and his prime minister, Khaled Bahah, under house arrest. The president was then given new demands to agree to which would have effectively legitimised the coup. Hadi and his entire government resigned, leaving the Houthis to announce their "constitutional declaration" and creating a "revolutionary committee" which superseded Yemen's state institutions.

Hadi fled to Aden, and the Houthis denounced him as a separatist. When he spoke about the unity of Yemen, the Houthis tried to justify their advance to the South of the country as a battle against Al-Qaeda and ISIS. Before reaching Aden, the Houthis occupied the Al-Anad air base, sixty kilometres from the city. These events took Hadi by surprise in their speed and intensity. He appeared not to have a plan or the capacity to fight back against this Houthi takeover. His only hope was regional or international assistance to save him from this dilemma and rescue the country from the Houthis.

As the Houthis were advancing towards Aden, the Yemeni foreign Minister Riad Yassin repeatedly called for military action in an interview with *Al Jazeera*. "We want direct military intervention, especially by the air force, to stop the advance of Houthis on the ground," Yassin said. He also dismissed attempts to reach a solution to Yemen's crisis through dialogue, alleging that UN envoy Jamal Benomar had given "legitimacy to the Houthi coup". Saudi Arabia moved heavy military equipment including artillery to areas near its border with Yemen. The nightmare scenario for the kingdom of Saudi Arabia, a critically important neighbour, was that Yemen would actually fall into the hands of its arch-enemy Iran, something the Saudis were not prepared to accept.

Brigade 39, loyal to overthrown Salih and allied with the Houthis, took control of the airport, leading to suspension of flights. Diplomatic missions of Hadi's Arab Gulf allies, including Saudi Arabia, the UAE and Kuwait, soon evacuated their diplomatic staff from Aden. The embassies had been moved to Aden, where Hadi set up a temporary capital following the coup.

The Houthi push towards Yemen's south pressed Saudi Arabia and its allies into action, and on 26 March 2015, they started Operation Decisive Storm, striking Houthi and Salih targets across the country. Foreigners were now involved in Yemen's civil war, which has since continued to destroy the country and starve its people. Salih saw the Houthi advance to Sanaa as an opportunity for him to get revenge on those he blamed for his removal, specifically Ali Mohsin and Hadi.

His plan might have worked, but the only problem with his manoeuvring was his inability to comprehend that he was no longer dancing on snakes, and the Houthis had become the cobra. The Houthis were mistrustful of Salih and were well aware of his great skills to play political games and his ability to survive. This time they wanted to use him but at the same time keep him in his place and deal with him if the situation required.

The Houthis by now believed that they were a powerful and unstoppable force and that Yemen was theirs for the taking. They believe that they have a God-given right to rule Yemen because they are the descendants of the Prophet through a bloodline. In a sense, they want to impose themselves on the rest of the population as the rightful rulers of Yemen. The Houthis, having removed most of those who played an influential role in ruling the Republic of Yemen for decades, see their opportunity to be the new leaders of the country; the biggest obstacle for them was the resistance when trying to take control of the south of the country.

CHAPTER 10

The Ongoing Civil War, Foreign Intervention, and the Humanitarian Crisis

Yemen's civil war, which started with the Houthi coup in 2014, became an international conflict with the intervention of Saudi Arabia on 26 March 2015. The Saudis head the Arab coalition, which includes the United Arab Emirates, and the Houthis are backed by Iran.

On 24 March 2015, President Abdroba Mansoor Hadi, having escaped from the Houthis, asked the GCC "to immediately provide support, by all necessary means and measures, including military intervention, to protect Yemen and its people from the continuing aggression by the Houthis supported by Iran".

Hadi fled to South Yemen and then to Saudi Arabia, and the international community granted his government status as the internationally recognised government (IRG), a government-in-exile in Saudi Arabia.

At the time of writing this book, the United Nations has described Yemen as the world's worst humanitarian disaster. Yemen is plagued by famine, COVID-19, and the increasing risk of further cholera outbreaks. To date, more than 250,000 people have been killed. The conflict has become a proxy war between the Iranian-supported Houthis, the Saudi-supported IRG, and the Southern independence movement assisted by the United Arab Emirates. The United Nations has tried unsuccessfully to negotiate a peace deal, and the antagonists have become increasingly entrenched and their positions seemingly irreconcilable. The intensification of the war has meant intensification in the rivalry between the Northern political class and the Southern one. The fighting has cost Yemen huge infrastructure damage estimated at $32 billion, and while it continues to rage, the costs are significantly increasing.

The Battle for Aden
The battle of Aden, the first major battle in the six-year conflict, was between the Houthis and Yemen army forces loyal to Ali Abdullah Salih on one side, and Yemen army units loyal to President Hadi and Southern Movement fighters on the other side.

It began on 25 March 2015 as pro-Salih and Houthi militia troops seized control of Aden International Airport, and Hadi fled the country by boat to Saudi Arabia. It took the pro-Hadi forces until 16 July to recapture Aden with the help of Arab coalition forces. By 22 July, the Southern forces were in full control of Aden, and the airport was immediately reopened. By late July, the Houthis were driven out of the South. But military confrontations in the South did not cease because there were further battles between pro-Hadi forces and Southern fighters (see chapter 11).

The Houthis' advance into Aden prompted Saudi Arabia to begin an air campaign to defeat them, both in the South and in other parts of Yemen. By 27 March the Houthis had encircled Aden and were in control of all land routes in and out of the city. The Saudi air attacks stopped a Houthi convoy from Shurqah, a coastal town. An explosion at an arms depot killed several people in Aden. The residents then raided the depot and took the weapons because the guards had abandoned their posts. The people also dusted off their personal weapons and formed their own units in the city's districts to fight the Houthis.

Clashes continued in Aden on 29 March as the Houthis pushed into the centre of the city. Control of the airport changed several times during the fighting. As well as being bombed by the Saudi air strikes, the Houthis came under fire from Egyptian warships which shelled their positions from off the Southern coast.

Several countries evacuated their citizens from Aden as the fighting worsened. China's People's Liberation Army Navy evacuated several hundred, including hundreds of non-Chinese citizens. A Turkish frigate also evacuated fifty-five Turks. The INS *Mumbai*, an Indian Navy destroyer, evacuated 441 Indian and other foreign nationals from Aden to Djibouti.

Médecins Sans Frontières and the International Committee of the Red Cross (ICRC) were successful in delivering 2.5 tonnes of medicine and a surgical team, respectively, by boat to Aden as the shops started running out of food. Water tanks in four districts were destroyed, and residents were hauling water in buckets.

"Aden is almost the only city in Yemen to be attacked by air, sea and land," said Nashwan Al-Othmani, a resident who spoke to the *New York Times*. "The siege has left little time to think about the political arguments dividing the country. No one seems to be clamouring for the return of Mr Hadi, whom the Saudis have vowed to restore as the legitimate president. There are some who accuse Hadi of bringing the war to Aden and then suddenly leaving."

On 1 April, the Houthis retook parts of the airport and advanced into Khormaksar district, the city centre, and the central Crater neighbourhood, but they were pushed back by overnight raids and strong Hiraki resistance, which prompted them to withdraw. They made their largest push on 6 April into Aden's Mualla district. Medical facilities in the city were reportedly overwhelmed, bodies cluttered the streets, and a number of buildings were set on fire. The Red Cross warned of a "catastrophic" humanitarian situation as fighting continued.

On 7 April, the BBC reported that Aden was a ghost town as the death toll rose. At least 185 dead and 1,282 wounded from the fighting were counted in hospitals in Aden since 26 March, according to the city's health department director, Al-Kheder Lassouar. "We are seeing a lot of people arriving dead at the hospital or dying in the hospitals," Robert Ghosen, the head of the ICRC in Aden, told the BBC. "The hospitals don't have the right supplies and the right staff. People are nowhere to be seen, they are hiding. The economy has completely stopped, the streets are littered with rubbish and rubble from damaged buildings. The city is full of armed people from different groups fighting. This is a big city and nothing is functional." Nizma Alozebi, a student from Aden, told the BBC that the violence had spread to residential areas and most shops. "People are afraid for their belongings and their safety. It's insanity," she said. Marie Claire Feghali, the spokesperson for the ICRC in Yemen, described a catastrophic humanitarian situation with air, naval, and ground routes in Aden cut off. "The war is on every street corner. Many are unable to escape," Feghali said. In the Sunni mosques, there were calls for the people to rise up against the invaders. Iran got involved in the conflict on the side of the Houthis. Two Quds Force officers from Iran were captured by the Southern fighters defending Aden.

As the fighting continued, control of Aden's districts, the airport, and the presidential palace changed hands several times. On 28 April, Houthi forces that took up positions at the University of Aden and the hospital in the Khormaksar district advanced in the area, capturing Hadi's family home and the German and Russian consulates. Just north of the peninsula, they also pushed west in an attempt to retake territory previously lost. The next day, the Houthis advanced towards the city centre. A large shopping mall in Khormaksar caught fire amidst fighting as the Houthis advanced through the neighbourhood, repulsing counter-attacks there and in the Mualla district. Eyewitnesses told Associated Press that the Houthi fighters and their allies searched house to house in Khormaksar, dragging some men out onto the street and shooting them, while warning residents by loudspeaker against harbouring anti-Houthi fighters. Houthi shells struck a boat loaded with refugees, killing forty.

A major counteroffensive against the Houthis was launched on 14 July. The Southern fighters, mainly from Aden, retook Aden International Airport and dislodged the Houthis from Khormaksar. They retook large areas of the port of Muallah near Aden and recaptured Crater. The anti-Houthi forces were assisted by the UAE, which landed troops and unmarked armoured vehicles in a small fishing harbour on the outskirts of Aden at the beginning of July.

On 17 July, it was announced that Aden had been liberated from the Houthis, but they did not give up without a fight. According to Médecins Sans Frontières, retreating Houthis killed about one hundred people in a single mortar barrage. The first aircraft to land at Aden's reopened airport, on 22 July, was a Saudi military transport bringing aid, weapons, and the commander of the Saudi navy. The first ship carrying aid from the World Food Programme docked in Aden and carried enough food to last 180,000 people a month. The ship had waited at sea for four months, unable to dock because of fighting in the port area.

Most of the fighting to liberate Aden was done by fighters from the Southern Movement and the residents of Aden. Many of Hadi's tribal loyalists deserted him early in the battle, after their president fled the country. The fighters in Aden were joined by fighters from Dhala, Abyan, Lahej, and Yafa with a strong determination to kick the Houthis out of Aden.

The anti Houthi forces launched an offensive outside Aden and drove the Houthis from the Muthalath al-Ilm, the Ya'wala, Al-Basateen, and Qariat al-Falahi neighbourhoods, as well as Lahij province. The Houthis were gone from South Yemen, but the civil war was just beginning.

Major General Jaafar Mohammed Saad, who played a prominent role with other colleagues in planning the operation that pushed pro-Houthi fighters out of Aden in July, was appointed as governor of Aden in October 2015. However, his tenure proved short-lived; he was assassinated in a bombing for which ISIS claimed responsibility on 6 December 2015. The next governor of Aden appointed by President Hadi was Aidarous al-Zubaidi, a strong Hiraki from the Dhala region who commanded a strong resistance army with his colleague Shelal Ali Shai in Dhala. They emerged as two important leaders in the struggle to defeat the Houthis and later, with the majority of the Hirak movement, set up the Southern Transitional Council (STC) in April 2017 after disagreements and an uneasy relationship with Hadi's government (see chapter 11). The victory against the Houthis in the South was seen by the Hirakis as a victory against the Northern regime that had humiliated them in the 1994 war. The military conflict with the Houthis brought the Hirakis closer together for the first time with real vigour to establish their own state in the South.

The Arab Coalition and the Houthis Fight for Control of Yemen
When the Arab coalition first intervened in the Yemeni civil war, it relied on air power to dislodge the Houthis from the South. The Houthis entrenched their positions in the North, and deadly air strikes which

often resulted in civilian casualties could not rid the North of the Houthis. Fierce fighting on the ground soon became a feature of the civil war.

In April 2015, the UN Security Council (UNSC) adopted Resolution 2216 under chapter VII of the UN Charter, authorising an arms embargo on the Houthi-Saleh forces and legitimising the coalition's military actions. The resolution was a road map for the undoing of the Houthi coup. They were the only party in the multifarious conflict mentioned by name, and the resolution had a formula for ending the Houthis' usurpation of power. Sadly, the resolution was never implemented. It stated:

> *Alarmed* at the military escalation by the Houthis in many parts of Yemen including in the Governorates of Ta'iz, Marib, Al Jauf, Albayda, their advance towards Aden, and their seizure of arms, including missile systems, from Yemen's military and security institutions,
>
> *Condemning* in the strongest terms the ongoing unilateral actions taken by the Houthis, and their failure to implement the demands in resolution 2201 (2015) to immediately and unconditionally withdraw their forces from government institutions, including in the capital Sana'a, normalize the security situation in the capital and other provinces, relinquish government and security institutions, and safely release all individuals under house arrest or arbitrarily detained, and reiterating its call on all non-State actors to withdraw from government institutions across Yemen and to refrain from any attempts to take over such institutions …
>
> *Demands* that all Yemeni parties, in particular the Houthis, fully implement resolution 2201 (2015), refrain from further unilateral actions that could undermine the political transition in Yemen, and further demands that the Houthis immediately and unconditionally:
>
> (a) end the use of violence;
>
> (b) withdraw their forces from all areas they have seized, including the capital Sana'a;
>
> (c) relinquish all additional arms seized from military and security institutions, including missile systems;
>
> (d) cease all actions that are exclusively within the authority of the legitimate Government of Yemen;
>
> (e) refrain from any provocation or threats to neighbouring States, including through acquiring surface-surface missiles, and stockpiling weapons in any bordering territory of a neighbouring State;
>
> (f) safely release all political prisoners, and all individuals under house arrest or arbitrarily detained; and
>
> (g) end the recruitment and use of children and release all children from their ranks.

After the resolution was passed, Saudi Arabia and the United Arab Emirates sent separate ground forces to Yemen. A naval blockade was also imposed. The Houthis began using banned anti-personnel landmines and started firing missiles and sending drones to Saudi Arabia.

As the hostilities intensified, so did the civilian casualties. Between March 2015 and March 2016, there were approximately 9,000 civilian casualties, including 3,218 killed and 5,778 injured. Millions more were displaced. The UN panel set up under UNSC Resolution 2216 reported that the Saudi-led coalition was responsible for twice as many civilian casualties as all other forces put together, virtually all as a result of airstrikes. The coalition naval blockades systematically kept out humanitarian cargo ships and prevented commercial access to fuel, food, and non-food items. The UN high commissioner for human rights, Ra'ad Al Hussein Zeid, condemned all sides for the high civilian toll. But while condemnation of the Saudis and Emiratis for their military actions in Yemen has been relentless and damning, Iranian support for the Houthis in the form of smuggled sophisticated weapons and technical and logistical support has drawn little criticism. Campaigns like that of Britain's Stop the War Coalition have never mentioned Iranian involvement in the war, and their one-sided condemnation is lamentable. Iranian military officers have confirmed the supply of arms to the Houthis through social media reports.

The first round of peace negotiations in Geneva in 2015 did not achieve anything because the two parties refused to sit together. Ceasefires were more honoured in the breach than in the observance. The next peace talks were held in Kuwait in April 2016, sponsored by the United Nations. Government forces and the Houthis took part, but AQAP and Islamic State were excluded. The agreed ceasefire was breached several times during the talks, and the initiative petered out in August. The UN efforts to end the war subsequently took the form of crisis management. In 2018 there was a hope that the Stockholm agreement could lead to peace. The undertakings set out in the agreement came in three parts: the Hodeidah Agreement, the Taiz Understanding, and a prisoner swap agreement. Taken together, these undertakings committed parties to (1) a ceasefire in the city of Hodeidah and the ports of Hodeidah, Salif, and Ras Issa, as well as redeployment of forces on both sides; (2) an opening of humanitarian corridors for the movement of aid via these ports; and (3) a prisoner swap aiming to release more than fifteen thousand prisoners and detainees. The parties also agreed to discussions towards creating a humanitarian corridor that would allow humanitarian aid into Taiz governorate. The agreement was largely a stopgap measure to stem the deepening humanitarian crisis.

The Yemen Data project reported that in 2016 alone, the coalition conducted 5,102 air strikes. The strikes intensified after talks collapsed. The widespread, indiscriminate aerial attacks which have continued to be a feature of the war were criticised by the international community. According to the UN panel of experts, at least ten detailed investigations revealed the coalition did not meet the requirements of international humanitarian law for proportionality and precautions, and some of the attacks could even constitute war crimes. The Saudi-led coalition had access to high-tech military equipment and was sold state of the art weapons by the United States and the United Kingdom, which included combat aircraft, bombs, assault weapons, ammunition, and other forms of material support. The United States also provided targeted intelligence for the bombing campaign and assisted in refuelling coalition bombers.

The Houthi-Salih alliance first got its weapons from the national stockpile. When these supplies ran out, the Iranians began supplying the Houthis. A report by the UN panel of experts included evidence from Conflict Armament Research, which analysed weapons seized from sailing vessels near the Horn of Africa and found a significant portion were manufactured in Iran. The areas in which weapons were intercepted suggested that weapons were flowing from Iran and Somalia to Yemen.

As the Houthis tightened their stranglehold over areas under their control in North Yemen, violations of human rights increased. They began recruiting child soldiers to fight on the front line.

The Houthis' human rights violations varied between killings, kidnappings, house raids, confiscation of properties, and arbitrary arrests at the checkpoints deployed in streets and roads between the provinces. The president of the SAM Organisation for Rights and Liberties, Tawfiq al-Humaidi, indicated that while women hold a special status in Yemen, they lost that with Houthis' control over Sanaa and other cities and are being subjected to gross violations of human rights, norms, and values. Female detainees were subjected to severe torture and cruel treatment, prompting many to try to commit suicide.

The Houthi-Salih Alliance

An alliance between the Houthis and ex-President Salih started in July 2016 when Salih wanted to reassert his power. He repressed the Zaidi community in the North when he was president, yet the Machiavellian Salih joined forces with the Houthis. But this was his final dance on the heads of snakes—a term he used to describe governing Yemen.

When he decided to break with the Houthis, Salih gave a televised speech in which he said he was willing to enter into a dialogue with the Saudi-led coalition. "Yemeni citizens have tried to tolerate the recklessness of the Houthis over the last two and half years but cannot anymore. I call on our brothers in neighbouring countries … to stop their aggression and lift the blockade … and we will turn the page."

Mohamed Qubaty, a former Yemeni ambassador, told *Al-Jazeera*: "Salih has been playing the Houthis for years. He did this when the Salafists started growing in power in the North. Initially he backed them, then he switched and supported the Houthis. Then he betrayed the Houthis. This is what he does."

The fact that all was not well with the alliance was obvious at a rally to mark the thirty-fifth anniversary of the establishment of the General People's Congress in August 2017, as thousands of tribesmen headed towards Sanaa's Al Sabeen Square. The Houthis only allowed Salih to make a short speech in which he confined his criticisms to comments about changes to the school curricula and books.

Clashes between army units loyal to Salih and Houthi fighters, which started on 1 December 2017, turned the streets of Sanaa into a battleground. Three days later, Salih was killed by a rocket-propelled grenade fired at his car. Saleh miscalculated the mood of the nation and definitely underestimated the strength of the Houthis and their determination to eliminate him. He was deluded to think he still possessed the charisma to instigate a revolt. This delusion did not materialise, and his speech did not instigate a rebellion in the North, even from his own tribe in Hashid. People in North Yemen saw him as a man of the past, but many do credit his courage for staying in Sanaa and making a historic speech against the Houthis. Offers were made from other states to take Salih and his family safely out of Sanaa, but he refused to accept them. Salih never stopped believing that Yemen could not function without his leadership, and this belief led to his downfall.

Hours after Salih's death, Hadi delivered a televised speech calling for Yemenis to unity against the Houthi rebels, describing them as "Iranian militias" and a "nightmare". There was no friendship between Salih and Hadi following Hadi's appointment as president. Hadi was closely connected to Ali Mohsin, and both of them suspected Salih was preparing his son to take power after his demise. This became a feud between them throughout the Arab Spring and thereafter.

There was extensive media speculation that Saudi Arabia and the UAE had been trying to get Salih to change allegiance for months after they became disillusioned with Hadi's leadership, and they looked for a new way to break the political and military deadlock. These attempts were unsuccessful.

The Saudis no longer had anyone in Yemen with whom to strike a deal to engineer their exit from the conflict. Their determination to crush the Houthis hardened after an Iranian-made missile was fired from Houthi positions at the international airport in Riyadh. They responded by mounting a three-week blockade of goods entering Houthi-controlled ports, prompting widespread shortages. With Salih out of the way, the Houthis quickly consolidated their control over Sanaa, increased their military capacity, and were now a potent danger to the Gulf states. They now have the military sophistication and ability to strike right at the heart of Saudi territory.

Saudi Arabia's Vietnam

Yemen quickly became Saudi Arabia's Vietnam, and the kingdom has not found a face-saving excuse to extricate itself from the conflict which it thought would end with a blitzkrieg lasting only three weeks. In her paper "The Saudi Intervention in Yemen: Struggling for Status", May Darwich, assistant professor in international relations for the Middle East at Durham University, argues that the intervention is driven by a will for status. "In the post 2011 order, the Kingdom has fought for its status as a regional power at both regional and international levels. In this context, the Saudi leadership responded to regime change in Yemen with a violent intervention to confirm its status as a leading power in the region."

Saudi Arabia announced that the goal of its intervention was "defending the legitimate government in Yemen" and "saving Yemeni people from the Houthi aggression". During the twenty-sixth Arab League Summit in Sharm el Sheikh in March 2015, King Salman vowed, "The campaign will continue until it achieves its goals for the Yemeni people to enjoy security." Another narrative evolved quickly as the primary rationale behind the Saudi decision—that of a war between the Kingdom and the Iran-backed Houthis, who belong to a Shiite sect. The Saudi identity narrative officially embraced the ideals of Islam, which prescribe solidarity and fraternity amongst Muslims and prohibit fighting or causing harm to brotherly Muslim people. Although the kingdom portrayed the Houthis as Shia "others", the humanitarian crisis is affecting the entire Yemeni population, which consists of a Sunni majority.

The Saudi-owned media and religious authorities portray Yemen as a battlefield for the Saudis to fight the Shiites, perceived as a threat to not only Yemen but also to the entire region. King Salman accused the Houthis of being backed by Iran and of causing sectarian division in Yemen. The kingdom has imposed tight control over the media to avoid any revelation that the operation has so far failed to defeat the Houthis, and it has used a heavy hand in prohibiting any challenge to the official narrative of a "just" and "necessary" war.

In the conclusion to her report, Darwich points out that the cost of the operation continues to mount for the Saudi kingdom, and there is still no agenda appearing to minimize the costs. The perseverance in this catastrophic war reflects the Saudi elites' aversion to perceived losses, especially in terms of status, and any attempt to solve the conflict without conveying the image of a Saudi victory is unlikely to succeed.

After more than six years of incessant shelling by air, land, and sea, the Saudis became painfully aware of the limits of their military power in Yemen. The Houthis have not ceased their attempts to control the whole of North Yemen, and fighting is continuing in Hodeidah, Taiz, Marib, and Al-Baida, leading to some losses in the Saudi armed forces and the forces of the IRG. No fundamental victory can be observed because the advances of the Houthis and their supporters have not ceased. Until now, the intervention has done nothing to change the balance of power between the different forces on the ground, and the Houthis appear to have the upper hand in military confrontations.

As the blockade and coalition bombing continued, the Houthis retaliated with a constant barrage of ballistic missiles fired over Saudi borders. The attacks against Saudi Arabia increased, and ballistic missiles and drones targeted Riyadh on an almost daily basis at the beginning of 2021. The airport was hit, leading to its temporary closure, and Aramco's facilities were also successfully targeted. The reality of Houthi control of Yemen has now become something of a nightmare scenario for the Saudis who simply cannot allow the Houthis to have such power in any future relationship with the kingdom. The Saudis have become desperate for a political solution that doesn't give the Iranians any foothold in Yemen in the same way as they have in Iraq and Lebanon. They see Iranian influence in Yemen as a potent danger to the regime in the kingdom of Saudi Arabia.

In 2018 a civil war within a civil war broke out, and the Southern Transitional Council, previously allied with Hadi's forces in the Arab coalition, eventually seized control of Aden with Emirati support (see chapter 11). It is the opinion of some commentators that the Emiratis do not support the legitimate government of Hadi because of the role played by the Muslim Brotherhood in this government. Their dislike for the Muslim Brotherhood, in the form of the Islah party, shifted their loyalties towards the STC in 2017.

The war against Al-Qaeda continued. A raid by security forces in the Al-Qaeda stronghold of Abyan resulted in the deaths of leaders of Al-Qaeda in Yemen, Murad Abdullah Mohammed Al-Doubli (nicknamed Abu Hamza al-Batani) and Hassan Baasrei. Shelal Ali Shai played a major role in the fight against Al Qaeda in the Arabian Peninsula and ISIS in Aden and beyond, supported by the STC and the Emiratis.

Attacks on Hodeidah intensified. In April the coalition bombed a residential housing area, killing fourteen civilians and wounding nine. On 8–9 June, heavy fighting began in Al-Durayhmi and Bayt Al-Faqih, ten and thirty-five kilometres from Hodeidah respectively. The United Nations warned that a military attack on or siege of the city could cost up to 250,000 lives, and they withdrew from the city. Around six hundred people died in the fighting. It took the warring parties until December to agree to a crucial ceasefire; the port was a lifeline for half the country. The Houthis and the Yemeni government agreed to withdraw all troops from Hodeidah, and both were replaced by UN-designated "local troops".

In June the presidency building in Sanaa was hit in a coalition air strike, resulting in the death of six civilians and the injury of thirty. The deadliest attack of 2019 occurred on 1 September when the coalition launched several air strikes on a university being used as a detention centre in the south-western province of Dhamar, resulting in seventy fatalities.

In November, almost a year after the signing of the Stockholm agreement, Oman became the mediator between Saudi Arabia and the Houthis, holding indirect, behind-the-scenes talks to end the war. The talks were now between the Saudis and the Houthis, whereas earlier talks were between the Houthis and Hadi's government. Reuters reported diplomats as saying that the Saudi-Houthi dialogue had been going on for about two months and appeared aimed at providing a framework for a resolution to coincide with the arrival of a new UN envoy to Yemen, the former British diplomat Martin Griffiths. The talks reportedly began in September after a Houthi attack on the world's largest crude oil facility in Saudi Arabia, which temporarily hit nearly 6 per cent of daily global production. November 2019 also saw the signing of the Riyadh Agreement between Hadi's government and the Southern Transitional Council (see chapter 11 and appendix 3).

In 2020, the Houthis continued to make significant gains in extending the areas under their control in the north of the country. They began their advance towards Marib and captured 2,500 square kilometres of territory, including the city of Naham and parts of the governorates of Al-Jawf and Marib, from Saudi-led forces. They also recaptured the entire Sanaa governorate. The coalition frequently denied claims of the Houthis' advances, but there was no doubt they were making significant territorial gains in the North. In March, Al Hazm, the capital of Al Jawf governorate, was captured along with the town of Taba Al-Bara and other areas in Marib's Sirwah District. The offensive continued eastwards towards Marib.

On 30 March, the Saudi-led coalition carried out an air strike on Sanaa. The attacks came despite requests by the UN secretary general António Guterres and others to maintain a ceasefire during the COVID-19 pandemic. In their statement, a group of regional experts also said that all political prisoners should be released from prisons, and efforts should be made to tackle the appalling healthcare system and stop the COVID-19 pandemic from spreading in Yemen. The International Organisation for Migration (IOM) reported that between 30 March and 18 July, over ten thousand people were internally displaced, citing fear of coronavirus.

On 5 April, at least five women were killed and twenty-eight were injured when shelling hit the women's section of Taiz's main prison. The shelling came from the part of the divided city controlled by the Houthis. The attack was condemned by the United Nations high commissioner for human rights (UNHCHR), Michelle Bachelet, who called it a breach of international humanitarian law.

In 2021 the Houthi targeting of Saudi Arabia continued, and the coalition successfully intercepted numerous Houthi drones destined for Saudi. The most successful Houthi attacks were on Saudi Aramco in Jazan province. The Houthis' attempts to capture Marib continued. In February they launched another offensive with the aim of capturing of capturing Marib city. After making steady advances in the governorate, there was a three-direction assault on the city with occasional ballistic strikes. According to the IOM, over 140,000 displaced refugees from western Marib fled fearing the Houthis' advance.

The battle for Marib did not stop when, in March 2021, US President Biden forbade the selling of American weapons to Saudi Arabia for offensive attacks against Yemen and removed the Houthis from the list of Foreign Terrorist Organisations. The Houthis were emboldened and intensified their assault on the city.

The governor of Marib, Sultan Al-Arada, has claimed that as many as eighteen thousand have died since early 2020, and the number of deaths continues to escalate. The United Nations Refugee Agency UNHCR said the escalation in hostilities in 2021 has led to the displacement of over 13,600 people (2,272 families) in Marib—a region that is hosting a quarter of Yemen's four million internally displaced people. In addition to stepping up their military offensive in a bid to capture Marib, the Houthis have dramatically increased their cross-border attacks, targeting Saudi cities, oil refineries, and key infrastructure with dozens of drones and ballistic missiles.

An unintended consequence of the war has been the expansion of Al-Qaeda and ISIS, especially in eastern Yemen. Amidst the chaos created by the collapse of the government and the clashes between the Saudi-led coalition and the Houthis, these groups have found fertile ground for expansion and increased their influence. On 2 April 2015, Al-Qaeda captured the southern port of Mukalla from government forces; it was dislodged a year later by UAE forces. Al-Qaeda and ISIS have their own agenda and fight both the Saudi-led coalition and the Houthis, so the resolution of this conflict is becoming increasingly complicated. The war has fragmented the country, created long-term instability, allowed extremists to thrive, and created the world's worst humanitarian crisis.

The Humanitarian Crisis

Since March 2015, the sea, air, and naval blockade over the Yemen imposed by the Saudi-led coalition has sparked a catastrophic humanitarian crisis. The air strikes targeted the infrastructure—airports, roads, factories, and power stations—in a country that was already unable to maintain a basic infrastructure without foreign aid. The attacks also targeted civilians, refugee camps, schools, places of worship, and residential buildings, which highly increased the war casualties and atrocities.

The first phase of the intervention involved a tight air and naval blockade to prevent weapons supply from reaching the Houthis. This phase also included air strikes to destroy Yemen's air and coastal defence and ballistic-missile capabilities. After destroying initial military targets, the coalition widened its scope to take out the infrastructure to hinder the Houthis' mobility. Yet this air war had high costs. The collateral damage, including civilian casualties and the resulting humanitarian crises, has been acute and has led to condemnation of the intervention in international forums.

Civilians and medical facilities often bear the brunt of the conflict. In 22 April 2018, the Saudi-led coalition carried out air strikes on a wedding in Hajjah, a town in north-western Yemen. The raids, with two missiles that hit several minutes apart, left at least thirty-three people dead and forty-one wounded; most of the people killed were women (including the bride at the wedding) and children. Ambulances were not able to get to the site of the attack at first because jets were continuing to fly overhead after the attack, and there were concerns about further air strikes. The Saudis have accepted that a mistake was made in the bombing but blamed Houthi militias and said that they would carry out internal investigations into any mistakes made and take appropriate action to remedy them. The British and US governments have also been blamed for militarily supporting the Saudis, and they have promised their own investigation. Both governments continued to support the Saudis against what they both say is Houthi-Iranian aggression.

On 12 June, a newly constructed cholera treatment centre run by the international medical humanitarian organisation Médecins Sans Frontières (MSF) in Abs was hit by an air strike. Markings on the roof of the compound clearly identified it as a healthcare facility.

More than 1,900 of the country's 3,500 health facilities are currently either not functioning or partially functioning with insufficient staff and equipment, leaving half the population without adequate healthcare. Yemeni forces, the Houthis, and the Saudi-led Arab coalition have attacked over one hundred medical facilities. Water and sanitation systems have also been destroyed.

Around 18 per cent of Yemen's 333 districts have no doctors, and many of those who are still working have been unpaid for nearly two years. There are now ten healthcare workers for every ten thousand people—less than half the World Health Organisation benchmark.

"Yemenis are not going hungry. They are being starved." This statement from the UN under-secretary general Mark Lowcock accurately describes the famine in Yemen, which is a human-made disaster brought about by more than six years of civil war. The areas worst affected by acute food insecurity are Marib, Taiz, and Al Jawf governorates in the North and Al Bayda, Abyan, and Hadhramaut in the South.

According to the United Nations, as of 5 November 2020 there had been more than 900,000 suspected cholera cases, and 2,192 associated deaths have been reported. More than half of the suspected cases are children. People have also been affected by malaria, dengue fever, shortages of clean drinking water, severe flooding, and locust swarms.

Yemenis now face the COVID-19 pandemic. The World Health Organisation's prediction of a worst-case scenario—namely that 93 per cent of a population of nearly thirty million would be infected with the virus—is about to become a reality. There is a serious shortage of medical and PPE equipment, lack of IC beds, lack of trained IC staff, the threat from other diseases such as cholera and diphtheria, malnutrition, food insecurity, and the problem of internally displaced people with a weak immune system who are at great risk of contracting COVID-19.

The first wave of the virus affected Yemen from April to August 2020. On 10 April 2020, Yemen recorded its first laboratory-confirmed COVID-19 case in the Southern governorate of Hadhramaut. By the end of May, cases and deaths had been reported in the governorates of Aden, Taiz, Lahj, and Sanaa. By June 2020, the coronavirus had spread across the country, pushing Yemen's ruined healthcare system to the brink. Many hospitals closed for fear of the virus, or for lack of staff and personal protective equipment. The second wave started in March 2021 on the sixth anniversary of the start of the war. The recorded cases of COVID-19 in the first two weeks of March were twenty-two times higher than the number of cases in the first two weeks of February. On 31 March, the internationally recognised government declared a health emergency in the areas under its control.

An estimated 4.3 million people have fled from their homes since the start of the conflict in 2014, and approximately 3.3 million remain displaced. The camps of internally displaced persons are fertile ground for the spread of COVID-19 and other diseases such as cholera and scabies. On 9 April 2021, the health minister announced that occupancy in intensive care units in quarantine centres had reached maximum capacity because of a sharp increase in the number of cases. On 7 May, officially declared cases of COVID-19 totalled 6,426 and deaths totalled 1,265. This is likely to be an underestimate owing to a severe lack of testing facilities and the questionable reliability of figures from the government and the Houthis, who control most of the North of the country. The mortality rate of 27 per cent is one of the highest in the world and five times the global average.

One of the greatest challenges in fighting COVID-19 is the collapsing healthcare system, which is buckling as the coronavirus pandemic hits an infrastructure already devastated by more than six years of war. The ongoing conflict means that many cases are untraceable. A report from the non-governmental organisation MedGlobal and the Center for Global Health at the University of Illinois in the United States said that ninety-seven healthcare workers had died from COVID-19, citing data collected by medical students and local doctors.

Lack of adequate food supplies leading to hunger, malnutrition, and famine is the greatest humanitarian tragedy caused by the war. In March 2020, UNICEF estimated that two million children under the age of five suffered from acute malnutrition. The magnitude of the crisis is illustrated by the fact that one child dies every twelve minutes. In May, UNICEF described Yemen as "the largest humanitarian crisis in the world", a country where 80 per cent of the population—over twenty-six million people—were in need of humanitarian assistance.

In 2018, Save the Children reported that over eighty-five thousand children had died since the beginning of the conflict as a direct result of famine. Since then, entire communities have been decimated by hunger. Nearly half of all Yemeni children suffer stunted growth because of malnutrition, which also impairs their cognitive development. Henrietta Fore, the head of UNICEF, described the lives of Yemeni children as "a walking nightmare". With an economic crisis—the Yemeni riyal has plummeted to an all-time low, and 80 per cent of the country's food is imported—skyrocketing food prices have plunged millions of families into crisis. Babar Baloch, UNHRC spokesperson, said that with rampant inflation and few livelihood opportunities, families can no longer afford basic meals. "To put food on the table, many displaced families are selling off belongings, pulling children out of school and sending them to work, begging on the streets, or eating just once a day."

In April 2021, Fatik Al-Rodaini, who runs Mona Relief, visited a dusty mountain village in Yemen where he found a bedraggled-looking family of seven sitting against the stone wall of their home, stooped over a boiling pot on an open fire. A smell like vinegar hung in the chilly February air. In the pot were leaves from a halas vine—the family's entire meal. Yemenis used to eat halas leaves only occasionally during periods of food scarcity. The bitter, leathery foliage, boiled in well water often tainted with sewage, can cause stomach ailments. But during the famine, the leaves have become the only thing keeping many Yemenis alive—even in a village just a few dozen miles from Sanaa.

A Yemeni family surviving on halas leaves. Source: Mona Relief.

Al-Rodaini set up Mona Relief in 2015, two months after war started. Mona Relief delivers foodstuffs and supplies to about 6,500 families. Al-Rodaini had seen leaf eating on his relief trips to more remote areas of Yemen. But seeing it so close to the capital left him horrified. "I feel the world is turning a blind eye to the largest humanitarian crisis," he said in an interview with *The Daily Poster.* "The suffering of this area is a living example of how the war has exacted a terrible and massive human cost."

In late 2019, a UN-commissioned report by the University of Denver, "Assessing the Impact of War on Development in Yemen," confirmed that more Yemenis had died of hunger, disease, and lack of health clinics than from fighting; the figure was estimated at 131,000 people. War, in comparison, was responsible for 100,000 deaths—a figure published by the Armed Conflict Location and Event Data Project (ACLED), which tracks confirmed fatalities of war.

Between 2015 and 2019, international donors gave the UN-led aid response in Yemen $8.35 billion, including $3.6 billion spending in 2019 that reached almost 14 million people each month with some form of aid. This was up from 7.5 million people in 2018.

However, aid agencies say that in 2019 and 2020, they spent vast amounts of their time and energy struggling to get approvals countrywide to provide assistance in accordance with humanitarian principles and without the authorities' interference.

Partly in response to the obstruction of aid, donor support to UN aid agencies collapsed in June 2020, particularly from Kuwait, Qatar, Saudi Arabia, the UAE, and the United States. As of 28 August, aid agencies received only 24 per cent of the $3.4 billion they requested for the year.

While funding the aid efforts, the United States, the United Kingdom, France, Canada, and others have sold arms to the Saudi-led coalition, worsening Yemen's humanitarian crisis. The United Kingdom has given £1 billion in aid to Yemen but has licensed £6.5 billion worth of arms to the countries bombing it.

The funding crisis has had a dire impact on Yemeni civilians, including the halving of food assistance to nine million people and the suspension of support to healthcare services, which the United Nations says has put the lives of millions on the line.

But there is money in Yemen to assist humanitarian efforts. A UN panel of experts reported in June 2017 that the Houthis had earned up to $1.14 billion from fuel and oil distribution on the black market and that fuel was "one of the main sources of revenue for the Houthis". However, for the warring factions, humanitarian aid is not a priority. All parties to the conflict in Yemen have stood in the way of humanitarian aid delivery and demanded that taxes be levied and aid rerouted so it would benefit their respective militias.

In September 2020, Human Rights Watch published a sixty-five-page report titled "Deadly Consequences: Obstruction of Aid in Yemen during Covid-19", which details systematic interference in relief operations by the Houthi authorities, Yemen's internationally recognised government and affiliated forces, the UAE, and the Southern Transitional Council.

The Houthis have a particularly egregious record of obstructing aid agencies from reaching civilians and diverting aid to their supporters and fighters. In 2019 and 2020, aid workers had to push back against Houthi officials insisting they hand over their cars, computers, and cell phones at the end of projects.

But obstruction of aid agencies in government-held areas in the south and east is also on the rise. In July 2020, Lowcock said that aid agencies reported an "increase in violent incidents, targeting humanitarian assets and [that] local authorities were adding new bureaucratic requirements".

Yemen's humanitarian crisis is not a by-product of Yemen's institutional and political failures. It is solely the result of a protracted military conflict, and only an end to the conflict will bring an end to the humanitarian crisis.

The country cannot fight a war on two fronts (the military conflict and the fight against famine and disease). Yemenis have different political agendas: the Houthis want to continue creating an Islamic state to fit with their version of Islam, whereas most Southerners want to be independent from the North and establish their own state. But all Yemenis are united in their common condition of poverty, hunger, and disease. Ending the fighting and solving the humanitarian problems together can help end the political stalemate and the pointless war which has no winners except those who trade in arms and the warlords who buy and sell people's lives.

Chapter 11

The Southern Transitional Council and the Struggle for Southern Statehood

In January 2017, the Arab coalition announced the launch of Operation Golden Arrow to retake the western coast and cut off a key Houthi-Salih alliance supply line. In February the strategic port of Mocha was captured by pro-Hadi forces. After the liberation of the South from the Houthis, disputes and disagreements between the Southern Movement and the internationally recognised government (IRG) eventually led to armed conflict. Even though the areas of Yemen not under Houthi control are now theoretically ruled by a power-sharing government in which the Southern Transitional Council (STC) and the IRG are equal partners, there is little cooperation between the two.

At the beginning of 2017, the United States upset Hadi's government with a ground operation in the Yakla area of Al-Bayda governorate which resulted in the death of around thirty civilians, and the government withdrew permission for the United States to run ground missions against suspected Al-Qaeda terrorists in Yemen following the raid.

Witnesses told Human Rights Watch that on 29 January, about thirty US personnel flanked by military dogs approached the home of a military commander, Abdul-Raouf Al-Dahab. Men in Al-Dahab's house heard people approaching and called out. When they got no response, they began shooting, one witness said. Those outside returned the gunfire. Another witness, who was in the house next to Al-Dahab's, said that the men in the house fired warning shots into the air and that the forces outside then opened fire on the home.

The US military said that its forces came under heavy fire "from all sides", including from "houses and other buildings" and from "armed women firing from prepared fighting positions". Human Rights Watch could not confirm that account, but civilians who directly participate in hostilities are subject to attack under the laws of war. The gunfire quickly escalated, with the villagers engaging in a firefight with the forces outside, witnesses said. As the fighting intensified, helicopters and other aircraft began firing on the village with light automatic cannons. Witnesses said that at least twenty houses were damaged.

By late April, tensions intensified between Hadi and the UAE, a member of the Saudi-led coalition, over the UAE's support for independence groups that sought a different agenda to that of the IRG, and a power struggle developed between the IRG, the STC, and the UAE. Hadi accused the UAE of using the war to occupy the South and build a larger web of influence on the important trade route of the Gulf of Aden. Senior members of the STC and the UAE questioned Hadi's alliance with the Yemeni Muslim Brotherhood, and this alliance made the participation of the STC in the IRG difficult because the Islamist ideology was totally at odds with the STC's secular ideology.

The UAE exerted its influence in South Yemen through its support for the Southern Transitional Council and through its local partner, the Al-Hizam al-Amni (Security Belt Forces), which it used to stabilise areas of South Yemen under its control. The Security Belt Forces consisted of tribes powerful in their local area. The UAE was aware that the Southern Resistance was the best organised group for it to partner with, and the one with the broadest appeal to the tribes. The Southern Resistance created a good working partnership with the UAE armed forces.

There were a number of disputes between the Southerners and the IRG. Security forces at Aden International Airport refused to allow prominent Southern Movement leaders to board a plane to Beirut on 20 April. The delegation included the chief of staff of the governor of Aden, Mansour Zeid; the deputy security director for Aden, Abu Bakr Jaber; and a number of administrators and tribal representatives. The group intended to meet representatives of the Berghof Foundation, a German NGO that specialises in preventing political violence. The standoff highlighted ongoing tensions between the Aden International Airport security director, Saleh Al-Amri, and forces allied to President Hadi. There was also an armed standoff between the Security Belt Forces and forces loyal to Hadi on 22 April 2017.

Preparations by the Hadhramaut Tribal Alliance (HTA) for an inclusive conference to shape the governorate's political vision began in mid-2016 after the liberation of Mukalla from AQAP. The Hadhramaut Inclusive Conference (HIC) took place in April 2017 in Mukalla with some three thousand participants. It managed to bring a diverse collection of influential social and political figures into the presidency committee, including erstwhile rivals such as Muhsin Basura, a key Islah party leader and national parliament member from Hadhramaut, and Ahmed Ba Mualim, the head of the STC in the governorate.

The background of the participants was diverse. Around 30 per cent came from the HTA, 30 per cent were from other political entities, 20 per cent were women and representatives from youth-focused non-governmental organisations, 10 per cent represented civil society organisations, and 10 per cent represented the Hadhrami diaspora.

After its first meeting, which called for greater autonomy, representation, and a greater devolution of power over the security sector, the HIC evolved into a permanent organisation which established an office in the Sahl and Wadi, and its secretary general, Tarek Al Akbari, joined the newly formed government as minister of education.

Hadi was upset by the holding of the conference and its deliberations and, on 27 April, responded by dismissing a number of UAE-linked officials in the South, most notably the governor of Aden, Aidarous Al-Zubaidi, and the minister of state, Hani Bin Braik, who also commanded the Security Belt Forces. Hadi was uncomfortable that many pro-Southern independence fighters were amongst the forces trained and supported by the UAE.

Hadi's decision to dismiss Al-Zubaidi and Bin Braik sparked wide protests across Southern Yemen. The protests showed amazing support for Al-Zubaidi, whose pictures were on banners carried by hundreds of demonstrators. On 4 May, Reuters described how convoys of buses and cars carrying hundreds of people from around Southern governorates arrived in Aden in a rally billed as a gathering of millions. "Hadi is going along partisan objectives and deepening divisions in the country," protestor Hamed Faraj told Reuters. He said many people believe that the dismissals showed the president was caving in to pressure from the Islamist Islah party, Yemen's branch of the Muslim Brotherhood, which also opposed the South's calls for independence.

Both Al-Zubaidi and Bin Braik were popular figures in the South, having risen to prominence as commanders of the Southern forces who played a key role in pushing the Houthis out of the South with the financial and military support of the UAE, which most directly aided Bin Braik in the formation of the Security Belt Forces (Al-Hizam).

The STC's alliance with Emirati forces has been beneficial in providing much-needed security in the South, but the Emirati forces have been involved in flagrant human rights violations against the civilian population. Before withdrawing most of its ground troops in 2019, the UAE financed, armed, and trained local Yemeni forces, including the Hadhrami Elite Forces and the Shabwani Elite Forces, to combat terrorist groups such as Al-Qaeda in the Arabian Peninsula (AQAP) and ISIS. Several reports compiled by Human Rights Watch reveal that these local forces, as well as the STC and the Security Belt, committed several abuses while ostensibly fighting Yemeni affiliates of Al-Qaeda and ISIS. These human rights violations included arbitrary arrests, detentions, torture, and unlawful killings. The Security Belt Forces have also been accused of a campaign of violence and marginalisation against Northerners in the South.

Human Rights Watch also reported the presence of a number of unofficial places of detention and secret prisons in Aden and Hadhramaut, including two detention centres run by the UAE and one run by Yemeni security forces with backing from the UAE. Survivors, relatives of victims, and detainees alike shared worrying accounts concerning atrocious crimes committed in these facilities by prison officials. These actions showed an ingrained disregard for international law from which the STC seeks recognition. Given that Yemen, the current de jure state in which these abuses are said to be occurring, is also a member of both the Arms Trade Treaty and the Convention Against Torture, there is a compelling link between the STC and these obligations to respect the provisions of these treaties.

Aden Historic Declaration, 4 May 2017

A turning point in the Southern nationalist movement's struggle for independence was 4 May. The factions of Hirak released the Aden Historic Declaration, which denounced Hadi's decision to dismiss Al-Zubaidi and Bin Braik and entrusted Al-Zubaidi with establishing a leadership for governing and representing Southern Yemen. Al-Zubaidi told the protestors that he intended to work with all parties to push for independence for the south. The declaration stated:

> The capital Aden is embracing the largest and unprecedented step in the political history of the South. This crowd represents the struggle of our peaceful Southern movement and its gallant resistance; these masses are here today to represent all the Southern people's needs, the needs which they have been struggling to gain for many years. There are many who have sacrificed their lives and those who are injured or maimed and those who are still imprisoned are fighting to reinstate the Southern State.

> The cause of the people of the South of is a just cause and has legal and political legitimacy which is recognized regionally and internationally. There are dangers that threaten the South and Southern cause. Those dangers were represented through the latest provocative decisions which only reflected the animosity towards the Southern people which repeat the practices of the aggressors of the 1994 war against the South.

> Those decisions did not only target the Southern leaders or their personnel but are aimed at the very substance and content of the Southern cause. The Decisive Storm and Hope saw a new phase in the history of the region and created a positive reality for the future of the South. With the help of the Arab Coalition we were able to liberate the Southern parts of the country and defeat the Houthi Saleh militias. Unfortunately those victories were not enough to win the Southern resistance a place in the partnership in political representation; on the contrary they were rewarded with marginalization from political participation and excluded from the governing body.

> The Muslim brotherhood in partnership with the governing body played a great role in excluding the Southern resistance. They went to the extent of placing a number of the members under investigation. This was aimed to dampen the hopes of the people in the resistance and lose the chance to take part in the political role in the

future. Another form of punishing the resistance came in the shape of stripping the people from the basic public services such as water supplies, electricity, health education and fuel supplies to the extent of cutting and stopping paying wages to civil servants including the police and army. In addition there is a continued, deliberate neglect of public institutions. The people of Aden, who fought bravely and took part in a war to liberate the country from the oppressors, do not deserve what they are receiving from the government. They are entitled to much better compensation.

Based on that and here from the great and brave city of Aden today, emerges the will of the people of the South. The people of the South expressed their position and desire to exercise their legal right to protect and fortify the Southern issue. This great crowd has come to restore victory and fulfil the aspirations of the people of the South.

We here take the opportunity to salute the people of Hadramawt and congratulate them in their success at the Hadramawt General conference, which is considered an integral part of the National Southern Movement. Given the importance of a political means to protect the Southern issue and its political project as well as achieve the aspirations of the people of the South and its sovereignty over its land and a liberated State, and building its free national democratic federal state the Southern people demand the following:

First: This declaration is called the Aden Historic Declaration and carries the legitimate right of the Southern People's will power.

Second: Leader Aidroos Al-Zubaidi, declared a national political leadership (chaired by him) to manage and represent the Southern leadership the leadership which is tasked to achieve its goals and aspirations, Al-Zubaidi has full authority to take the necessary measures to implement the requirements of this declaration.

Third: The masses promise that the South is a home and an identity and is a based on a system of compatibility and national partnership.

Fourth: The Southern resistance and the Hirak are partners supported by the deep relationship with the UAE and the Kingdom of Saudi Arabia through the joint sacrifices they pledged in order to overcome and stop the Iranian expansion and the fight against terrorism in the region.

Fifth: The above points to be implemented from date of issue the 4th May 2017.

Emboldened by the support he received from all sectors of society in South Yemen who demonstrated against his dismissal as governor of Aden, Al-Zubaidi announced the formation of the Southern Transitional Council on 11 May, effectively creating a third government in Yemen. The Houthis set up a de facto state in the North, and the IRG was based in the temporary capital Aden, although most of its ministers and Hadi resided in villas provided by the Saudi government in Riyadh.

In a televised speech, Al-Zubaidi said that the newly established council was willing to continue working with the Saudi-led Arab coalition—which also involved the UAE—to battle terrorism in the county, despite the coalition's recognition of Hadi as the sole legitimate leader of Yemen. The STC released a statement pledging to "pursue the mission of liberating" South Yemen. It aims to "run the Southern provinces" and "represent them inside and outside" the country.

The STC was presided over by Al-Zubaidi himself; Hani bin Braik was announced as his vice president, but he rejected the move and considered the formation of the council an act that "targets the country's interests, its future and social fabric".

The GCC backed Hani bin Braik on his position and also rejected the move. By 31 May, the UAE reportedly came to exert indirect control over Aden International Airport after clashes erupted between the airport's UAE-backed security director, Saleh al-Amri, and his deputy, al-Khader Kurdah, who supported President Hadi's government. In the wake of the Qatari diplomatic crisis that broke out in early June,

Qatar was expelled from the Saudi-led military coalition. On 15 June, the UN Security Council adopted a presidential statement on the importance of keeping all Yemen's ports functioning, including Hodeidah port, as a critical lifeline for humanitarian support and other essential supplies.

The fact that the STC and Al-Zubaidi were now the key players in the struggle for Southern statehood was clearly illustrated by the fact that the Southern Movement endorsed Al-Zubaidi's leadership and stated, "Commander Aidarous Qassim al-Zubaidi is authorised to announce a national political leadership (under his leadership) to manage and represent the South, and this leadership is responsible for representing and leading the South to achieve its goals and aspirations, going on to grant him the power to do so by whatever steps necessary to implement the articles of the Aden Historic Declaration." The STC born out of the struggle of the Southern Movement is now a major political and military organisation fighting for Southern statehood.

The Southern Transitional Council

Since it was set up in May 2017 the Southern Transitional Council (STC) has acted as a government-in-waiting by setting up a bureaucratic institutional structure and opening offices in America and Europe. On its EU website, the STC describes a leadership council of twenty-four persons and its component departments: political affairs, information, legal affairs, guidance, mass action, rights and freedoms, martyrs and wounded affairs, culture, finance and economy, and organisation. The basis of the formation of the STC is the Southern Movement, which had already been in existence since 2007 with its own political structures and organisations. The leadership council consists of some governors of the South Yemeni governorates (Al-Dhali, Shabwa, Hadhramaut, Lahij, Socotra, and Al-Mahra), ministers of the government, and representatives of the Southern Movement. Over the long term, the various departments of the council will build state structures in South Yemen.[25]

The website (https://stc-eu.org/en/sueduebergangsrat/) states that on 30 November 2017, the National Assembly was formed from 303 representatives covering the entire spectrum of political and civil society in South Yemen. Currently, no institutionalised electoral system or regulations on political parties exist in South Yemen, owing to the fragile situation in the country and the war. However, the Southern Movement is a grassroots movement supported by large sections of the population, which is evident from the high turnout in demonstrations. The STC pursues a participatory approach and gives access to all decisions taken in the council. Positions were distributed following suggestions and a consensual decision-making process. The positions in the leadership council and in the National Assembly were distributed to persons who play a vital role in the political, civil, cultural, and charitable life in their local communities. In 2018, the first offices of the STC were established worldwide. Attempts have been made to establish a cogent network

---

[25] The presidential council of the STC consists of twenty-six members: Hamid Lamlas, governor of Shabwah; Aidarus al-Zoubaidi, president of STC; Ahmed bin Breik, former governor of Hadhramaut, Ali Al-Kathiri, representative from SLA party; Murad al-Hallemy, minister of transport; Niran Suqi, jurist; Saleh Al-Awlaqi, Southern parliamentarian; Fadhl Al-Ghadi, governor of Dhale; Lutfi Bashareef, minister of communications; Abdurahman Shaikh, deputy of Aden; Lutfi Shatara, journalist; Ameen Saleh, activist; Mona Basharaheed, professor of literature; Ahmed Al-Socotry, governor of Socotra; Ali Ashaibah, brigadier general and activist; Abdullah Arefarar, representative of Mahra and Socotra; Hani Bin Breik, vice president of STC; Aqel Al-Attas, activist; Nasser Al-Khobbaki, governor of Lahij; Adnan Al-Kaaf, deputy of Aden; Abdurrab Al-Naqeep, representative of YafeaWest–southern Abyan; Salem al-Awlaqi, activist; Nasser Assadi, brigadier general and activist; Abdulhadi Shayif, economist; Sahair Ali, professor of law; and Ahmed Bamuallem, Brigadier General and representative from Hadramaut.

of political decision-making bodies in the form of STC National Assemblies in Aden and Shabwa which address important local issues such as food shortages and provision of services to refugees in the South

The STC's vision is described in the following terms:

> With a deep understanding of the fundamental problems of the Southern cause, the Southern Transitional Council (STC) represents the will of South Yemenis to regain their own state, as well as their expectations for solving the Southern cause. The STC strongly believes that any solution which is not compatible with the will and the aspirations of South Yemenis will fail and further destabilize the already unstable region. Therefore, the council is willing to cooperate with all regional and international stakeholders to bring about a solution of the Southern cause, so that conflicts in the region can be avoided in the future. That is why the council aims at good relations with North Yemen after South Yemen's independence. Particularly, the STC hopes for constructive cooperation with the UN special envoy to Yemen, in order to bring about a joint solution for the Southern cause. The independence of South Yemen will lead to long-term stability in the strategically significant region of the Bab al-Mandab and the Gulf of Aden.

The STC accused the Hadi administration of mismanagement from 2012 to 2014. It claims that the provision of electricity, water, salaries, and civilian life as a whole deteriorated to unprecedented levels, and the rehabilitation of government institutions, which did not function effectively when Salih was in control of the South, has also been neglected. It has ambitious visions of restoring Aden and the South to their former glory but is mindful of the harsh lessons learnt during the time of the PDRY about internecine conflict and the dangers of blindly following an uncompromising ideology. One of its main problems is the lack of capital to restore essential services and promote the development of the South. As of December 2021 the STC has not been able to carry out most matters of state beyond international diplomacy. Both in Saudi Arabia where he has an official residence and in Aden, Al-Zubaidi has met scores of diplomats, the UN special envoy to Yemen, and representatives of aid and humanitarian organisations. The STC is also developing its media presence through the Internet and a newsletter.

Since its formation, it has received financial and military support from the UAE, which is not averse to its demands for the independence of the South. Military activities in the region, as well as talk of investment plans, have strengthened rumours regarding the UAE's strategic interests and goals in the region. Analysts believe that an independent South Yemen would be a huge strategic asset to the UAE in terms of military defence base locations, economic and trade opportunities, and resource availability.

The STC, in an essential partnership with the UAE, is trying to win the hearts and minds of the people through the provision of services which, it points out, the IRG has not been able to provide.

Despite the emergence of the South in general and the STC in particular as a genuinely significant player and stakeholder in the Yemeni conflict, it continues to be considerably sidelined as an issue by international policymakers. Their tendency to focus almost solely upon Hadi's internationally recognised government and the Houthi movement reflects a longstanding disregard for South Yemen both internally (within Yemen) and externally (by international actors).

After Martin Griffiths's appointment as the UN's special envoy, the STC attempted to cooperate with him, but when he did not include the STC in peace talks because of negative pressure from President Hadi, it called on the local leaders and people of the South to follow the STC's lead and peacefully protest and refuse to abide by the requirements set out in any peace agreement which they were not consulted in making. In its call, the STC made it clear that "we have not been the cause of this war, but it has been imposed upon us, and we have become a major party in it, and it cannot be stopped without us".

Today, the Southern Transitional Council has a significant presence in all Southern territories. Flags of the former PDRY are flown from Aden to Hadhramaut, often alongside those of the Arab coalition as a gesture of gratitude for their ongoing support. Whilst the STC has achieved a modest early step towards independence, its cause is clearly at the mercy of international politics that is still broadly aligned with President Hadi and a united Yemen. The United Nations, as is evident from the peace talks it sponsored, insists on one Yemeni state. Southern independence movements are constantly described as "secessionist" even though the Houthis control more than 80 per cent of the North and there is no Yemeni state from which to secede.

Southern Political Movements

While the STC has grabbed the limelight as the major political movement in the South since the Houthi coup in 2014, it is certainly not the only political organisation in the South calling for an independent South Yemen. It has come into conflict with other pro-independence groups and is clearly not welcome in Mahrah governorate where traditional tribal rulers suffered at the hands of the socialist government during the time of the PDRY and are now making a successful political comeback.

While the Southern Movement (Hirak) has let the STC play the leading role in advancing the case for Southern statehood both politically and militarily,[26] the loose association of political groupings is still very much alive (see pg. xx). The movement's vision is "to liberate Southern land from the occupying North Yemeni military forces and transform the calls of the Southern people of Yemen for a free and independent Southern state into meaningful action. This will be achieved by peaceful dialogue with all relevant stakeholders, reaching an agreement to revive the independent South Yemen (South Arabia) state on its original borders prior to 1990. These are put into action by exercising the people's right to self-determination through a referendum with a choice for independence by way of agreed secession". While the majority of political groupings affiliated with the Southern Movement reject violence, the armed struggle is not completely ruled out.

---

[26] While the Houthis have one army command structure and one leader, it gives them an advantage to execute the war to their advantage. The Southern forces and the legitimate government are divided, and there is very little joint cooperation between them and too many leaders with no unified command structure. After the Houthi coup, the National Army weakened, and the Houthis were able to amalgamate some of the troops and senior army officers into their militias as well as getting possession of almost all army hardware . President Hadi's current forces were once part of the National Army, are now called the Yemeni National Army, and are mostly loyal to Ali Mohsin, the president's deputy. The Republican Guards are now under the command of Tarik Salih, the nephew of the deposed president Ali Abdullah Salih. The Shabwani Popular Movement and Hadrami Elite forces are supported by the Southern Transitional Council. In addition, the Security Belt Forces are the military wing of the STC, which also has a number of brigades in Dhala, Hodeidah, and Aden. It is also important to note that forces of the government and the STC have to answer to the coalition commanders. The Riyadh agreement was intended to amalgamate the different factions in one army with one command structure, but this agreement had failed to materialise six months after it was signed and agreed to by all parties.

Hassan Ba'oum.

The Supreme Council of the Revolutionary Movement for the Peaceful Liberation and Independence of the South, established in 2007 by Hassan Ba'oum, aims to establish an independent state in South Yemen. The movement is known for its anti-Saudi and anti-UAE stances. It has repeatedly called for the expulsion of the Arab coalition from Yemen's Southern provinces, calling it "an occupation force". When the STC rescinded its self-rule declaration in July 2020 (see pg. 145), Ba'oum called for the formation of committees to communicate with Southern leaders, including military and academic personalities, who believe in liberation and independence.

The Southern National Coalition was set up by Al Shaik Ahmed Saleh Al Easy. It supports the internationally recognised government and opposes the STC. It was established to counteract the influence of the STC in Hadhramaut, Shabwa, Abyan, and Aden. On 17 August 2020, it organised a demonstration to voice rejection of the monopoly of popular representation in the Southern governorates by the STC. It also expressed its condemnation of all measures of normalisation of relations with Israel.

The Yemeni Socialist Party (YSP), the former ruling party in South Yemen, was established in 1978 by Abdul Fattah Ismail, Ali Nasir Muhammad, and Ali Salem Al-Beidh. It was a successor of Yemen's National Liberation Front, which ousted the British from South Yemen in 1967. Originally Marxist-Leninist, the party gradually evolved into a democratic socialist opposition party when North and South Yemen united in 1990 (see part one, pgs. 54-57). The general secretaries of the YSP were Abdul Fattah Ismail (1978–80), Ali Nasir Muhammad (1980–86), Ali Salem Al-Beidh (1986–1994), Ali Saleh Obad (Moqbel; 1994–2005), Yasin Said Numan (2005–15), and Abdulraham Al-Saqqaf (2015–present).

The General Council of the Sons of Al Mahrah and Soqotra was established in 2021 by Sultan Abdullah bin Isa Al Afrar. Sultan Al Afrar is a member of the family that ruled the sultanate of Mahrah and Qishn until its abolition in 1967. The council's main goal has been to create a federal region within the borders of the former sultanate. It seeks to restore the sultanate's linguistic, cultural, social, geographical, and historical independence and homogeneity, as well as to increase its own role in political decision-making in Al Mahrah after its historical exclusion and political marginalisation. The council opposes Saudi Arabia's policy of controlling the governorate indirectly through development and relief projects, as well as its military presence. It also opposes Emirati involvement in the governorate, and unlike most Southern movements, it supports Yemeni unity.

The Southern Assembly (TAJ) was established in July 2004 by Abdo Al Naqeeb. The movement has subsided since the establishment of the STC, but its leadership has recently become active again. Their aim it to establish a Southern Arabian state.

Dr Abdul Galil Shaif and Karen Dabrowska. Source Author.

Friends of South Yemen (FOSY) was established in June 2020 by Dr Abdul Galil Shaif (the author of this book) and Karen Dabrowska to campaign for an independent South Yemen through contacts with politicians and providing information about South Yemen through its website, www.friendsofsouthyemen.org, and its Facebook page, which is updated daily. FOSY produces a monthly newsletter and organised an international online conference on "The Case for Southern Statehood". A booklet of the conference proceedings has been published. FOSY has also produced a documentary on the case for Southern Statehood and has put forward the only road map for ending the war and fostering development (see pg. xx). Its chairman has been a prominent speaker at many international Zoom conferences on Yemen.

The Conflict between the STC and the IRG

Conflict between the STC and IRG was inevitable. Their only common objective was the ousting of the Houthis from the South, and as soon as this happened, relations deteriorated steadily and finally resulted in armed clashes.

President Hadi was suspicious of Al-Zubaidi and Hani bin Braik because they both held strong sympathies with the Southern Movement and supported Southern independence. If this was achieved, the IRG would be surplus to requirements because the Houthis have gained control of more than 80 per cent of the North and are ruling through a de facto government which, with Iran's support, is entrenching itself more and more in Sanaa and proving almost impossible to dislodge.

When Al-Zubaidi was governor of Aden, he and Bin Braik rose to prominence as the commanders of the forces of the independence movement that, with the IRG and the Arab coalition, pushed the Houthis out of the South. The UAE assisted Bin Braik in the formation of the Security Belt Forces.

Hadi and Al-Zubaidi had different backgrounds and political allegiances. Al-Zubaidi was an air force pilot in the PDRY, and Bin Braik was head of a faction of the Yemeni Socialist Party (YSP) named the Zomra, which fled to North Yemen in 1986 after the defeat of its leader Ali Nasser Mohammed at the hands of Ali Salem Al-Beidh's Toghma faction. Hadi fought on the side of the Salih regime in the summer of the 1994 war of secession and formally led Salih's war effort as his defence minister. After the war, he was named vice president of the "united" Yemen—part of Salih's charm offensive to woo the South.

In the 1994 war, Al-Zubaidi fought with the forces of Al-Beidh. After the war, he set up the Movement of Self Determination (HATM), which aimed to destabilise the Salih regime's hold on the South through assassinations and attacks against military targets. HATM was active between 1997 and 2001 and in 2011. Al-Zubaidi subsequently commanded a number of pro-independence forces which gained control of the provincial capital of Al-Dhale, Al-Zubaidi's home province, in 2015.

Protests in support of the STC continued in South Yemen. In July 2017, thousands of Yemenis demanding an independent state rallied in the streets of Aden waving the flag of the formerly independent South in their third protest since May. The protesters chanted "Independence is our objective" as they marched.

STC president Aidarous Al-Zubaidi. Source: STC.

The conflict between the IRG and the STC intensified. Amidst tensions between the Southern Transitional Council and the Hadi government in Aden, the STC announced on 21 January 2018 that it would overthrow the Yemeni government within a week unless President Hadi sacked his entire cabinet, including Prime Minister Ahmed Obeid bin Daghr, for "rampant corruption" and "waging a misinformation campaign against the Southern leaders using state funds".

"The Southern Resistance Forces (SRF) declare a state of emergency in Aden and announce that it has begun the process of overthrowing the legitimate government and replacing it with a cabinet of technocrats," a statement issued by the STC said.

The government responded by banning protests in Aden, but the STC organised an anti-government rally for 28 January 2018. Gun battles erupted when security forces loyal to the Hadi government attempted to prevent pro-STC demonstrators from entering the city. The STC captured the government headquarters in Aden. The government ordered its own troops to return to base following fierce clashes across Aden, and the STC declared it was in control of the city on 30 January. The two sides exchanged prisoners the next day. Since that time, the STC has continued to challenge the authority of the IRG in the South.

Fighting, kidnappings, assassinations, carjackings, bombings, and other hazards made Aden a difficult operational environment for relief actors, and most organisations have operated without international staff in Aden since mid-2015.

In June 2019, the UAE scaled down its military presence in Yemen but stated it would continue fighting "terrorist organisations" in Southern provinces and other areas. Hadi was incensed with the UAE, accusing it of acting as an occupying force as opposed to a liberation force, and condemned the UAE's support for the STC. At the end of October, the UAE announced that its troops had left Aden and returned home, handing over control to Saudi Arabia. But the UAE still maintained a presence in the South, especially on the island of Socotra where it financed a number of humanitarian and development projects and built military facilities.

Writing in the Middle East Institute's 15 February 2020, newsletter Ibrahim Jalal[27] pointed out that the UAE may have withdrawn from Yemen, but its influence remains strong. It has also retained control over several non-state armed groups, thought to total around ninety thousand fighters across the liberated territories, which it supports by providing direct training, capacity building, logistics assistance, and salaries. In the east it has the Shabwani and Hadhrami Elite Forces, and to the west it has the Joint Forces, including the Guards of the Republic, which brand themselves as the National Resistance. It has the Security Belt Forces in the South and the Abu al-Abbas Fighters in the south-west. The UN's Yemen Panel of Experts' 2020 report concluded that the UAE has had operational control of most of these groups since their establishment, although the Yemeni government has claimed otherwise.

The next major flare up occurred on 1 August 2019, when the Houthis launched an attack on a Southern military ceremony in Aden. A medium-range ballistic missile was used to kill dozens in the camp, including a well-known and senior commander of the Southern movement, Muneer al-Yafee, aka Abu al-Yamama. The attack triggered widespread anger in the South, with the STC levelling blame at the Hadi-affiliated Islah party, accusing it of complicity in the attack. In response, a four-day battle took place between STC forces and those loyal to the Saudi-backed Hadi government. Dozens were killed in the infighting, which came to an end with the Southern forces taking control of all government buildings and military camps within the city. including the symbolic presidential palace.

The Riyadh Agreement

Saudi Arabia initiated negotiations to resolve the conflict between the IRG and the STC after the STC's moves to expel Hadi loyalists from Aden and other areas in the South.

On 5 November 2019, a power-sharing agreement was signed in Riyadh between the IRG and the STC. The document set forth a range of points and dispensations, most importantly providing for power-sharing between North and South and the return of Prime Minister Moeen Abdelmalek to Aden to set up state institutions. It also included three annexes covering a range of political, economic, military, and security issues, the implementation of which would be overseen by Saudi Arabia. (For the full text of the agreement, see Appendix 3.)

The agreement provided for various procedures to put state institutions into operation, the most important of which were the following.

1. Strengthening the role of Yemeni state institutions and bodies both politically and economically.

2. Reorganising military forces under the command of the Defence Ministry.

3. Reorganising security forces under the command of the Interior Ministry.

4. Commitment to full citizenship rights and an end to regional and sectarian discrimination and division.

5. An end to current media campaigns between the two sides.

6. A unified military effort under coalition leadership, restoring security and stability to Yemen.

7. Confronting terrorist organisations.

---

[27] Ibrahim Jalal, "The UAE May Have Wwithdrawn from Yemen, but Its Influence Remains Strong", MEI@75, 25 February 2020.

8. Forming a committee under Saudi leadership and coalition oversight to monitor implementation of the agreement and its annexes dealing with political and economic arrangements, military arrangements and security arrangements.

9. STC participation in the government delegation to the negotiations to find a final political solution to the Houthi coup.

10. As soon as the document is signed, President Hadi will issue directives to state institutions to implement the agreement.

An unrealistic two-month timetable for full implementation of the agreement was set and then promptly broken, and military confrontations between the STC and IRG forces continued for control of territory in Abyan and Shabwa governorates. In Aden, the troubled relationship between the STC and Saudi forces worsened, and the STC forces tried to prevent the Saudis from moving into certain areas. On 9 January 2020, a new timetable was set for withdrawal of military forces to pre-August positions and the gathering of heavy weapons in Saudi-managed sites. It looked as if progress was being made, but the STC had little faith in the process and removed its operational matériel away from Aden and into its rural strongholds.

The agreement was honoured more in the breach than in observance, and there were armed clashes between government and STC forces. The Riyadh Agreement was becoming increasingly irrelevant to the situation on the ground. Towards the end of April 2020, Saudi Arabia sponsored direct negotiations in Aden between the military representatives of the government and the STC. The government was severely criticised for its performance, the two sides traded accusations and insults, and the STC claimed that the government of Maeed Abdul Malik lacked legitimacy. It announced that the implementation of the Riyadh Agreement was subject to the return of STC leaders who were prevented from leaving Saudi Arabia.

The Riyadh Agreement was designed by the Saudis, as the main sponsors, to bring an immediate end to the military confrontation in Abyan and Shabwa between the STC and the IRG led by Hadi. However, this agreement had many limitations in its implementation. The STC and the government have used the agreement to try to win public support in the South, but their failure to achieve anything on the ground has made it somewhat redundant. Publicly both groups blame each other for the lack of implementation, but in reality differences persist, and the potential of another military conflict remains on the table. It would be in the interest of both groups to build mutual trust and bring about some solutions to the current stalemate.

The STC has definitely achieved international recognition through the agreement as part of the government and appointing a governor and a chief of police in Aden connected to the group. The legitimate government continues to be in charge of government funds and is using its authority to make it hard for the STC to maintain control of the areas they are in charge of.

Despite fighting in the same coalition against the Iran-aligned Houthis, the UAE continues to support the STC and doesn't trust Hadi or his government after accusing them of aligning with the Islah party, a powerfully connected party throughout Yemen, whom the UAE view as ideologically close to the Muslim Brotherhood.

Both the STC and the government are getting support from one Gulf state or another, and in a sense they are weakening each other hoping that one side will soon crumble for the benefit of the other. In reality the only beneficiary of this continuing feud are the Houthis.

The STC has made many attempts to convince the Saudis that they are the genuine partner with them to defeat the Houthis militarily, but so far the Saudis are not convinced and hence continue to support the IRG throughout South Yemen.

The STC has to some extent remained silent about the Houthi advance into Marib because they believe this advance would definitely weaken the IRG and expose its inability to govern. The Saudis are well aware of the situation and have so far ensured that Marib doesn't fall into Houthi hands.

The Houthi advance into Marib and possibly Shabwa may be far more dangerous for the STC and the South in the short term. The government, in contrast, believes that if they can hold off the Houthi advance to take Marib and maintain their control of Shabwa, they can then begin the process of stabilising the economy and improving needed services in the south. That would weaken the STC.

There are definitely some differences emerging within the Arab coalition between the Saudis and the Emiratis on the question of which group to support in the Yemen crisis.

The talks aimed at resolving the differences between the IRG and STC came at a difficult time and achieved little. On 10 April 2020, Yemen recorded its first laboratory-confirmed COVID-19 case in the Southern governorate of Hadhramaut. By the end of May, cases and deaths had been reported in the governorates of Aden, Taiz, Lahj, and Sanaa. By June 2020, the coronavirus had spread across the country, pushing Yemen's ruined healthcare system to the brink. Aden also suffered from devastating floods.

Declaration of Self-Rule by the STC

On 26 April 2020, the STC announced that it was establishing self-rule in the parts of South Yemen under its control. It was an adventurous decision that changed the political landscape in Yemen and showed that despite its collaboration with the IRG, the STC's main objective was the establishment of an independent state in the South. Participation in the IRG was a means to secure this end. The declaration showed that the Saudi- and UAE-led coalition had collapsed because Saudi forces were fighting against the STC, though these two countries continued to give the impression that they were on the same page in Yemen as they were both against the Houthis.

The council cited several issues that pushed its leadership to announce self-rule. Amongst other things, it stated that the Yemeni government had not paid the salaries of government employees and the security forces, the fighters on the frontlines had been neglected, and the support for the injured and families of "martyrs" had been stopped. According to STC leading figures, the declaration of self-rule is irreversible because it lays the groundwork for realising independence from Yemen's north. Saleh Alnoud, a spokesperson of the STC, said, "We don't make it a secret that people want to establish an independent state … the STC will try to achieve the goals for the Southern cause as much as possible." He considered the continuation of Yemen's unity as "inconceivable".

The declaration of self-rule was expected and followed from the announcement of the historic Aden Declaration (see pg. 132). It was also hinted at in STC literature and the announcement by Bin Braik that the STC intended to establish its own Ministry of Defence. This was in total opposition to the Riyadh Agreement, which called for unifying military forces in the South and including them under the Ministry of Defence of united Yemen.

Ahmed bin Braik, chairman of the Southern Self-Administration Committee, issued a decree mandating all state institutions and administrative apparatus in Southern governorates to deposit their revenues into an STC-controlled, consolidated account at Bank Al-Ahli Al-Yemeni, otherwise known as the National Bank of Yemen (NBY). On 5 May, the STC ordered public customs and tax offices operating in the Free Zone, Al-Mualla, and Al-Zait areas of Aden port to deposit revenues at the NBY instead of the

Aden central bank, where they are legally mandated to go. In enforcing the redirection of public revenues, the STC closed the central bank offices at the Aden port facilities, confiscated YR639 million worth of existing customs and tariffs, and transferred these to the NBY.

But not all the governorates were happy with the declaration. As *Inside Arabia* pointed out in its article on 12 May 2020, the STC still faced huge local opposition in many Southern provinces, as well as international rejection. "The Council does not enjoy a strong presence in Hadramout, Shabwa, Al-Mahra, Abyan, and Socotra. Following the declaration of the self-rule, the governors of these provinces released separate statements denouncing the 'meaningless' words of the STC. Out of the eight provinces in the south, the STC has a considerable presence in three—namely, Aden, Lahj, and Dhale."[28]

The self-rule declaration renewed the conflict with the IRG. On 11 May, Hadi government forces attacked the STC positions in the capital of Abyan province, Zinjibar. An STC official, Nabil Al-Hanachi, stated that they managed to "stop the attack and kill many of them". The renewed fighting between the two sides brought additional risks to the already fragile Riyadh Agreement, which sounded fine in theory but was not being implemented on the ground.

In an attempt to resolve the conflict, Al-Zubaidi visited Riyadh on 19 May to discuss the prolonged impasse with the Hadi government. The talks went on until 26 May, as the Saudi Crown Prince Mohammed bin Salman was facing a challenge to resolve the conflict between the Hadi government it sponsored and the STC, backed by the UAE. The conflict between the two sides reflected rising differences within the Saudi-led coalition, giving rise to a "war within a war"—the war that the two are fighting against the Houthi rebels, who are gaining the upper hand.

STC Control of Socotra

The STC, confident and emboldened after the declaration of self-rule, flexed its military muscle, and on 21 June 2020, it seized full control of the island of Socotra, deposing Governor Ramzi Mahroos, who denounced the action as a coup. The move was carried out by a small number of fighters with no bloodshed.

The IRG condemned the action as a full-fledged coup and accused STC forces of attacking government buildings in gang-style behaviour. The deposed governor of Socotra accused the coalition and the UAE of turning a blind eye to the takeover of the island. The STC reportedly expelled dozens of Yemenis from the Northern governorates who lived on the island, transporting them in small boats.

The once peaceful island, situated near strategic shipping lanes linking Asia to Europe via the Red Sea and Suez Canal, and famed for its rare and picturesque biodiversity, is a weak spot for all parties involved in the Yemen conflict, all of which have attempted to sneak their way into the hearts of the local population.

The Socotra Archipelago, in the north-west Indian Ocean near the Gulf of Aden, is 250 kilometres long and comprises four islands and two rocky islets which appear as a prolongation of the Horn of Africa. The main island covers most of the archipelago. The site is of universal importance because of its biodiversity, with rich and distinct flora and fauna: 37 per cent of Socotra's 825 plant species, 90 per cent of its reptile species, and 95 per cent of its land snail species do not occur anywhere else in the world. The site also supports globally significant populations of land and sea birds (192 bird species, 44 of which breed on the islands while 85 are regular migrants), including a number of threatened species.

The marine life of Socotra is also very diverse, with 253 species of reef-building corals, 730 species of coastal fish, and 300 species of crab, lobster, and shrimp. But the conflicts on the island are

---

[28] "STC's Declared Self-Rule in South Yemen Sets Path to Future of Civil Strife", *Inside Arabia,* 12 May 2020, https://insidearabia.com/stcs-declared-self-rule-in-south-yemen-sets-path-to-future-of-civil-strife.

preventing it from benefiting from its tourism potential as a UNESCO World Heritage Site. At the end of October, UNESCO decided to send a mission to the island amidst concerns over increasing threats to the archipelago's unique biodiversity. A nature reserve is now under the control of the STC. Yemen's delegate to UNESCO, Muhammad Jumaih, discussed plans to carry out a report on the state of the reserve with Mechtild Rossler, the director of the UNESCO World Heritage Centre. The Socotrans have resorted to using wood as fuel owing to a gas shortage, which they blame on the STC. The *Socotra Post* reported that twenty-one local and three international lawyers have joined a human rights group working to file a lawsuit against Hadi's government regarding its failure to fulfil its duty to protect the sovereignty of the archipelago as the UAE consolidates its influence.

Although Socotra is part of Yemen, the central government has done little to improve the lives of the people on the island, which has been plagued by widespread poverty and economic underdevelopment. The UAE has been luring Socotrans with promises of economic benefits, residents are provided free healthcare and work permits in Abu Dhabi, and many have been given UAE citizenship, all in return for naval facilities, but the island's rare flora and fauna and clear waters are at risk if such plans go ahead. Any unfettered increase in human and cargo traffic could be devastating for the environment.

According to ABNA News Agency on 27 October 2020, the head of the STC militia in Socotra, Rafat Al-Thaqali, met two officers, Lieutenant Mohammed Salem Ahmed Al-Jamhi and Lieutenant Khamis Saleh Saeed, on the islands of Abd Al Kuri and Samaha, where the UAE wants to establish military bases. UAE military leaders have also held extensive meetings with STC leaders on Socotra. The UAE is reportedly also trying to persuade citizens to sell their land to them. It is trying to acquire land through its delegate Abu Mubarak, who has already bought large areas.

Scores of Yemeni tribal leaders and dignitaries have called for the removal of the STC forces and the checkpoints they established. STC forces have reportedly shot at demonstrators, causing tension. ABNA reported that the people in the Sarhin area accused the UAE of pushing the STC to seize their land to achieve its military interests, and there were a number of violent clashes between the residents and STC forces. In June the UAE reportedly established a joint operations room with the Israeli navy in the strategic Ras Quttainan area after displacing the people who lived there. Issa Salem bin Yaqut, an Oman-based senior sheikh of Socotra, continues to campaign fiercely against the UAE's presence, which he condemned in his testimony before the US Congress in October 2019.

Military activity on the island, the building of military bases, and conflict between the locals, the STC, and the Emiratis have resulted in a lethal mix, and Yemen's only haven of peace and natural wonder is now set to become an environmental and cultural tragedy as the traditional way of life is threatened by outsiders trying to use the island to serve their own interests with scant regard for the wishes or welfare of the local inhabitants.

The UAE has tried to win the hearts and minds of the islanders over six years, with aid amounting to $110 million. The donor organisations include the Emirates Red Crescent (ERC), the Khalifa Bin Zayed Al Nahyan Foundation, the Sheikh Sultan Bin Khalifa Al Nahyan Humanitarian and Scientific Foundation, the Abu Dhabi Fund for Development (ADFD), and the Abu Dhabi Waste Management Centre. This aid has shored up key sectors of the government including roads and transport, education, water and health, construction, and energy, amongst other areas.

The STC Rescinds the Self-Rule Declaration and Suspends Participation in Riyadh Agreement Consultations

The STC's self-rule declaration shocked both Saudi Arabia and the UAE. Both countries put pressure on the STC to backtrack, and the declaration was rescinded on 29 July 2020. Saudi Arabia said it had proposed a plan to "accelerate" the implementation of the Riyadh Agreement. Ahmed Al-Lamlas was appointed as Aden's new governor.

Saudi Arabia's state news agency announced that Yemen's prime minister would now form a cabinet within thirty days, representing North and South Yemen equally and including STC representatives. It was agreed that military forces would leave Aden governorate, forces in neighbouring Abyan province would separate and return to previous positions, and a ceasefire agreed to in June should continue, the Saudi announcement said.

Saudi Arabia's "efforts have succeeded in bringing together the Yemeni government and the Southern Transitional Council in accepting the proposed mechanism by the kingdom to implement the Riyadh agreement", the Saudi deputy defence minister, Prince Khalid bin Salman, wrote on Twitter. "The efforts in bringing together Yemeni political leaders … and reaching consensus on the mechanism for implementing the Riyadh Agreement shows the possibility of resolving Yemeni differences through dialogue without the use (of) military force," he added. The UAE welcomed the Saudi initiative and urged all Yemeni forces to cooperate in the fight against the Houthis, according to a Foreign Ministry statement carried by the state news agency WAM.

But the UN special envoy to Yemen, Martin Griffiths, commented that the window of opportunity to reach an agreement was limited.

On 25 August 2020, the STC sent an official letter to Saudi Arabia as the sponsor of the Riyadh Agreement between the STC and the Yemeni government. The letter said the STC confirmed the suspension of its participation in the ongoing consultations to implement the agreement, noting that the suspension decision came for the following reasons.

1. The continuing and increasing pace of military escalation by the forces affiliated with the Yemeni government in the governorate of Abyan, and their failure to comply with the agreed ceasefire. The forces have carried out more than 350 documented violations, resulting in a toll of more than 75 people—martyrs and wounded soldiers—from the Southern Armed Forces since the declaration of the ceasefire on Monday, 22 June 2020.
2. The continuation of the military build-up operations towards the South, with significant participation of elements affiliated with Al-Qaeda and ISIS, who got embedded within the Yemeni government forces in Abyan.
3. Ignoring the families of the martyrs or treating the wounded who gave their lives and blood for the cause of the South and the Arab project.
4. Delays in paying the pensions and salaries for several months, especially allocations for the military and security sectors, plus settling the status of military and civilian retirees as well as the civil sector employees, particularly the teachers.
5. Forces affiliated with the Yemeni government continued to target civilians in Shabwa governorate, Hadhramaut Valley, and Al-Mahrah through systemic assassination, repression, arrests, enforced disappearances, and torture inside prisons.
6. The collapse of public services in the Southern governorates, and the failure to have any intentions towards real solutions to alleviate the citizens' suffering.

7. The continuing collapse of the currency, the failure to provide cash liquidity in the Southern governorates, and the inflation of goods and services prices which caused consequent tragic repercussions for the citizen.

The STC's Policies, Strategies, and Future Prospects

In the conclusion to their report "Back to the Future? (A Report on the STC and Secessionist Activities within Southern Yemen)", Max Donbenko, Skylar Benedict, Enzo El Adem, and Alex Forster make some important points about the policies, strategies and future prospects of the STC.

- Understanding the STC and Southern Independence issue requires a knowledge of Yemen's historical divide. North and South Yemen have long been separate entities and have developed along different social, cultural and religious lines. These are still prominent in the areas today. Alleged Northern repression of South Yemen since unification in 1990 fuels secessionist sentiment within the South and support for the STC.

- The emergence of the STC is significantly linked to Al-Hirak. However, the aims and structures differ significantly as a result of the civil war context. The STC appear to be fulfilling a vacuum left by Hadi's unpopularity in the South, catalysed by the firing of Al-Zubaidi as Governor of Aden in 2017.

- The STC is pursuing a clear strategy to present itself as a legitimate body in both the civil and military sense. Its commitment to re-establish services and infrastructure long neglected in the South is evidenced in particular by the rhetoric of the Aden Declaration. However, the reliance on UAE support for doing this is extensive and it is likely the latter is involving itself in South Yemen as part of its strategy to increase its influence in the Gulf.

- The STC's control over South Yemen is far from complete. Complex and overlapping loyalties, and localized power structures in Yemen, are at the root of this. However, the Council remains by far the largest Southern actor, and the only one with the potential to fully unite South Yemen. Its reliance on the UAE is comprehensive, however. Albeit for different reasons, both Saudi Arabia and the United Nations express an ambivalence towards the STC's legitimacy, focusing attention upon Hadi's internationally recognised government. For the UN, this may be as a result of Security Council Resolution 2216, which recognises the sole legitimacy of Hadi's government.

- The current categorisation of the STC in international law is probably as a non-state actor, elevated somewhat above a simple militia. Whilst they fail to fulfil crucial elements required to be categorised as a de jure or even de facto state, this does not prohibit their possessing of international rights and obligations. Their obligations in conducting war are set out by Additional Protocol II to the Geneva Conventions. It can be argued that both the STC and the UAE have broken international law as a result of torture networks within South Yemen discovered in 2017.

- Looking ahead, there are a number of potential outcomes for the STC; the volatile nature of Yemen's civil war and the unpredictability of its actors make it impossible to predict an exact end result. That the Southern cause will "fizzle out" is unlikely because of the combination of the longstanding resentment of Southerners towards North Yemen and the extensive support offered to the STC by the UAE. It is possible that South Yemen will eventually achieve statehood; more likely, however, is a "limbo" state of de facto or contested statehood. Finally, federalism is also a potential solution for the South. This would mean that the South consensually remained a part of Yemen, but with significant regional autonomy.[29]

Missed Opportunities to Advance the Case for Southern Statehood

The chairman of Friends of South Yemen (FOSY), Dr Abdul Galil Shaif, pointed out that the STC missed three important opportunities to advance the case for Southern statehood: in 2015 when the Houthis were kicked out of Aden, in 2017 when the STC was set up, and in 2020 when it rescinded the self-rule declaration. Disillusionment with the STC prompted Shaif to set up FOSY (see page xxx).

In 2015 the Houthis, having overthrown Hadi's government, decided to invade South Yemen so they could exert political and military control over the whole of Yemen. But the Southern movement (Hirak) and its local Adeni supporters who were adamant about establishing their own state in the South fought back, and with Emirati forces, part of the Saudi-led coalition, they drove the Houthis out of Aden after they had been in the city for at least one month. Hadi immediately appointed Al-Zubaidi as governor of Aden and other Southerners to leadership positions throughout the South. These Southern governors could have taken control of state institutions. Hadi fired Al-Zubaidi and other Southerners because of the influence of Islah with the presidency. Their inaction was a missed opportunity to take over state institutions while they were in authority.

The formation of the STC in Aden 2017 inspired hope that an independent state in the South was no longer a mirage. The movement had huge support throughout the South, and the weakening authority of Hadi's government, which had become a government in exile based in Saudi Arabia, placed the STC in an ideal negotiating position on the regional and international stage. But once again it failed to step up to the plate, and its weakness in taking decisive political action during the last five years enabled Hadi to make political and military inroads into Hadhramaut, Shabwa, and parts of Abyan. Though the STC are nominal allies in a Saudi-led military coalition fighting the Houthis, the rivalry between the STC and Hadi's government has led to a civil war within a civil war, and the historic struggle between the South and the central government continues, opening old wounds.

Pressure from the Saudis prompted the STC's declaration of self-rule in Aden in 2020, a move designed to influence the coalition to put more pressure on Hadi, to be abandoned in the hope that the Riyadh Agreement, always honoured more in the breach than in the observance, would finally be implemented. This lost the STC credibility within its own ranks and with the Southern population. Southerners saw themselves cheated out of their own state while others felt that ending the military conflict meant accepting that independence is a long process and that kicking the ball into the long grass may be the only option feasible for the present.

The STC Joins the New Government

In return for rescinding the self-rule declaration on 29 July, the STC agreed to abide by the Riyadh Agreement, and a new government should have been formed within thirty days. This did not happen. STC leaders were ensconced in their residences in Riyadh, and its head, President Al-Zubaidi, was addressing meetings in Aden through video calls.

As the political stalemate continued, Yemen was in the grip of the world's worst humanitarian crisis, eloquently described by Tim Loughton, the chair of the British All Parliamentary Group on Yemen, as the most lethal and complex cocktail: an extended and seemingly insoluble civil war with international

---

[29] Max Donbenko, Skylar Benedict, Enzo El Adem, and Alex Forster, "Back to the Future? (A Report on the STC and Secessionist Activities within Southern Yemen)", Adalah Yemen October 2018, https://www.adalahyemen.com.

ramifications; various other human-made disasters; numerous natural disasters and potentially catastrophic environmental ones; an economic meltdown; and now, on top of it all, a deadly pandemic that Yemen was not prepared and equipped to deal with.

Negotiations over the formation of a new government took five months. On 7 October, Al-Zubaidi called for the secession of South Yemen from the North, claiming it was the only solution to the country's unrest. Speaking during a meeting with the Russian ambassador to Yemen, Vladimir Dedushkin, in Riyadh, where he was residing, Al-Zubaidi said, "The people of the south have a live and present issue, for which no temporary or transient solutions can be found. There is no solution to that conflict, except by returning to its roots and causes, represented by responding to the demands and aspirations of the people of the south, to restore their state and identity."

The new power-sharing government between the STC and the IRG was finally announced in December 2020 with the following Southern ministers: Minister for Civil Service and Insurance, Dr Abdulnaser Al Wali, orthopaedic surgeon and assistant Professor in Aden University; Minister for Agriculture and Fisheries, Brig. Salem Al Socotri, a military figure from Socotra who had been Socotra's governor in 2016–17; Minister for Social Affairs and Labour, Dr Mohammed Al Zaawari from Sabbaiyha, Lahj Province, who was an active leader in the Southern Movement Al Hirak Al Janoubi; Minister of Transport, Dr Abdul Salam Homaid, a former general manager of Yemen's Petroleum Company, a deputy in the Ministry of Oil and Minerals, and chief of the economic department and Minister of Public Works and Highways; Manea Binyamin, an engineer from Hadhramaut.

On the last day of 2020, a year that continued to brutalise war-torn Yemen, twenty-six people were killed and over one hundred were injured as ministers in the newly formed government disembarked from an aircraft in Aden on their return from Saudi Arabia. This horrific attack was a deliberate attempt to turn a moment of hope to one of despair. The UN special envoy to Yemen, Martin Griffiths, said, "A transgression of such magnitude potentially amounts to a war crime. This cabinet is a signal of hope that reconciliation is possible."

In the article "How I Narrowly Escaped Death at Aden Airport", Hussam Radman described the terrorist attack.

> Only a limited number of journalists and government officials were supposed to be present at Aden International Airport on December 30, 2020. However, to our surprise, hundreds of citizens had flocked since the early hours of the morning to welcome the new cabinet members, and some to celebrate the return of former Aden security director and prominent Southern Transitional Council (STC) figure, Major General Shalal Ali Shaye'a, to the interim capital. Large crowds gathered at the airport's main gate in a festive atmosphere.
>
> The airplane's doors reopened at 2:00 p.m., and I shouted to my colleagues to resume direct coverage. Five minutes and just 20 meters saved us from certain death. A loud explosion rocked the airport lounge, where we were supposed to go to carry out live coverage on television. All eyes and cameras turned toward the scene of the explosion. We heard gunfire and, for a while, we thought a booby-trapped bomb had gone off, followed by armed clashes. This was the most frustrating moment in my life, and I thought: "Are we truly this infiltrated?"
>
> Before we could wrap our heads around what was happening, a second explosion went off, forcing everyone to run east. A few seconds later, there was a third explosion, confirming to everyone that these were the result of missile strikes. Panicked, everyone, including officials unable to maintain their poise, ran for their lives.[30]

The new government faced tremendous challenges: guaranteeing security and ensuring cooperation between the internationally recognised government and the Southern Transition Council (STC). Security analysts commented that it was difficult to fathom how the new government could move to Aden from

---

[30] Radman Hussam, "How I Narrowly Escaped Death at Aden Airport", Sanaa Centre for Strategic Studies, January 2021.

Riyadh without proper precautions, including keeping the date of its arrival flight secret. Well-wishers should not have been allowed on the tarmac, and the entire cabinet should not have been travelling on the same flight. Coalition forces have to be criticised for stationing Patriot missiles eight kilometres from the airport and not protecting it.

Mohammed Gamal, a resident of Aden, said the people were afraid of further attacks. "In the past year, when the government was working out of Saudi Arabia Aden was safe. If the return of the government brings back attacks on the city we hope they can leave it and let us enjoy peace."

Friends of South Yemen (FOSY), in an official statement, has called on the Arab coalition to set up a compensation fund for the victims of the explosion and their families and to arrange for treatment in neighbouring countries, if required, for those who have been injured. President Abdroba Mansur Hadi ordered the formation of a committee "to investigate the repercussions of the terrorist act", but the STC refused to take part in the committee. The deputy head of communications for the STC, Mansour Saleh, said, "The Houthis are the main culprits in this crime and they will benefit the most from its consequences. But other parties might be involved in the attack including elements from the Yemeni government and those affiliated with the Muslim Brotherhood who have been opposed to the agreement." No group has claimed responsibility, and the Houthis have denied involvement.

The new government has also been severely criticised because there are no women for the first time in two decades and no representatives from the Tihama region. Tahani Saeed, a founding member of the Yemeni Women's Pact for Peace and Security (Tawafuq), said, "Yemeni women are dying and suffering because of Yemen's civil war, yet we are denied a role in helping forge a solution. Over the past six years, the conflict in Yemen has had a profound impact on women and girls. Over a million pregnant women and new mothers are now acutely malnourished. According to UNICEF one woman and six newborns die every two hours from complications during pregnancy or birth. Along with starvation, Yemeni women are suffering from rising levels of gender-based violence. Since the war began, violence, including domestic abuse and child marriage has increased by 63 percent. COVID-19 has only made matters worse."

Twelve MPs from the Tihama region (Hodeida, Rayma, Mahwit, and Hajjah governorates) sent a letter to Hadi protesting that the region has no representatives in the new government. "Tihama region represents 23 percent of Yemen's population but the region is neither represented in parliament and Shura Council Presidencies nor in the Advisory Board of the Presidency," MP Sakhr Al-Wajih said. "If we do not get our rights to be treated just and equal like other regions we will have to use our right to withdraw from attending cabinet sessions and not grant parliamentary approval to the new government." Everyone who is someone in regional and international politics—the United Nations, the European Union, the GCC, the Arab Parliament, the United Kingdom, Saudi Arabia, the UAE, Bahrain, Jordan, and Egypt—welcomed the new government.

Al-Zubaidi played a pivotal role in securing the implementation of the Riyadh Agreement, which was signed in November 2019. Those who criticise him for taking this approach have clearly stated that his loyalty to the Arab coalition has blinded his judgement on the critical issue of Southern statehood. In contrast, he believed that Southern statehood will be achieved as part of a long-term process that requires cooperation with major international and regional powers. Some may disagree with his strategy in delivering a political solution for the South, but one certainly needs to recognise that the current crisis is complex and requires skilled negotiations at the highest level, taking into account the many and powerful players—especially the external players—in the conflict.

European and regional capitals have a strong interest and a major role to play in ensuring the success of the government and preventing the Yemeni state's collapse. Britain, with US support, is uniquely positioned to spearhead this effort because it enjoys some credibility with actors across the Yemeni political spectrum. FOSY proposed an immediate donor conference be established, with European and regional states significantly increasing their funds to help the new government establish itself. It needs urgent funding and technical capacity for major infrastructure projects (such as in energy, water, and garbage disposal) and reconstruction in areas affected by the war. Through such projects, donor countries could insist on the establishment of standards (e.g., transparency in planning, procurement and disbursement of funds). Donors could also expand existing programmes that seek to create jobs for many unemployed people by improving and expanding local infrastructure. FOSY expressed its concern that without this immediate support, the new government could collapse before it begins.

The success of the new government depended on the support of the international community and on Saudi Arabia, the guarantor of the implementation of the Riyadh Agreement. The government's coffers were empty, and no budget had been drafted since 2014. Some six hundred thousand civil servants have lost their jobs. Those remaining are paid weeks, sometimes months, late. The Coordinating Council for Retired Military and Security Personnel in South Yemen threatened to take control of the presidential Al-Maashiq Palace, the airport, and other facilities if six months' salaries were not paid and other salary arrears were not rectified. The failure to resolve numerous problems and the conflict between the STC and the IRG continued during the first six months of 2021.

CHAPTER 12

The Future of South Yemen

The return of the new government to Aden was not auspicious. The attempt to kill its members by bombing the aircraft which carried the new team failed, but on its return, the government accomplished little and is in great danger of collapsing. Speaking at the end of June 2021, Yemen's foreign minister Ahmed Awad bin Mubarak admitted that Yemen was on the brink of collapse. However, he expressed his belief that the legitimate authority (the internationally recognised government) succeeded in securing livelihood in liberated areas, including Shabwa, Hadhramaut, Marib, and Mahra, despite challenges.

Areas of conflict and control in Yemen, May 2020.

The international community did not provide adequate funding for humanitarian assistance to save Yemenis from famine and medical disasters. Cuts in international aid have had a dire impact on Yemeni civilians, including the halving of food assistance for nine million people and the suspension of support to healthcare services, which the United Nations says has put the lives of millions on the line.

FOSY's chairman, Abdul Galil Shaif, speaking at a conference organised by the Next Century Foundation on regions of conflict in the Middle East, said that it is essential humanitarian assistance goes hand in hand with supporting development.

> Waiting for the war against the Houthis to end before supporting development is a strategy which has failed during the past six years. The new government must act very quickly with a clear economic and political programme that addresses some of the very acute problems faced by their citizens particularly those relating to salaries, services and currency stability. The government programme should have been prepared before ministers landed in Aden. The Prime Minister and his ministers must not delay any further and adopt it as an immediate priority. There is incredible potential to build a successful economic and political alternative in the liberated South of the country but we need to act immediately without any further delay. The new government needs to understand that unnecessary delays and poor statecraft and bureaucratic misrule, will only inflame tensions and fuel mistrust.

On the economic front, things are going from bad to worse. Yemen's GDP in 2015 was $43 billion. In 2020 it was $21 billion, cut by more than half, whereas the population has grown from 25 to 30 million. Yemen's riyal hit a new record low at the beginning of June amidst deadlocked diplomatic efforts to end the war and rising tensions between the IRG and the STC.

On 21 July 2021, the International Rescue Committee expressed concern about the rapidly growing level of humanitarian needs in Yemen as the exchange rate fell to 1,000 YER per US$1 in the south of the country for the first time. The devaluation is rendering it impossible for ordinary citizens to afford basic necessities, including food. Throughout the south of the country, it is not that food is unavailable but that it is completely unaffordable. After six years of conflict and economic crisis, many Yemenis have exhausted their savings and sold off all valuable assets like property or livestock. Families are making decisions no family should have to, such as skipping meals or subsisting on cheap foods like bread. Women and girls have reported being forced to ask to borrow food on credit from shopkeepers, which exposes them to exploitation and harassment. The rate of forced and early marriage of girls has more than doubled since the war started, with as many as two-thirds of Yemeni girls married while they are still children.

Essential finance to enable the government to function was not forthcoming from the international community, and the government's inability to provide essential services caused serious problems. Salaries of government employees and pensions, including those of army veterans, remain unpaid. Essential services such as water and electricity are working below par if at all, and the government has not announced its political and economic programme. Amidst a loss of basic services, Yemenis have had to swap houses for tents, gas for firewood, and jobs for aid.

A high-level STC delegation headed by Al-Zubaidi visited Moscow at the end of January 2021 at the invitation of the Russian foreign office. At the time of Al-Zubaidi's arrival in Moscow, the STC's official website released a statement saying that he "renewed the path of independence and the restoration of the Southern state with full sovereignty." Such language called into question the STC's willingness to abide by the power-sharing agreement. Some commentators saw this move by the STC as a warning to the Gulf states and Western states that another partner was possible in the form of an old ally to the South. The visit to Russia was more of a propaganda stunt to increase the pressure on Hadi to give the

STC more power. The Russians are not keen to re-establish the strong relations the Soviets had with the South during the time of the PDRY.

In a comment posted on the Gulf International Forum, Giorgio Cafiero, the CEO of Gulf State Analytics, wrote,

> Moscow's actions make clear that even if it is not formally or overtly favouring a split of Yemen along North-South lines, it has its own interests in strengthening its ties to the STC amid a period of extreme uncertainty in Yemen as the war continues. Indeed, as Russia seeks to establish itself as a major player in the Red Sea, the Soviet past in Southern Yemen makes this part of the Arabian Peninsula an area where, from the Russian government's perspective, Moscow has a natural opportunity to regain clout that it once had during the Soviet era. The Kremlin sees itself playing a stabilizing role in Yemen by fostering ties between the STC and other actors in the civil war. With its growing influence, Russia aims to advance its own geopolitical, economic, and energy interests in Southern Yemen while also enhancing the Russian brand in the wider Arab/African regions as a power which is adept at brokering resolutions to multifaceted conflicts.[31]

In February, US president Joe Biden ended arms sales to Saudi Arabia and the UAE, but the war continued as the Saudi defence minister pledged his country's support for Yemen. America has promised to continue assisting Saudi Arabia if the country's security is threatened. Biden also removed the Houthis from the list of US designated foreign terrorist organisations, owing to pressure from aid organisations who were convinced that this designation would hamper the delivery of humanitarian assistance. The United Kingdom did not follow in America's footsteps and continues to sell weapons to Saudi Arabia. Biden also appointed diplomat Timothy Lenderking as the US special envoy for Yemen. Since his appointment, Lenderking has held consultations with most of the parties to the conflict.

It is important to note that while the United States will protect its interests with the Gulf states, particularly Saudi Arabia, because of its own economic interests, it has made overtures to the Houthis, including behind-the-scenes negotiations directly with them, but also between the Houthis and the Saudis. There are two fundamental reasons for this: the Houthis' strong resistance and their presence and strength on the battlefield, and the fact that the Houthis are strongly opposed to Al-Qaeda and have fought pitched battles with fundamentalist groups, including the widely despised Al-Qaeda in the Arabian Peninsula and ISIS, to gain control of territory. This explains why the United States is willing to negotiate with the Houthis—even though it would never normally countenance talks with a group that has an Islamist ideology.

Despite commendable efforts to broker a peace agreement, Lenderking returned to Washington on 1 August 2021 after meeting a dead end on the Yemen crisis. A statement by the US State Department said that during his trip, Lenderking met senior officials of the Yemeni and Saudi governments, the Gulf Cooperation Council, the international community, and the office of the UN special envoy. He expressed concern that the Houthis continue to refuse to engage meaningfully on a ceasefire and political talks and stressed that only through a durable agreement between the Yemeni parties can the dire humanitarian crisis in the country be reversed. He also called for an end to the stalemated fighting in Marib.

The battle for the strategic city of Marib, a centre of the oil industry, which started in February 2020, continues. The United Nations high commissioner for refugees (UNHCR) in Yemen warned that more than one million displaced Yemenis are at risk due to the ongoing fighting. The UN agency said on Twitter that tens of thousands of displaced Yemenis in Marib could be forced to flee because of the fighting. "Since the beginning of 2021, the escalation in hostilities has led to the displacement of over

---

[31] Giorgio Cafiero, "Making Sense of the Southern Transitional Council's Latest Visit to Russia", comment posted on Gulf International Forum, 8 February 2021, https://gulfif.org.

13,600 people (2,272 families) in Marib—a region that is hosting a quarter of Yemen's 4 million internally displaced people," the UNHCR said.

If this city falls to the Houthis, they will have total control of North Yemen. A senior Houthi official said attacks on Saudi targets, which intensified in the last months of 2020, would continue until the Saudi war and the tight air and naval blockade come to an end. In an interview with Lebanon-based Al-Mayadeen television news at the beginning of March, Mohammed Al-Bukhaiti, a member of the Houthi Supreme Political Council, said the new US administration asks Yemenis to halt their attacks but does not ask the Saudi invaders to lift the crippling siege imposed on Yemen. He stressed that the Houthis were ready to discuss a political solution after the end of the aggression and the siege. "The blockade on Yemen is more dangerous than direct military aggression."

The Houthis seem to have interpreted their removal from the terrorist list as a green light to push forward with their war strategy, and they are continuing with their attacks on Marib even though the Saudis have started making peace overtures and agreed to stop military operations inside Yemen if the rebels stopped attacking Saudi Arabia. Attempts were made to secure the reopening of Sanaa airport, and the Houthis carried out maintenance work on the runway and other facilities.

After US pressure to find ways to end the war in Yemen, Prince Faisal bin Farhan Al Saud said the ceasefire is envisioned "for the entire conflict", including allowing for the main airport in Yemen's rebel-held capital, Sanaa, to reopen. "It is up to the Houthis now," Prince Faisal added, stressing his country would continue to "protect" its borders, citizens, and infrastructure and face the Houthi "aggression with the necessary response. The Houthis must decide whether to put their interests first or Iran's interests first". The Saudi proposal would also allow for fuel and food imports through Hodeidah, Yemen's main port of entry, and restarting political negotiations between the government of President Hadi and the Houthis. The Hadi government supported this proposal, but the Houthis perceived it as a Saudi weakness and a military success for them and declined the offer, demanding much more in return. They also intensified their military onslaught on Marib and Al-Bauda.

During his farewell briefing before his term came to an end on 16 June, the UN special envoy to Yemen, Martin Griffiths, who has been replaced by Hans Grundberg, told the United Nations that the Houthis' leader, Abdel-Malek al-Houthi, had insisted there must first be an agreement on reopening Sanaa airport and the key Hodeidah port; only after that was done would the Houthis begin negotiations on a ceasefire, a first step towards reviving peace negotiations. He painted a bleak picture of mediation and said that the two parties have not overcome their differences. The Houthis continue their military attack on Marib, increasing the pressure on Saudi Arabia to negotiate with them. They have met strong resistance, providing some breathing space for Hadi. Should the Houthis occupy Marib, their negotiating position will be much stronger, giving them extra leverage and control. They may even enter the South again through Shabwa, or they may try to take over Hodeidah again.

For UN mediation to be successful in Yemen, a series of conditions have to be met. The Security Council has to provide the new envoy with a clear mandate to work on, but above all it has to be united in its support for the mediation efforts and its interest in solving the conflict and ending this pointless war. The mediator also depends on the permanent members to back an agreement with guarantees—such as the UN or third states deploying troops—and threaten transgressors with sanctions and penalties. When these conditions are not met, the UN envoys find it difficult to negotiate viable agreements, and current failures in Yemen are a clear indication.

The current UN peace process in Yemen lacks the urgency and seriousness required and the question after almost seven years of war is how UN mediation efforts can become more effective. FOSY proposed possible routes. First, a change is needed in the UN resolution which is not fit for purpose. Second, the mandate of the UN envoy should not be limited to mediating between the local parties in a civil war; instead, from the outset it should also provide forums that allow for the reconciliation of the competing interests of relevant regional and great powers, or at least enable the UN to influence the rules of engagement in the conflict. Third, any power-sharing agreements should be sufficiently inclusive; the negotiations should bring together actors who are truly representative of the political forces and constituencies on the ground—the Southerners have so far not been listened to by the international community in the same way as the other local players. Fourth, any proposed agreements should give these parties sufficient incentives to abide by the deal. Fifth, the UN mediators should avoid taking sides in favour of one group or the other, because that undermines agreements and UN credibility. They should also be prepared to take action against those local players who make financial gains from the war, through travel bans or freezing of accounts abroad.

The European Parliament has also passed a long resolution on Yemen but has done virtually nothing to ensure its implementation (see Appendix 4).

Clearly, a negotiated settlement appears out of reach as long as the Houthis continue the intensification of their military attacks on Marib, Shabwa, Dhala, and Yafa. They see that the balance of power changes rapidly in their favour, and they can count on sustained foreign backing from Iran. In other words, as long as the Houthis feel they are gaining the upper hand on the ground by making military gains, UN mediation becomes more difficult; the Houthis believe that their strength on the ground will determine their strength at the negotiating table.

The Yemen war, in its seventh year as this book went to press, was continuing on two fronts: the anti-Houthi front consisting of the IRG and the Saudi-led Arab coalition and the conflict in the South between the STC and the IRG (see pg. 138). On 16 March, demonstrators broke into the Maashiq Presidential Palace in Aden amidst public anger over the lack of services, poor living conditions, and depreciation of the currency. Saudi forces evacuated members of the cabinet, including Prime Minister Maeen Abdulmalik Saeed, to a military building situated near the palace grounds. Many of the protestors were carrying the flag of the PDRY.

These protests prompted the Saudi Ministry of Foreign Affairs to condemn the "storming" of the Al-Maashiq Palace in the "strongest terms", calling on the Yemeni government and the STC to an urgent meeting in Riyadh. The new government in Aden appealed to the coalition and the international community to swiftly support it economically so it could meet the "accumulated obligations". In a statement, the government stressed the need to "urgently support it before an economic collapse, whose effects will be significant at all levels". Riyadh has repeatedly promised to provide support to the new parity government in order to restore the deteriorating conditions of the people, improve their living standards, and make the government's efforts in this path successful. However, since the arrival of the new government in Aden, these promises have not been fulfilled, according to both government sources and the new governor, Hamed Lamless, who is also a member of the STC.

Meanwhile, a separate demonstration broke out in the eastern city of Sayoun in Hadhramaut province after dozens of people stormed a government complex in protest against dire living conditions and continuous increases in prices. Forces affiliated with IRG fired shots in the air to disperse the crowds while protestors burned car tyres in the streets nearby. The STC condemned the government forces' response to the protests.

The Saudis have a significant presence in Mahrah which is not welcomed by the local people. Yemen's second largest but least populated Yemeni governorate, bordering Oman, has managed to avoid the ravages of war which have devastated the rest of the country during the past six years.

But this oasis of calm, which has provided a safe haven for some 250,000 internally displaced people, is threatened with instability as Saudi Arabia increases its military presence and plays an increasingly active role in the governorate's affairs, much to the chagrin of local residents who have protested against their involvement.

With barely 120,000 inhabitants, Yemen's most easterly province has for several years been the subject of interest for Saudi Arabia and the UAE as part of their military intervention in the country. The UAE's efforts between 2015 and 2017 to build influence in the governorate and create an elite force were eventually rebuffed by local opposition to foreign interference. Mahris have a unique history of running their own affairs as well as a common vision of sovereignty within a federal system that has kept them remarkably unified. Saudi Arabia controls the governorate's airport, border crossings, and main seaport and has established more than a dozen military bases around the province, where it has stationed thousands of its own troops and Yemeni proxy forces imported from other Southern governorates.

"The deep-seated sense of local identity has spurred a growing opposition movement to the Saudi presence in Mahrah—an opposition movement Oman has actively supported," the Sanaa Center for Strategic Studies said in a report on the governorate. "While this opposition began as peaceful demonstrations, there have been clashes with Saudi forces, with the Saudi air force carrying out airstrikes against Mahri tribesmen."[32]

FOSY's Three-Stage Road Map to Resolve the Crisis

Concerned that Yemen is like a rudderless ship with a number of captains motivated by their own selfish interests, on 24 March the FOSY proposed the first road map to resolve the current crisis.

> Stage One (2021–22): Ending the war immediately and laying the foundations for peace: The first step must be the effective implementation of the Riyadh Agreement which resolved the conflict between the Internationally Recognised Government (IRG) and the Southern Transitional Council (STC), leading to the formation of the current power sharing government. Despite FOSY's reservations about elements in this agreement it appears to be the only way forward available. It is critical that this government is given the opportunity to build trust between the two parties and ensure that the people in the liberated areas see some improvements in their living standards. Although it is fair to say that so far this government has failed to put forward a political and economic plan and improve people's lives.
>
> - Peace talks held under the auspices of the UN Special Envoy should start immediately to build trust between the warring parties (the Houthis and the IRG/STC) to agree an immediate end to the war. Saudi Arabia, the UAE, Iran, the USA, the UK and other states should engage in the talks supporting all sides to reach a peace settlement.
> - Imposition of UN sanctions, especially on politicians and tribal leaders who are making money out of the war and refuse to engage positively in peace talks. The threat of financial and travel sanctions against those Yemeni politicians would yield positive results in FOSY's opinion.
> - Formation of an international body to support economic development in North and South Yemen with a move away from reliance on humanitarian assistance. The power sharing government should focus on the payment of salaries, the provision of essential services and the presentation of a united front to reach a peace settlement with the Houthis.
> - Injection of funds into the Central Bank for development to be used under international supervision and strict accountability and transparency measures. The government should immediately administer and put measures in place to bring in income from oil, gas, fisheries, taxes and customs directly into the Central Bank to prevent corruption and strengthen the local currency.
> - Talks, preferably under UN auspices, between all political groups in the South to achieve national reconciliation and agree on the way forward for the Southern region and future relations with the North. The head of the STC,

---

[32] Casey Coombs, "Al-Mahra: Where Regional Powers Define Local Politics", Sanaa Centre for Strategic Studies, December 2020. The Sana'a Center for Strategic Studies is an independent think tank that seeks to foster change through knowledge production with a focus on Yemen and the surrounding region.

Aidarus Al-Zubaidi, and President Hadi could play a leading role in this initiative. The Houthis, the General People's Congress and Islah can also hold a national reconciliation conference to build trust.

Stage Two (2022–25): Transitional stage with a possible two region solution, one region in the North of Yemen and the other in the South of Yemen: Yemen could have two constitutionally recognised autonomous regions, the Northern region and the Southern region, each with its own parliament, political parties, elections, executive, ministries, legislative and judicial powers, budget, internal security forces and police. A central administration headed by President Hadi would be responsible for defence, foreign policy and the allocation of an equitable share of national revenue to the Northern and Southern regions.

- Two autonomous regions should be set up under UN auspices with a new constitution. There should also be a strengthening of the role and responsibilities of local government with minimum disruption to the current governorate structure. The governorates in the North will form the Northern autonomous region and the governorates in the South will form the Southern autonomous region. Elections to local governments must be held with international observers present.

- A focus on long term development projects and investment is needed. Yemenis living abroad must be encouraged to return and invest in their country. Improving the security situation in the two regions of Yemen will encourage and attract investors to return to their country.

- Southerners should eventually hold a Southern conference evaluating the experience of two autonomous regions, successes and failures, and building trust between all Southerners on the way forward. The Northern political elite can also initiate their own national conference and evaluate their successes and failures and build trust among themselves too.

- The two regions must cooperate politically and economically to heal the scars of war and serve all their people under international scrutiny. They must also hold elections under the constitution so the people can choose their future leaders.

Stage Three (2025–30): Decision on the future of Yemen based on the evaluation of the two region solution: Following the evaluation of the transitional stage of the two region solution a watershed in Yemen's history should come, when the people themselves decide whether to continue with the two autonomous regions or opt for two independent states. FOSY proposes one referendum in the North and one in the South to determine the future of the two regions.

There is every possibility that the Southerners through their referendum will want to establish their own state. There is income from oil, gas, fisheries and taxes and a strategic location which can revive their economy. No money will be required from external sources if proper state functioning institutions are developed. A UN-organised referendum on the independence of the South is required to enable this state to be re-established. Two states living side by side is better than one state destroying itself. If the South chose independence close economic co-operation with the north would be required.

The alternative to the South voting for independence is a continuation of the two regions under central authority. All past attempts to resolve the crisis have failed. The situation for the ordinary people of Yemen is desperate, so a new initiative is desperately needed. We urge all interested parties and honest brokers to give our proposal their serious attention.

The road map was widely publicised and sent to President Joe Biden, Prime Minister Boris Johnson, the British Minister for the Middle East and North Africa, James Cleverly, British MPs, the EU, and Arab ambassadors in London. It was published in full in several Arab newspapers and FOSY received many messages of congratulations on this unique initiative. FOSY also produced a documentary film *The Case for Southern Statehood* providing a penetrating flash of insight into the history of the South's struggle for self-determination.

FOSY also made a significant input into the following statement submitted by the Next Century Foundation to the forty-eighth session of the UN Human Rights Council:

By the end of this year, some 233,000 people will have died in the Yemen Arab Republic as a result of the war, including 140,000 children under the age of 5. That projection is in a U.N. commissioned study by the University of Denver. The report underscores the disintegration of a country that was already among the world's poorest before the war began in 2015. If the war continues through 2022, 482,000 people are estimated to die. If it lasts until 2030, the death toll will rise to an estimated 1.8 million, including 1.5 million children. War in the Yemen Arab Republic has continued into its seventh year. A key fault line that acts as a stumbling block when peace negotiations are attempted is the question of whether the outcome of any referendum for independence for South Yemen should be determined by a vote by all Yemenis or just by South Yemenis. Calls for secession from Southern independence activists and fighters date back to the unification of North and South Yemen in 1990 and have been exacerbated by the current conflict. A peaceful transition to stable governance can only be secured through a dialogue between all sides of the conflict on the future of Southern Yemen.

The Next Century Foundation suggests that such a dialogue may look towards a referendum on establishing an autonomous zone in Southern Yemen. Yemen remains divided between factions that include the internationally recognised government-in-exile and the Ansar Allah (Houthi) movement, which operates as a de facto government from Sana'a and controls most northern governorates. Southern independence fighters, represented by the Southern Transitional Council (STC), which is supported by the United Arab Emirates, currently control the key city of Aden and have been in a tentative military alliance with the internationally recognised Hadi government in order to confront Ansar Allah. However, this alliance, though currently functioning, has turned sour at several points in the war, for example the STC declared self-governance in 2020 without giving recognition to the Hadi government.

Peace in Yemen is impossible without acknowledgement of the STC's calls for independence from the north. The STC has far greater control of the South's eight governorates, including the port city of Aden, than the UN-recognised Yemen government. "To ignore the will of the people is a recipe for only more instability," the head of the presidential council of the STC, Major General Aidarus al-Zoubaidi said. Humanitarian efforts and attempts to lift the country out of its deepening economic crisis are unlikely to succeed without stable government, which is currently dependent on political autonomy in the South.

The alternative to constitutional autonomy, that of a referendum on partition, is liable to worsen the conflict. It is the responsibility of the international community to mediate a dialogue between all those party to the conflict and promote an amicable arrangement for autonomy in the South. The Next Century Foundation believes that endorsing autonomy in South Yemen would be a vital step forward on the path to peace in Yemen as a whole and would help bring a decisive end to the conflict.

The Next Century Foundation recommends that parties to the conflict work towards an arrangement for maximum autonomy for South Yemen without resulting in partition, which may lead to further conflict. We further suggest that the autonomous zone has control over most areas of governance, including control over its own armed forces, as the presence of central government forces in South Yemen is likely to exacerbate the conflict. The central government may provide financial support and manage foreign relations, but most governance would occur locally. Such an arrangement may be formed through a referendum in Yemen, or through national dialogue between all conflicting parties. The Next Century Foundation strongly believes that this is the optimal solution for all groups, but the establishment of stable governance and peace in Yemen must be supported by all international and national stakeholders to be successful. The international community must come together to support the peace process in Yemen and provide robust solutions towards an amicable system of autonomy in South Yemen in order to prevent the continuation of sectarian and nationalist division in the country, spiralling the state into a decade of war and humanitarian crisis.

Continuing Conflicts, STC Indecision, Deteriorating Human Rights Situation

In April 2021, the IRG relocated to Riyadh; later the same month, the prime minister travelled back to Hadhramaut and not Aden. The Saudis called on the leader of the STC, Aidaroos Al-Zubaidi, to return to Riyadh for talks about resolving the crisis, but Al-Zubaidi did not leave Aden and sent a group of negotiators to the talks. Al-Zubaidi, under pressure from his supporters, could not return to Riyadh because this would diminish his support base in the South. In the meantime, the Emiratis have allowed STC leaders to return to the South after a long absence, which in itself is an indication that the UAE government realises that the absence of STC leaders from Aden strengthens their rivals, the Muslim Brotherhood.

There was nothing to celebrate on the thirty-first anniversary of the unity of Yemen on 22 May. In his speech, President Hadi seemed to be rearranging chairs on a sinking ship. He called on the political elite to focus on confronting the Iranians' agenda and the Houthis, their proxies. Referring to the Houthi attack on Marib governorate launched more than a year ago, he said, "It reflects the group's sick mentality—the Houthi militias are trying to impose their rules, goals and false beliefs on people through force majeure, blood and destruction." He also condemned the Southern forces without naming them, saying they want to spread hatred and strife by calling for separation. "We believe Yemeni unity is a noble goal. The federal state project included in the outcomes of the National Dialogue Conference has laid the foundation for a correct path that guarantees rights and partnerships and establishes a stable and secure future," Hadi said, adding that he directed the government to establish security, activate state institutions and restore services such as electricity, water and education.

Al-Zubaidi announced in a statement that the "restoration" of the Southern state is nearing, adding that the STC "opened all doors in front of the people's cause and the extraction of the adversaries' recognition of a fully sovereign independent federal state" that is based on the pre-unity border of 21 May 1990. The STC will refuse any unilateral decisions taken by the Yemeni government. According to STC sources, the council joined the government in signing the Riyadh Agreement to open a pathway for its goal of restoring the South Yemeni state, and it considers that the agreement with the government does not entail backing down from its main goal of the restoration of that state. In an act of defiance to the government and the Saudis, Al-Zubaidi appointed Shelal Ali Shai as head of the counterterrorism unit on 28 May 2021. In June the STC took over the offices of the official state-run Yemeni news agency SABA in Aden and ordered it to be renamed the Aden News Agency for the State of the Arab South.

The STC is consolidating its presence in Aden. It attempted once again to storm the palace of Al-Ma'ashiq during a new round of talks on the implementation of the Riyadh Agreement. The Saudis have made it clear they want the IRG to return to Aden and are becoming increasingly frustrated by the current stalemate as the government they are backing is unable to reconcile with an increasingly belligerent STC. But the STC can't have it both ways. Either it remains part of the IRG, or it declares independence unilaterally.

Relations between the STC and the IRG are going from bad to worse. Both sides pay lip service to the Riyadh Agreement, which is still the only game in town for resolving the conflict between them, but each side accuses the other of failing to comply with the terms of the agreement.

In mid-July 2021, it looked as if the conflict could turn into an international crisis. A statement by the Yemeni official government's team tasked with applying the Riyadh Agreement said that the STC is not committed to implementing what was agreed to and is responsible for delaying the government's return to the interim capital to resume its duties. The STC accused the IRG of being responsible for the delays and, in a letter to the Security Council, said it was ready for the internationalisation of the dispute and the ensuing political repercussions. Both sides accused each other of making unauthorised appointments to government positions. Saudi Arabia sent two planeloads of troops and armoured vehicles to Aden. The STC threatened to prevent the Yemeni government from meeting in the South and arrested the leaders of fighters allied with the IRG.

The United States, France, and Britain are becoming exasperated by the never-ending bickering between the IRG and the STC. The STC's letter to the Security Council was prompted by their warnings of escalation in Southern Yemen through attempts to stir up political tensions against the backdrop of the continued delays to the implementation of the Riyadh Agreement. In July Britain appointed a new envoy, Richard Oppenheim, to the IRG without the rank of ambassador, suggesting it is losing faith in this government; Oppenheim replaced Ambassador Michael Aron.

While the STC and IRG argue and resort to armed clashes when words fail them, peace talks aimed at ending the civil war now in its seventh year are going nowhere, clearly illustrating the United Nations' scandalous catalogue of failures. UN envoy Martin Griffiths made a last-ditch attempt to convince the Houthis to accept a UN-brokered peace plan and stop their assault on Marib before his term of office came to an end in June 2021. Griffiths called on the IRG and the Houthis to make bold concessions to end months of political deadlock and reach a peace agreement. His words fell on deaf ears. Yemen's information minister, Moammar Al-Eryani, said that the latest Houthi attack in the Red Sea, foiled by the Arab coalition, shows the rebels are still threatening international maritime traffic and breaching existing agreements.

Al-Qaeda in the Arabian Peninsula (AQAP) continues to raise its ugly head in the South. In June seven soldiers from the Security Belt Forces (SBF) were killed and twenty-five were wounded by a blast from a booby-trapped motorbike that was blown up remotely. AQAP also claimed responsibility for attacks in Abyan and Shabwa earlier in the year.

Another worrying development is the deteriorating security situation in South Yemen. On 26 May, Oxfam confirmed the death of its colleague Fathi Mahmoud Ali Salem Al-Zurigi in Aden after a shooting incident on Monday, 24 May. Fathi, a Yemeni citizen aged forty-two, was travelling with another Oxfam colleague and a contracted driver when they were caught in what appeared to be crossfire at a checkpoint in Southern Yemen, travelling to Aden. The three men were taken to hospital, where Fathi succumbed to his injuries.

The STC's human rights record has been condemned by international and local human rights organisations. *The New Arab* reported that the STC has been blamed for a wave of kidnappings of military leaders in Aden. The STC has denied any involvement in these incidents.

A statement released by the self-styled Free Southern Resistance Council said the chairman of that council, Sheikh Muhammad Sheikh Al-Saeedi—known as Abu Osama—was kidnapped at the end of May in an attack involving two vehicles. The movement strongly condemned the kidnapping, pointing fingers at the STC. "We call on the security and local authorities in Aden to reveal the fate of Sheikh Abu Osama, and we in the Council of Free Resistance draw the attention of the international community and its humanitarian organisations to what is happening in Aden in terms of violation of all international conventions and treaties and moral and humanitarian values," the statement posted to Facebook said.

After international pressure, the STC released the journalist Adel al-Hasani, who was seized after he helped secure the release of two European journalists detained for about a week in mid-September in Mocha. The SAM Organisation for Rights and Liberties, a Geneva-based NGO, said in a statement, "Southern Transitional Council militia are violating human rights on the island of Socotra since they took control of the island on June 19, 2020."

In its report on Yemen for 2020, Amnesty International stated that all parties to the conflict continued to detain and torture hundreds of individuals targeted solely for their political, religious, or professional affiliations or for their peaceful activism. Parties to the conflict have also targeted journalists and human rights defenders, many since 2016. Detainees were held in unofficial detention centres and in dangerous conditions. For example, in Aden, the STC held detainees in a tin building and an underground cellar in Al Jala camp. According to the organisation Mwatana for Human Rights, at least thirteen people were arbitrarily detained in Al Jala camp, and seventeen were tortured between May 2016 and April 2020.

Commenting about the current situation, Dr Abdul Galil Shaif said the political climate is like a festering cesspool. The stalemate shows the need for a road map, such as the one published by FOSY (see pg. 156) to end the war and foster development. Shaif emphasised, "It is unbelievable in these economic circumstances how the people of Yemen are surviving. We don't want charity. We need to be working on a reconstruction and economic development programme to build roads, bridges, ports, airports, schools, hospitals and power plants and improve our public services. The stronger and more developed our economy is and the more people's lives improve the less likely they will be to fight and destroy the country. Less talk and more action is needed. Our leaders ought to realise it is harder to build than to destroy, easier to talk than to agree, and better to live in peace than be at war."

Seven years of war have broken Yemen and fractured the country's political landscape. In 2016, it was possible for peace talks in Kuwait to be held between Hadi's government and the Houthis. Such a two-party approach is no longer possible. Today, mediators have to shuttle back and forth amongst Hadi, the Houthis, and the STC, as well as the Saudis and Emiratis.

The anti-Houthi front is profoundly divided. It consists of Abdroba Mansour Hadi's IRG, the different political parties, and the forces of Ali Abdullah Salih's nephew, Tareq Saleh, who operate along the southern parts of the Red Sea coast (as do Salafi units). Officially, the anti-Houthi forces also comprise Southern independence activists including the Southern Transitional Council (STC), whose main interventions have been in opposition to the Hadi government.

Forces of the Southern Transitional Council. Source: Qais Saeed.

The naval blockade of the major Red Sea ports of Hodeida, Salif, and Ras Isa—all under Houthi control—has had the most devastating consequences for Yemenis. This blockade prevents the majority of the country's population from receiving the supplies of food and fuel that are essential to their survival, because Yemen relies on imports for about 90 per cent of its basic staples and most of its fuel. This is one of the major causes of the disastrous humanitarian situation and the outbreak of famine in some areas in 2021.

In May 2021, the World Food Programme stated that Yemen continues to be the world's worst humanitarian disaster, with many families displaced multiple times in six years of conflict. The WFP said nearly fifty thousand people in Yemen are already living in famine-like conditions, and five million are in immediate danger. Every ten minutes, a child dies from preventable diseases such as diarrhoea, malnutrition, and respiratory infections. Nearly thirteen million Yemenis depend on WFP emergency food assistance. They receive rations of flour, pulses, vegetable oil, sugar and salt, or vouchers or cash to purchase food.

Priority is placed on areas with the highest rates of food insecurity, and on providing rapid support to families displaced by conflict, such as the ongoing situation in Marib governorate. However, amidst a challenging operating environment, and in the face of reduced funding, the WFP was forced to halt monthly food assistance in the northern areas of the country in April, and it instead switched to providing aid every two months. The agency will require $1.9 million billion to prevent famine in Yemen.

In 2021 donors contributed nearly $947 million for the famine prevention efforts, with large-scale support coming from the United States, Saudi Arabia, the United Arab Emirates, Germany, and the European Union. The WFP said in a statement that its ability to maintain this level of response until the end of the year hangs in the balance. Sustained, predictable, and flexible funding is required immediately; otherwise, any progress will be undone, and needs will rapidly rise in what is an unpredictable and challenging operational environment.

Yemen also has a major refugee problem. At the end of 2020, the number of registered refugees and asylum seekers targeted by UNHCR for assistance stood at some 136,700 individuals. Of those, some 47,300 (35 per cent) were registered in Sanaa/Amanat al-Asimah, and some 65 per cent were registered in Southern governorates, largely Aden, Hadhramaut, Lahj, and Shabwah. Most of the refugees and asylum seekers are Somalis, followed by Ethiopians. Countrywide, 40.3 per cent of refugees and asylum seekers are female, and 18.7 per cent are children under eighteen.

Recently released data have shown that the Arab coalition has conducted at least 22,766 air raids in Yemen and up to 65,982 individual air strikes since it began its bombing campaign in 2015, with roughly one-third hitting non-military sites, including schools, residential areas, and hospitals. The data, published by the Yemen Data Project, details the latest information on the impact of the coalition's six-year bombing campaign. The aerial campaign led to the death of 8,759 civilians and injured another 9,815. The data includes figures up until 10 March 2021.

As of early 2021, Yemen is divided into cantons subject to varying levels of authority by a diverse range of groups and individuals. War, in the form of air strikes, ground battles, and the punishing blockade, dominates life in the country. Kleptocrats old and new benefit from a war economy that exacerbates the poverty of a population whose living standards have collapsed. Yemen continues to suffer from the world's worst humanitarian crisis, and the new country that has taken shape after the Salih era could not be further removed from the dreams of the revolutionaries in 2011. If Marib falls to the Houthis, there could be major consequences for Shabwa, a rich Southern city that currently has some Northern regime presence and could give the Houthis some control over the Bab El-Mandeb.

Confronted with a seemingly endless war, and led by religious fundamentalists on one side and members of the former kleptocratic elite on the other, Yemenis simply hope that a solution can be found to end the fighting. Meanwhile, those who can work in their communities, running projects and creating new forms of organisation that will hopefully form the basis for a new Yemen that will bear some resemblance to the dreams of the Arab Spring a decade ago.

The "Back to the Future" report states,

> The volatility of the Yemeni conflict, the unpredictability of its parties and the relative strength of the STC means the future of South Yemen remains somewhat unclear. It is posited that there are three broadly defined potential outcomes for South Yemen. Firstly, the secessionist cause may "fizzle out", leading to a unified Yemen once again—however, this seems unlikely given the development of circumstances and sentiments. Contrariwise, the South may succeed in seceding from Yemen, forming a new independent South Yemeni state; again, there are multiple obstacles to this. Finally, an intermediate conclusion may be reached, where the South obtains de facto autonomy but not unambiguous statehood: this may either be the result of a federalisation of Yemen, or, alternatively, of the failure of the South to attain substantial recognition from other states following a declaration of independence.[33]

---

[33] Max Donbenko, Skylar Benedict, Enzo El Adam, and Alex Forster, "Back to the Future? (A Report on the STC and Secessionist Activities within Southern Yemen)", Adalah Yemen—Justice in Yemen, October 2018.

Postscript

When this book went to press, Yemen was witnessing one of the bleakest periods in its long and troubled history. By the end of 2021, some 233,000 people will have died in the Yemen as a result of the war, including 140,000 children under the age of five.

Zubaidi meets ambassadors of the five permanent members of the UN Security Council.

The United Nations has described the country as experiencing the world's worst humanitarian crisis. In August 2021, Henrietta Fore, executive director of UNICEF, reported that 21 million people – including 11.3 million children – need humanitarian assistance to survive. Some 2.3 million children are acutely malnourished, and 400,000 children under five suffer from severe acute malnutrition. One child dies every ten minutes from preventable causes, including malnutrition and vaccine-preventable diseases. Two million children are out of school, and one in six schools can no longer be used. Two-thirds of teachers—over 170,000—have not received a regular salary for four years due to the conflict, placing four million additional children at risk of dropping out as unpaid teachers quit and find other ways of providing for their families.

Gross domestic product has dropped 40 per cent since 2015. One-quarter of the population rely on civil servant salaries which are paid erratically, if at all.

In his report to the UN Security Council on 23 August 2021, Khaled Khiari, assistant secretary general for the Middle East, Asia, and the Pacific, said that no progress has been made by the parties in Yemen to reach a political agreement to settle the civil war, which is now in its seventh year.

"It is imperative to resume an inclusive, Yemeni led political process to reach a negotiated solution to the conflict," Khiari said, referring to a 2015 peace plan, which called for a nationwide ceasefire, the reopening of Sanaa airport, the easing of restrictions on fuel and goods flowing through Hodeidah port, and the resumption of face-to-face political negotiations.

But the Houthis have rebuffed calls to stop their deadly military offensive on Marib. They submitted their conditions—the so-called Marib initiative—to Omani mediators. The initiative calls for the formation of a joint command for Marib, joint security forces, and joint technical committees. The Houthis have also demanded shares of oil and as well as the reoperation of the export pipeline that extends from Marib to the Houthi-held Ras Issa port on the Red Sea, the release of their loyalists from detention centres, and freedom of movement for their members to and from Marib.

These are conditions which the Saudis have refused to entertain so far, as has the internationally recognised government (IRG). Yemeni observers noted that the Houthis are demanding they be given control of Marib, which they have been trying to occupy militarily for over a year.

America's recently appointed envoy to Yemen, Timothy Lenderking, returned from a trip to Saudi Arabia at the beginning of August 2021 stating that he had met a dead end on the Yemen crisis.

The Houthis are continuing their occupation of over 80 per cent of the North and are consolidating their de facto administration in areas under their control. The IRG has failed to come to grips with worsening economic conditions and has very limited support from the public. The Southern Transitional Council (STC) controls Aden and the surrounding areas and has not allowed the IRG to function operationally from Aden. Government ministers are outside the country in the majority with occasional visits to Mukalla, Marib, and Shabwa. No progress has been made in the implementation of the Riyadh Agreement intended to resolve the conflict between the STC and the IRG, and the people in the South continue to be deprived of essential services such as electricity, water supply, and army salaries, which are seriously in arrears.

Al-Qaeda's Yemeni branch congratulated the Taliban on their takeover of Afghanistan and vowed to continue its own military campaigns. "This victory and empowerment reveals to us that jihad and fighting represent the (Islamic law)-based, legal, and realistic way to restore rights (and) expel the invaders and occupiers," Al-Qaeda in the Arabian Peninsula (AQAP) said in a statement. AQAP fighters in Yemen's central governorate of Al-Bayda and the southern province of Shabwa celebrated the Taliban's return to power in Afghanistan with fireworks and by firing gunshots in the air. The hard-line Sunni Muslim group has taken advantage of Yemen's war since 2014, bolstering its presence in Southern Yemen. In reality there is no unified Yemen as I write this book; it exists only in theory. The country has three governments, three central banks, and two exchange mechanisms, yet the international community pretends otherwise. The absence of any real governance is creating a vacuum that would, in my opinion, end up being filled by extremist groups like ISIS.

In my opinion, the Houthis have been emboldened by the Taliban's takeover of Afghanistan, and they may well be thinking that they can take over the South of Yemen in the same way. It is also possible that the Houthis will make a deal with Saudi Arabia, and the South will be abandoned by its Gulf allies. The Houthis have confirmed that negotiations with the Saudis are progressing with the positive mediation and intervention of Oman. The Southerners, in contrast, have been largely ignored and left with an uncertain future.

In answering the question posed by the title of this book, *South Yemen—Gateway to the World?* the answer is that Aden has the potential to be the gateway to the world, but its leaders have failed to turn this economic potential for the benefit of their people.

Aden in South Yemen is in a strategic location with a port in the middle of one of the world's most critical choke points, the Bab-el-Mandeb Strait between Djibouti and Yemen. Great powers see this strategic location as the gateway to the world, however the leaders of South Yemen failed miserably to utilise its economic importance.

Throughout history, South Yemen has been fought over as a prize by great and regional powers alike in the belief that Aden, with other connected South Yemeni islands, can be used as a gateway to the vital Suez shipping lane and as an important corridor to world trade.

But the internal feuding and negative international intervention failed to turn the islands into a Gibraltar of the East. Despite its location in the middle of one of the world's busiest shipping lines through which millions of barrels of oil and gas pass per day, neither the South Yemeni state established in 1967 nor the unified state established in 1990 has truly been able to utilise Aden's strategic potential.

The British colonial system did attempt to make Aden a vital artery of world trade, and Aden port became one of the busiest in the world, but sadly this economic success did not materialise in anything meaningful for the people of the South.

With Yemen currently embroiled in a bitter civil war and lacking economic development, it remains unlikely that the potential of Aden will be realised in the short term. Local leaders, regional powers, and the international community currently see Aden as a base for power political projection in the short to medium term.

The geopolitical strategic location of Aden from 1967 to 2021 has not been used economically to build the country. Instead, South Yemen has become an attractive magnet for external actors interested in expanding their influence in the Arabian Peninsula and using every tool possible to ensure continuous political turbulence and division.

During the period of the cold war, the territory of today's Yemen was a theatre of geopolitical rivalry, where the interests of superpowers and regional actors clashed. During the conflict in North and South Yemen, external entities played an important role as they drove the dynamics of these conflicts, counting on achieving their own strategic objectives. It is equally important to note that South Yemen could have developed to become an international hub and a gateway to the international community if its leaders had the vision to realise this.

There has always been a conflict in South Yemeni politics between the left wing and the right wing of the Yemeni Socialist Party (YSP). The problems this caused were not solved but reproduced themselves with greatly political and military consequences, leading to the tragic events of 13 January 1986, when Ali Nasser tried unsuccessfully to liquidate his opponents in a violent coup which greatly weakened the YSP and prompted the South to unite with the North.

This move was certainly not the universal panacea the leaders naively hoped for, and the Southerners were marginalised by the Northern regime, with their resources exploited and their rights trampled on. In 1994 they were defeated in a war of secession as they tried to re-establish the Southern state. The Southern leaders rushed into unity in 1990, and the lack proper planning to engineer unification in 1990 led to a brief separation and rebellion that was crushed by the Northern army supported by some Southerners, including the current president of Yemen. The Southerners through the Hirak movement saw this defeat as an invasion of the South by Northern forces and the end of unity entered into by a voluntary agreement.

The 2015 war against the South, which followed the Houthi coup of the North in 2014, revealed that the Houthis were not content to take over the North but also invaded the South, including Aden, and as a consequence they wanted to continue with unification by force. But their defeat in the South was a clear indication that the Southerners no longer want unity, and their resistance to yet another occupation this time proved decisive. The Houthis realised that the Southern people and the political and religious culture of the South was not a conducive environment for them to stay. In reality the country is divided, and a seven-year war continues to rage with no central functioning government. In my opinion, the Yemenis are united only in their share of the same experience of devastation, destruction, and economic misery. For President Hadi and his government, and for many of the Northern elite, a six-region federation is the key to maintaining unification and the start of a new social contract that would give the Southerners their share of resources and more autonomy. This, after all, was the outcome of Yemen's National Dialogue Conference, in which only a small part of the Hirak (Southern) Movement was involved—most of the Southerners refused to participate. But with the introduction of federalism, the key dissidents were the Hirak movement in the South and the Houthis in the North, who both believed the NDC was a raw deal for them. The Hirak movement was unaware that the Houthis were planning a complete takeover if things didn't go their way.

In this context, the Houthis embarked on a war against the NDC proposal when they stormed the presidential palace in September 2014 and arrested President Hadi. This was clearly a coup d'état against the new president and his government—an exercise of political and military takeover not seen in Yemeni politics for a long time. This coup took everyone by surprise, particularly the regional states and the international community. The Hirak movement could have done the same in the South but was more concerned about the possible takeover of the South by the Houthis and was less organised politically and militarily. It is highly likely that Ali Abdullah Salih assisted the Houthis in their takeover of the capital and also encouraged the Houthis to invade the South in an effort to re-establish his credentials and recreate his own power base within the Houthi authority. No doubt Salih also wanted to get revenge from Hadi and Ali Mohsin for what he saw as their betrayal of him.

In the ongoing conflict, Hirak in Aden is no longer under the control of old socialists like Ali Salem Al-Beidh or Haider Al-Attas. It's a coalition of Southern political forces combined under the auspice of the Southern Transitional Council, with some still remaining outside this scope but all attempting to orchestrate the secession from Yemen's Northern elite. This is a position which the internationally recognised government opposes.

They continue to raise the demand for an independent South to achieve a just solution to Southern grievances, citing the fact that before 1990 their state was alive and kicking. Recently the Friends of South Yemen (FOSY) presented a plan to the UN Security Council that proposes a way out of the war with a two-region solution, two governments, and eventually a referendum on Southern statehood.

FOSY highlighted the increasing grievances and repression the Southerners have endured since unification of the two states, which ignored the regional disparity in population and resources and was unable to deal with Southern grievances. The call for independence by the Hirak movement and now the STC has been an expression of protest that some Southerners perceive as legitimate. It is fair to note that the STC is currently in a difficult political position, with pressure from their supporters to initiate steps to bring about a Southern state and pressure from the international community to work within the current UN solution. No doubt their inability to take any meaningful steps is losing them public support and confidence in the South.

The STC could become a political party for the South, incorporating the Hirak movement and splinter groups and providing much-needed leadership for the South, whose development has been stifled by continuing disputes with the IRG.

The formation of a presidential council has been mooted because the Saudis have become exasperated with the IRG (whom they have been supporting) and the inability of the STC and the IRG to work together. But even if President Hadi is sidelined, it is doubtful the STC and IRG will ever be able to work together or agree on common objectives.

The IMF said Yemen will receive about $665 million worth of reserves to help ease the acute economic crisis, and Qatar has made a $165 million cash donation. A GCC Marshall Plan could also provide a much-needed Arab solution to the crisis. Through prudent use of these funds, the South could capitalise on its strategic location and revitalise its economy—the port, the Aden Free Zone, and the fishing and tourist industries. Yemen has oil and gas reserves and continues to sell these products but very little information is available on who benefits from these revenues.

The future of Yemen under the current circumstances is often viewed with despondency and despair. Fragmentation and divisions have increased significantly over recent years, not only in the Southern governorates but also throughout the country. Yemen's politicians have failed to advance any peaceful meaningful proposals. Mending rifts amongst the divided nation in Yemen can be done only by a much more effective role played by the United Nations and recognition of the realities on the ground.

Yemen is certainly on the road to further devastation and could be divided into a number of states if common sense does not prevail. Any political process (including the frequently interrupted Yemen peace talks) shaping Yemen's political future must take the circumstances on the ground extremely seriously.

The Southern issue and the Southern aspirations of establishing autonomy can no longer be postponed by the international community and regional states if they want to avoid a repeat of their mistakes regarding the transition period with the Houthis in 2014. At that time, the Houthis were able to advance to Sanaa easily, and the main reason was that outsiders ignored the reality of the political and military situation on the ground and did not see the Houthis as a real and practical threat to the political process in Yemen. In fact, their disregard of the Houthis' military and political strengths, and the failure of international intelligence information, led to the speedy overthrow of the legitimate government. This was a strategic miscalculation that has had huge, negative implications for the country, and it could be repeated in the South of Yemen. The international community also made the same mistake in their calculation of the Taliban advance into Kabul in 2021. This is one more reason why the international community and the region should consider a peace process that properly engages Southerners in any future outcome and prevents further wars and conflicts.

The STC's ambition for self-determination requires them to have a sound plan for achieving a Southern state. Their current foreign policy plan is unclear, and the eastern governorates, including Shabwa and Hadhramaut, seem to some extent to align themselves with the legitimate government, drifting away from their supportive position of the Hirak movement in 2015. Regional pressure on the STC has made the STC's immediate goal to somehow shift towards a federal arrangement as part of a transitional phase—a step not necessarily supported by its rank file members.

The STC has shown some flexibility by engaging in negotiations with the IRG through diplomatic means by signing the Riyadh Agreement, which in a sense does give it a formal seat at the governance table and possibly some recognition in future diplomatic negotiations.

It is my opinion that although this agreement is a fundamental shift from the STC's aim for a separate state, it does give the STC an opportunity to be part of an internationally recognised government, push for a suitable settlement to their cause, consolidate the Southern movement by bringing together Southerners through a conciliation initiative, and court international support.

The STC have recently initiated a reconciliation process in an attempt to bring Southerners together under their umbrella, but so far those who oppose them have initially refused to participate, leaving an uncertain future for the STC and South Yemen. The STC has military control over Aden and those governorates close to the city but lacks a hegemonic position within South Yemen overall.

So far the STC has been unable to achieve a similar position to that of the National Liberation Front's hegemony over South Yemen in their anti-colonial struggle in the late 1960s. The STC's position on a separate Southern state is opposed by Southerners in the IRG and Islah, who want to preserve their own power base and do not share the STC's vision for independence but support a federal state. In my opinion, this opposition to the STC is orchestrated by the opposition groups, particularly in the eastern part of the South, to politically and militarily prevent overall STC hegemony in South Yemen. This is a major obstacle for the STC to overcome.

A historic meeting between the President of the Southern Transitional Council Aidrous Al-Zubaidi and the ambassadors of the five permanent members of the Security Council was held in Riyadh on 22 November 2021. It showed the international community now considers the inclusion of the STC as essential in its endeavours to secure a lasting peace in Yemen.

Discussions focused on the implementation of the Riyadh Agreement as well as the latest developments on the ground. Zubaidi highlighted the cause of the South and stressed the need "for an active presence of the STC in all stages of the upcoming political process to stop the war and bring peace to the region."

He also drew the ambassadors' attention to the role of the STC and its forces in countering terrorism and smuggling operations across the coasts of the South, securing international shipping corridors in the Bab El-Mandab, the Gulf of Aden and the Red Sea, as well as confronting the Houthis.

They discussed ways and methods of addressing the worsening economic crisis and restructuring the state systems and institutions, especially the economic, financial and supervisory institutions as well as the judiciary and political institutions.

As was stated in the introduction, it is likely that the people of South Yemen will continue their struggle for an independent state—which could take the form of a unilateral declaration of independence without international recognition.

Bibliography

Brehony, Noel. *Yemen Divided: The Story of a Failed State in South Arabia*. London: I. B. Tauris, 2013.

Carapico, S. *Civil Society in Yemen: The Political Economy of Activism in Modern Arabia*. Cambridge: Cambridge University Press, 1993.

Cafiero, Giorgio. "*Making Sense of the Southern Transitional Council's Latest Visit to Russia*". Comment posted on Gulf International Forum, 8 February 2021. https://gulfif.org.

Coombs, Casey. *Al-Mahra: Where Regional Powers Define Local Politics*. Sanaa Centre for Strategic Studies report, December 2020.

Darwich, May. *The Saudi Intervention in Yemen: Struggling for Status*. Insight Turkey, 2018, https://www.insightturkey.com/articles/the-saudi-intervention-in-yemen-struggling-for-status.

Donbenk, Max, Benedict Skylar, El Adem Enzo, and Forster Alex. "Back to the Future? (A Report on the STC and Secessionist Activities within Southern Yemen". Adalah Yemen—Justice in Yemen, October 2018. https://www.adalahyemen.com.

Elyah, Moosa, Luuk van Kempen, and Lau Schulpen. "Adding to the Controversy? Civil Society's Evaluation of the National Conference Dialogue in Yemen". *Journal of Intervention and State Building* 14, no, 3 (2020).

Garallah, Mohammed. *Successful Separationists in a Unity Fan Society: Al-Hirak Al-Janubi Social Movement in the Republic of Yemen*. Thesis, Naval Postgraduate School, Monterey, California, 2013.

Halliday, Fred. *Yemen's Unfinished Revolution; Socialism in the South*. London: MERIP Reports, 1979.

Halliday, Fred. *Arabia without Sultans*. London: Penguin, 1974.

Human Rights Watch. Report *Human Rights in Yemen During and After the 1994 War*.

Human Rights Watch. Report *In the Name of Unity: The Yemeni Government's Brutal Response to Southern Movement Protests*.

Inside Arabia. *STC's Declared Self-Rule in South Yemen Sets Path to Future of Civil Strife.* 12 May 2020. https://insidearabia.com/stcs-declared-self-rule-in-south-yemen-sets-path-to-future-of-civil-strife.

Jalal, Ibrahim. *The UAE May Have Withdrawn from Yemen, but Its Influence Remains Strong.* MEI@75, 25 February 2020. https://www.mei.edu/publications/uae-may-have-withdrawn-yemen-its-influence-remains-strong.

Kostiner, Joseph. *Yemen: The Tortuous Quest for Unity 1990–1994.* London: Chatham, 1996.

Lackner, Helen. *People's Democratic Republic of Yemen: Outpost of Socialist Development in Arabia.* Political Studies of the Middle East. London: Ithaca, 1985.

Lackner, Helen. "How Yemen's Old Order Snuffed Out the Country's Hope for a New Dawn". *Jacobin,* 18 March 2021.

Molyneux, Maxine, *State, Politics and the Position of Women Workers in the People's Democratic Republic of Yemen 1976–1977,* Geneva: International Labour Office, 1982.

Saif, Ahmed Abdel-Karim. *The Politics of Survival and the Structure of Control in the Unified Yemen 1990–97.* MA dissertation, Department of Politics, University of Exeter, September 1997.

Shaif, Abdul Galil. *Revolutionary Politics in South Yemen 1967–1986.* PhD thesis, University of Sheffield, 1990.

Shaif, Abdul Galil. *1994: The Yemen Civil War, a Crisis of Leadership.* Self-published pamphlet, 1995.

Schmitz, Charles. "Yemen's National Dialogue". MEI Policy Paper, February 2014.

Stookey, Robert. *South Yemen—A Marxist Republic in Arabia.* London: Croom Helm, 1982.

Whitaker, Brian. *The Birth of Modern Yemen.* E-book available at al-bab.com.

Zimmerman, Katherine. "Yemen's Southern Challenge: Background on the Rising Threat of Secessionism". Report for www.criticalthreats.org.

Appendix 1

The National Liberation Front's National Charter

The National Charter called for the liberation of South Yemen from colonialism and the complete dismantling of the British military bases. It called for the abolition of sultanate government and Yemeni unity. It is the only political document before 1967 which gives an analysis of the NLF's political programme. Its critique of the existing colonial system had by then become more apparent.

The charter states,

The armed insurrection which has swept the South as an expression of the will of our Arab people and as the fundamental means of popular resistance to the colonialist presence, its interests, its basis and its institutions of exploitation, does not only aim to expel the colonialists from the area. This revolutionary movement is the expression of a global conception of life which aims basically at the radical transformation of the social reality created by colonialism through all its concepts, values and social relations, which are founded on exploitation and tyranny and to determine the type of life which are people aspires and the type of relations which it wants to see installed on the local, regional, national and international levels.

The charter went on to emphasise the need for a united Yemen and explained that Yemen was an integral part of the Arab homeland and that it had historically been a single unit through shared struggle and fate. It called this unity a necessity imposed by the revolution. It is interesting to note that the subject of unity had always been on top of the agenda during the time of revolution. Both the September 1962 Revolution which ousted the Iman in North Yemen and the October 1963 revolution in the South pledged to unify Yemen as one state. The amalgamation of the two parts of the homeland was viewed by Arab nationalists as a necessary step towards unification of the entire Arab nation. The concept of unity is enshrined as the major objective of both revolutions. Both state constitutions interpret the two revolutions as aspects of the struggle for a single Yemeni democratic state.

On the economic and political level, the National Charter set forth a series of measures whereby the principles of independence and social justice would be rooted in the new Yemeni economic system. The charter called for an enlarged public sector and concentrated on the great gap which existed between Aden and the underdeveloped rural areas which had been neglected by colonialism. It called for the construction of a much-needed economic infrastructure. In general, its economic programme was based on the following four principles.

1. Complete economic liberation from foreign exploiting capitalism and colonialist companies.
2. The building of a national economic on a new and healthy basis compatible with the principles of social justice and achieved through popular control over primary products and means of production.
3. Through planning and guidance of material, human and scientific means to achieve this aim according to a general plan for economic and social development.

4. The belief that the private sector can play an important role in the country's development provided it avoids exploitation and monopoly and limits itself to the areas allocated to it by law; these are that it can operate alone, in association or in coordination with the public sector, according to the development plan and general economic organisation.

The National Charter was radical in its opposition to capitalism. But it did not adhere to a socialist programme. In the charter, there was a challenge to the existing colonialist system. It did not seek to promote a nationalised economy but obviously restricted the economic role of the private sector. It seemed that the charter did not bind itself to any particular ideology but was influenced both by capitalism, in the sense that it still saw an important role to be played by the petty bourgeoisie, and by socialism, in the sense that it saw the economy as being guided by an overall development plan.

The charter went on to emphasise the fundamental importance of the alliance between the workers and peasants as the guarantor social progress. In its discussion on internal affairs, the charter stated,

Social development and progressive transformation from the present backward stage to the state of socialist construction requires that all the working popular forces carry out their responsibilities in construction.

Here the charter demonstrated the influence of Marxist politics in its call for socialist construction and for the exploited classes to transform Yemeni society. Although it used strong language, it actually failed to suggest how such socialist construction could be accomplished—for example, failing to mention nationalisation.

Appendix 2

Proclamation of the Democratic Republic of Yemen

Aden, 21 May 1994

In the course of recent national history, Yemeni unity was a goal for achieving security, stability and social progress, and for upholding the national esteem of the Yemeni people. Out of a sincere wish to achieve those ends, we worked voluntarily to establish unity on 22 May 1990 between the two states of Yemen and implant it in the life of society. In order to remedy the deep-seated problems which Yemen was facing in all fields, and working in the spirit of the aims of the Yemeni revolution and in harmony with contemporary worldwide developments, we sought democracy and reform as a basis for reshaping the old regime in the two parts of the country and building the unified Yemeni state.

From the first day, and throughout the years of unity, there were persistent attempts, remarkable national efforts, continual dialogues, but in reality none of those goals was not achieved. On the contrary, the ineffectiveness of co-ordination, the failure of the processes for transforming democracy, and devotion to the dictatorial military regime under the control of the Yemen Arab Republic impeded implementation of the unity agreements and completely devastated political life. The life and security of the people, the stability of the state and the running of the administrative system collapsed utterly. The manifestations of patronage and corruption spread and the ownership and revenues of state institutions were handed over to supporters of influential people in a system which then accumulated a deficit in the general budget. That, together with the inflation rate and price rises, brought the level of social services for the people close to ruin.

Meanwhile, acts of repression and political terrorism spread through the country. The leadership of the state and its cadres vied for power with representatives of the Yemen Socialist Party and national and opposition personalities, and systematically carried out the destruction of the military and civilian institutions which the Socialist Party had brought to the single state until they became part of it. That was the reality, especially in the south of the state. The powers and prerogatives of all its [the Socialist Party's] cadres and representatives in the commands and organisations of the state were suspended, and all processes of economic and social development were brought to a standstill, especially in the southern provinces. Thus the state was deprived of all its functions and became unable to perform its constitutional tasks at the level of the whole state. In order to halt that alarming deterioration in the life of the state and society, the Socialist Party, together with all upright citizens, made every effort during the continuous dialogue with the President, the leaders of the General People's Congress and the Yemeni Assembly for Reform (Islah), and at the numerous signings of agreements with them, to remedy the country's problems. The [Socialist] Party's initiative was its appeal to establish the government alliance, seeking national unity and power-sharing by various representatives of the political forces; to widen the political dialogue to achieve national agreement and the signing of the Document of Pledge and Accord; and to show concern for the legitimacy of the national society. And yet, all its efforts brought failure because of the wilful insistence and systematic destruction of those by the President and his influential retinue who assisted in an astonishing way in tyrannical decrees and terrorist military operations which also extended to citizens of foreign states and their embassies with the aim of putting pressure on them and the robbery of their [positions?] and the dropping of hints of the exigency of the danger and scrutiny of the support on fanatical fundamentalist movements, and spreading their influence in various organs of the state, and supervision/scrutiny of their training camps and exporting terrorism abroad and the formula for the country's foreign relations of a type which was deceptive, insincere and for hire at a cheap price.

The process of preparing to place the country in the furnace of a destructive civil war has gathered pace since the beginning of this year. This may be laid at the feet of the head of state personally by the declaration of war against everyone in his notorious speech in Sabaean Square on April 27 last, in which he called for the establishment of civilian courts for all his opponents from the Yemen Socialist Party and the National Dialogue Committee and all Yemeni political forces. That speech was followed a few hours later by the large-scale attack on the Third Brigade at Amran, on the southern units that had transferred to the north on unification, followed by the attack on the Ba Suhaib Brigade in the northern governorate of Dhamar, and before them, the elimination of the Fifth Brigade in Harf Sufyan. On 4 May (Ayyar) the war of total annihilation began against all the southern and eastern provinces that had comprised the People's Democratic Republic of Yemen – which had participated in establishing the single state – followed by the declaration of a state of emergency in the country and the dismissal of senior officials among the southern leaders in the state presidency and government.

Despite what this war has wrought, and despite measures and decisions taken in total violation of the constitution and legitimacy, the leadership in Sana'a is bringing this war to 'Anad in the south, striking civilian targets and villages and the homes of citizens and killing women and children and plundering property, turning honour to disgrace, and arrogantly rejecting the appeals of Yemen's political and social forces and of the leaders of Arab and foreign states for a ceasefire and a return to dialogue. Thus the family of the House of Ahmar and their allies bear the historic responsibility for burning the bonds of brotherhood, resisting unity and, in reality, deciding upon separation, completing their previous obstruction in implementing unity. The country in effect remained divided, despite the declaration of its unity, when the administrative and judicial systems, the currency, the army, the ports and airlines remained separate as they had been before unification, and unity did not exist except in the form of a flag and national anthem, and nothing else.

In the behaviour of the Sana'a leadership the attitudes of the past remained and the legacy of historical backwardness which prevails and dominates their political practices—revenge, annexation, [possessiveness], blood feuds and monopoly of power. In reality, the arbiters of Sana'a rely on a worn-out philosophy and sterility of government based on the principles of exercising power and securing it as regards establishing state institutions which reduce the power of the president, military power as a basis for control, bloody repression and corruption as a means for suppressing and stifling opposition, squabbling between the tribes as a means for keeping them occupied, backwardness as a way of imposing subservience, and the introduction of various forms of social divisiveness in wages which are all higher among the branches of the tribes, the nomads and those districts which have established the historical right to a backward regional power, which has deprived the people of the right to equal citizenship. On this graded ladder the sons of the southern and eastern regions found themselves fourth-class citizens.

Arising out of all those efforts and humiliations and the effective fragmentation of society and homeland, and emanating from the constitutional responsibility to defend the rights of the citizens in the constituencies that granted us their votes, the delegates of the people from the party bloc of the southern and eastern provinces and representatives of the parties and political forces and social personalities, and in the spirit of the Document of Pledge and Accord decided upon at the national meeting, announce the establishment of the Democratic Republic of Yemen on the following basis and principles:

1. We announce the establishment of an independent sovereign state called the Democratic Republic of Yemen. Its capital is Aden and it is part of the Arab and Islamic umma.

2. Yemeni unity remains a basic objective; because of its broad national alliances and the strength of national unity, the state strives to restore Yemeni unity on democratic and peaceful foundations.

3. Islam is the religion of the state and the shari'a is the main source of legislation.

4. The political system is built on the foundation of political and party pluralism.

5. The <u>constitution of the Yemeni Republic</u> is considered to be the constitution of the Democratic Republic of Yemen.

6. The <u>Document of Pledge and Accord</u> is the basis of establishing and building the state of democratic Yemen and its political and economic system.

7. Commitment to the charters of the Arab League, United Nations, the International Declaration on Human Rights and the recognised rules of international law. Also commitment to all the regional and international agreements and treaties, and to the preservation and protection of the interests of all states and international companies in the domain of the state.

8. Commitment to a policy of good neighbourliness and strengthening the ties of brotherhood and friendship with all the brotherly and friendly states, and especially the neighbouring states and non-intervention in internal affairs.

9. To establish the organisation of the state on the basis of administrative decentralisation as the foundation for organising the democratic relations between entities of the state.

10. To protect general liberties and respect human rights and the freedom of opinion, labour and the press, according to the basis of democracy and its peaceful accompaniments.

11. Economic policy is established on the basis of freedom of economic activity and the mechanism of the free market while ensuring the protection of all interests and an equilibrium between them.

12. To hold general parliamentary and local elections within a year of the proclamation of this document on the basis of political and party pluralism.

13. The Provisional Assembly for National Salvation is composed of 111 members in the following manner:

    a) members of parliament representing constituencies in the southern and eastern governorates

    b) representatives of political parties and organisations

    c) persons with national, social and religious standing

14. The Provisional Assembly for National Salvation assumes the following tasks:

a) selection of a president for the assembly;

b) selection of the chairman and members of the presidential council to undertake the tasks of the state presidency;

c) selection of a provisional government;

d) preparation of the permanent constitution of the Democratic Republic of Yemen in accordance with the Document of Pledge and Accord;

e) preparation of the law on local government;

f) preparation of the law on elections;

g) preparation for the holding of parliamentary and local elections in accordance with Article 12 of this document;

h) undertaking all legislative functions on the election of the new parliament.

Consequently the Democratic Republic of Yemen calls upon all brotherly and friendly countries to recognise its state, in accordance with international legislation. We all confidently hope that these countries will favourably assess the position of this state and its leadership, which has always been characterised by wisdom, prudence, judiciousness, and adherence to democracy, general liberties and human rights.

Appendix 3

The Riyadh Agreement

The two sides of this agreement,

Who met under the auspices of King Salman bin Abdulaziz Al Saud in the Kingdom of Saudi Arabia from 20/8/2019 to 24/10/2019, in response to the Kingdom's call for dialogue to discuss differences, prevail with wisdom and dialogue, renounce division, stop sedition, and unite ranks:

The Coalition for Supporting Legitimacy in Yemen is committed to the three references: the Gulf Cooperation Council Initiative and its operational mechanism, the outcomes of the National Dialogue Conference, and Security Council Resolution 2216 and the relevant resolutions and the decisions of the Riyadh Conference.

Confirming the role of the Coalition for Supporting Legitimacy in Yemen, led by Saudi Arabia, responding to the request of His Excellency the legitimate, elected President Abdu Rabu Mansour Hadi to protect Yemen and its people from the continued aggression of the Houthi militia backed by the Iranian regime, and to build on the political, military, security, relief, and developmental successes, and on top of all these restore control to most of Yemen's territory.

Out of the necessity to activate state institutions, the two parties declare their full commitment to the following:

1. Activating the role of all Yemeni state authorities and institutions, in accordance with the political and economic arrangements contained in Annex I of this agreement.

2. Reorganising the military forces under the command of the Ministry of Defence, in accordance with the military arrangements contained in Annex II of this agreement.

3. Reorganising the security forces under the command of the Ministry of Interior, in accordance with the security arrangements contained in Annex III of this agreement.

4. Upholding the full citizenship rights of all Yemeni people, to reject regional and sectarian discrimination, and to reject division.

5. Stopping abusive media campaigns of all kinds between the parties.

6. Uniting efforts, under the leadership of the Coalition for Supporting Legitimacy, to restore security and stability in Yemen and confront terrorist organisations.

7. Forming a committee under the supervision of the Coalition for Supporting Legitimacy in Yemen, led by Saudi Arabia, to follow up, implement, and achieve the provisions of this agreement and its annexes.

8. The participation of the Southern Transitional Council in the government delegation to consultations on the final political solution to end the coup of the Houthi terrorist militia

backed by the Iranian regime.

9. Upon the signing of this agreement, His Excellency the President of Yemen will issue his directives to all state agencies to implement the agreement and its provisions.

Annex I: Political and Economic Arrangements

1. The formation of a government of political competence seating no more than (24) ministers whose members are appointed by the President in consultation with the Prime Minister and the political components, provided that the ministerial portfolios shall be equal between the southern and northern provinces, within thirty days of the signing of this agreement. Those selected for the ministerial portfolio should be recognized for their integrity, competence, and experience, and did not engage in any hostilities or incitement during the events in Aden, Abyan, and Shabwa. Members of the government will be sworn in by the President the day after its formation in Aden.

2. His Excellency the Yemeni President shall appoint, on the basis of the criteria of competence and integrity, and in consultation, a governor and director of security of Aden governorate within fifteen days of the signing of this agreement, and the appointment of governors of Abyan and Al-Dhale'a within thirty days of the signing of this agreement in order to improve the efficiency and quality of work.

3. The Prime Minister of the current government will begin his work in the interim capital Aden within 7 days of the signing of this agreement to activate all state institutions in the various liberated provinces to serve Yemeni citizens, and work on the payment of salaries and financial benefits to employees of all military sectors. The state's security and civil affairs shall be in the provisional capital Aden and all liberated governorates.

4. His Excellency the Yemeni President shall appoint, based on the criteria of competence and integrity and in consultation, governors and security directors in the rest of the southern governorates, within 60 days of the signing of this agreement.

5. Management of state resources, ensuring the collection and deposit of all state revenues, including oil, tax, and customs revenues in the Central Bank of Aden, spending under the budget adopted in accordance with Yemeni law, and submitting a transparent periodic report on its revenues and expenses to parliament for evaluation and monitoring, and the contribution of regional and international experts and specialists to provide the necessary advice.

6. Activating the Central Authority for Oversight and Accountability and strengthening it with honest and professional figures and reconstituted the National Anti-Corruption Authority and activating its oversight role.

7. Restructuring and activating the Supreme Economic Council and strengthening it with competent, experienced, impartial and independent individuals, and associated with the Prime Minister to support fiscal and monetary policies and fight corruption.

Annex II: Military Arrangements

1. The return of all forces – which moved from their main positions and camps towards Aden, Abyan, and Shabwa governorates since the beginning of August 2019 – to their former positions with all their personnel and weapons, and to be replaced by security forces belonging to the local authority in each governorate within 15 days of the signing of this agreement.

2. Assembling and transporting medium and heavy weapons of various types from all military and security forces in Aden, within fifteen days from the date of the signing of this agreement, to camps within Aden identified and supervised by the leadership of the Coalition for Supporting Legitimacy, and removal of these weapons is allowed only under approved plans and under the direct supervision from the Leadership of the Coalition for Supporting Legitimacy in Yemen. These weapons include in particular tanks, armored vehicles, artillery, Katyusha rockets, heavy mortars, thermal rockets, and heavy and medium-caliber armed vehicles.

3. Transfer of all government military forces and Transitional Council military formations in Aden governorate to camps outside Aden governorate, determined by the leadership of the Coalition for Supporting Legitimacy in Yemen, within thirty days of the signing of this agreement, and directing them under approved plans and under the direct supervision of the leadership of the Coalition for Supporting Legitimacy in Yemen, excluding the First Presidential Protection Brigade, which is tasked with protecting the Presidential Palace and their surroundings and securing the movements of His Excellency the President, and providing security protection to the leaders of the Southern Transitional Council in Aden under the supervision of the leadership of the Coalition for Supporting Legitimacy in Yemen.

4. Unifying the military forces contained in paragraph (3), numbering them and including them in the Ministry of Defence and issuing the necessary decisions, and distributing them in accordance with the plans adopted under the direct supervision of the leadership of the Coalition for Supporting Legitimacy in Yemen, within 60 days of the signing of this agreement.

5. Reorganising the military forces in the governorates (Abyan and Lahj) under the command of the Ministry of Defence, with the same measures that were applied in Aden province, within 60 days of the signing of this agreement.

6. Reorganising the military forces in the rest of the southern governorates under the command of the Ministry of Defence, with the same measures that were applied in Aden province, within 90 days of the signing of this agreement.

Annex III: Security Arrangements

1. Police forces in Aden governorate are responsible for securing the governorate while reorganising government forces and the formations of the Transitional Council according to need and the security plan, and for selecting their elements according to competence and professionalism and work on their training, and to be linked to the governorate security chief and numbered as security forces of the Ministry of Interior, within 30 days of the signing of this agreement.

2. Reorganisation of special forces and counter-terrorism forces in Aden governorate, selection of new elements of the Legitimacy forces and the formations of the Transitional Council, and work to train them, appoint a commander, and number them as security forces under the Ministry of Interior, taking into account the confidentiality of terrorism combat elements, to carry out counter-terrorism operations and to participate in securing Aden, within 30 days of the signing of this agreement.

3. Reorganisation of the forces responsible for protecting installations in a unified force under the name "Installations Protection Force" within 30 days of the signing of this agreement, as follows:

The members of the Force are selected on the basis of the competence of the current military forces protecting installations, from the legitimacy forces, or formations of the Transitional Council.

This force is to fully protect the civilian installations, the government headquarters, the central bank, the ports of Aden, Aden airport, the refinery and the headquarters of the branches of ministries and state institutions in Aden.

This force is linked to the Ministry of the Interior and is designated as its security force.

4. The Installation Protection Force, within 90 days of the agreement, will protect the remaining civilian and vital installations in the rest of the liberated governorates, the ports of Mukalla, Al-Dhabba, Al-Mocha and Balhaf facility.

5. Unifying and redistributing the security forces, numbering them, including them under the Ministry of Interior, and issuing the necessary decisions, within 60 days of the signing of the agreement.

6. The reorganisation of security forces in Abyan and Lahj governorates under the leadership of the Ministry of Interior with the same measures that were applied in Aden province, within 60 days of the date of the agreement.

7. Reorganisation of security forces in the rest of the southern governorates which are not on the lists of the Ministry of Interior under the leadership of the Ministry of Interior, with the same measures that were applied in Aden province, within 90 days of the signing of the agreement.

Appendix 4

European Parliament Resolution of 4 October 2018 on the Situation in Yemen (2018/2853[RSP])

The European Parliament,

—having regard to its previous resolutions on Yemen, in particular those of 25 February 2016(1) and 15 June 2017(2) on the humanitarian situation in Yemen, and of 9 July 2015(3) and 30 November 2017(4) on the situation in Yemen,

—having regard to the report published by the UN Human Rights Council Group of Regional and International Eminent Experts on Yemen on 28 August 2018 on the situation of human rights in Yemen, including violations and abuses since September 2014,

—having regard to the joint statements by Vice-President of the Commission / High Representative of the Union for Foreign Affairs and Security Policy (VP/HR) Federica Mogherini and Commissioner Christos Stylianides of 13 June 2018 on the latest developments around Hodeidah, Yemen, and of 4 August 2018 on the airstrikes in Hodeidah,

—having regard to the annual report of the UN High Commissioner for Human Rights of 24 September 2018 on the situation in Yemen,

—having regard to the Council conclusions of 25 June 2018 on Yemen,

—having regard to the statement by the President of the UN Security Council of 15 March 2018,

—having regard to the statement of 6 September 2018 by the Special Envoy of the UN Secretary-General for Yemen,

—having regard to the statement by the World Food Programme Executive Director of 19 September 2018,

—having regard to the Rome Statute of the International Criminal Court,

—having regard to the UN Security Council resolutions on Yemen, in particular resolutions 2216 (2015), 2201 (2015) and 2140 (2014),

—having regard to Rule 123(2) and (4) of its Rules of Procedure,

A. whereas the ongoing conflict in Yemen has entered its fourth year and more than 22 million people need humanitarian support; whereas over 17 million people are food insecure, among whom more than 8 million people are severely food insecure and at risk of starvation; whereas the current fragmentation of the conflict is a clear sign of the erosion of state unity; whereas the situation in Yemen also carries grave risks for the stability of the region;

B. whereas the conflict started in 2015 when Iranian-backed Houthi rebels ousted the country's internationally recognised president, who subsequently brought in a multinational coalition led by Saudi Arabia to fight the rebels and those troops allied to them;

C. whereas since November 2017, the Saudi-led coalition has established a blockade on all imports to the Houthi-controlled territory, with the exception of urgent humanitarian and relief materials; whereas according to the OCHA, Yemen has received only 21 % of its fuel requirements and 68 % of its food import needs since the blockade began; whereas, in certain cases, Houthi rebels have blocked the delivery of essential medical supplies, food and humanitarian aid to government-controlled cities;

D. whereas in June 2018 the coalition led by Saudi Arabia and the United Arab Emirates (UAE) started an offensive to take the city of Hodeidah; whereas Save the Children has reported hundreds of civilian casualties in this operation; whereas Hodeidah is Yemen's most important port and is the transit point for as much as 70 % of the country's critical food and humanitarian aid; whereas, according to the UN, nearly 470 000 people have fled Hodeidah Governorate since early June 2018; whereas a further attack on Hodeidah would have devastating consequences for civilians; whereas parties to the conflict are obliged to allow and facilitate the rapid and unimpeded passage of humanitarian relief, including medicine, food and other items necessary for survival;

E. whereas the ceasefire negotiations led by the UN Special Envoy for Yemen, Martin Griffiths, resulted in a temporary cessation of the offensive; whereas the collapse of the latest attempt to hold peace talks in Geneva led to a resumption of hostilities on 7 September 2018; whereas since the offensive started, civilian deaths have increased by 164 %; whereas, in spite of the international pressure to achieve a stable and inclusive political solution to the crisis, the parties to the conflict and their regional and international backers, including Saudi Arabia and Iran, have failed to reach a ceasefire or any type of settlement, and the fighting and indiscriminate bombings continue unabated;

F. whereas on 9 August 2018, an air strike perpetrated by the Saudi-led coalition hit a school bus in a market in the northern province of Saada, killing scores of people, including at least 40 children, most of whom were under the age of 10; whereas this attack was followed two weeks later, on 24 August, by a new Saudi-led coalition strike killing 27 civilians, mostly children, who were fleeing the violence in the besieged southern city of Hodeidah;

G. whereas the Saudi-led campaign and the intense aerial bombardments, including indiscriminate attacks in densely populated areas, exacerbate the humanitarian impact of the war; whereas the laws of war prohibit deliberate and indiscriminate attacks on civilians and civilian targets such as schools and hospitals; whereas, having regard to the findings of the Group of Independent Eminent International and Regional Experts (GEE), such attacks may amount to war crimes and the individuals who commit them may be prosecuted for these crimes; whereas the Saudi-led coalition's investigations into alleged war crimes in Yemen have lacked credibility and failed to provide redress to civilian victims;

H. whereas since March 2015, more than 2 500 children have been killed, more than 3 500 children have been maimed or injured and a growing number of children have been recruited by armed forces on the ground; whereas women and children are particularly affected by the ongoing hostilities; whereas according to UNICEF, nearly two million children are out of school, which compromises the future of an entire generation of children in Yemen as a result of limited or no access to education, making them vulnerable to military recruitment and sexual and gender-based violence;

I. whereas in August 2018 a report compiled by the UN High Commissioner for Human Rights concluded that there are 'reasonable grounds to believe' all parties to the conflict in Yemen may have committed war crimes; whereas forces on both sides of the conflict have been accused of firing heavy weapons into built-up areas and highly populated areas, including strikes on hospitals and other non-military structures;

J. whereas the war has led to the destruction of infrastructure and the collapse of Yemen's economy, and caused widespread disruption to basic commodities and the supply of utilities, sanitation and clean drinking water; whereas the regular payment of salaries of up to 1,4 million non-military Yemeni public workers effectively ceased at the end of 2016;

K. whereas preventing the use of UN flights for international media and human rights organisations impedes independent coverage of the situation in Yemen and contributes to the global neglect of the conflict;

L. whereas gender-based sexual violence has increased exponentially since the start of the conflict; whereas the already limited capacity to address sexual and gender-based violence in the criminal justice system has collapsed, and no investigations have been conducted in relation to practices such as abducting and raping women, or threatening to, as a way of extorting money from their families and communities;

M. whereas human rights defenders have faced relentless harassment, threats and smear campaigns from all parties to the conflict; whereas women human rights defenders, journalists and activists have faced specific repression on the basis of their gender;

N. whereas Houthi de-facto authorities have conducted a systemic campaign of harassment, arbitrary and abusive detentions, and forced disappearances and torture against human rights defenders, journalists and religious minorities; whereas 24 Yemenis from the Baha'i minority, including one child, are facing charges that could result in the death penalty, for nothing other than their beliefs and peaceful actions;

O. whereas Houthi rebels have been accused of causing mass civilian casualties during their siege of Taiz, Yemen's third largest city; whereas they have waged a war of attrition against civilian populations in government-controlled areas; whereas they have also deployed banned anti-personnel landmines and recruited children;

P. whereas Kamel Jendoubi, Chairman of the GEE that issued a Report to the Human Rights Council on the Situation of human rights in Yemen on 28 August 2018, is the victim of a smear campaign aimed at intimidating the GEE and casting doubts on its findings;

Q. whereas Yemen has signed the Rome Statute of the International Criminal Court but has yet to ratify it; whereas several provisions of the Rome Statute, including those related to war crimes, reflect customary international law;

R. whereas in February 2018 Russia vetoed a UN Security Council resolution highlighting Iranian involvement in the conflict;

S. whereas there is an international arms embargo in place against the Iranian-backed Houthi rebels and, according to the 18th EU Annual Report on Arms Exports, EU Member States have continued to authorise transfers of arms to Saudi Arabia since the escalation of the conflict, in violation of Council Common Position 2008/944/CFSP of 8 December 2008 defining common rules governing control of exports of military technology and equipment(5); whereas in the past year, some EU Member States have partly or totally suspended arms transfers to Saudi Arabia and the UAE; whereas Parliament has repeatedly called on the VP/HR to launch an initiative to impose an EU arms embargo on Saudi Arabia, in line with Common Position 2008/944/CFSP;

T. whereas the majority of strikes carried out by US forces in Yemen are lethal drone strikes; whereas the decision to add certain persons to the target lists of drone operations is often made without court warrants or orders; whereas the targeting and subsequent killing of certain individuals can under certain circumstances be seen as extrajudicial killing;

U. whereas the war in Yemen has opened up space for extremist groups, including al-Qaeda in the Arabian Peninsula (AQAP), to extend their reach, thereby threatening the wider region; whereas a stable, secure Yemen with a properly functioning government is critical to international efforts to combat extremism and violence in the wider region and beyond, as well as to peace and stability within Yemen itself;

V. whereas stability in the wider region is of critical importance for the EU; whereas the EU is committed to a comprehensive and strategic approach encompassing all relevant regional actors; whereas finding a political solution to the conflict under the auspices of the UN peace initiative in Yemen should be a priority for the EU and the international community as a whole;

W. whereas the EU remains committed to continuing to deliver life-saving aid to all people in need in Yemen; whereas at the same time, the EU shares the concerns of the UN and other donors about the continuing shrinking of humanitarian space; whereas from 2015 until now, the EU has contributed more than EUR 233 million in humanitarian funding to Yemen;

1. Condemns in the strongest terms the ongoing violence in Yemen and all attacks against civilians and civilian infrastructure; emphasises its concern over the conflict that is continuing to degenerate into one of the gravest current humanitarian, political, and economic crises; reminds all parties involved, including their regional and international backers, that the deliberate targeting of civilians and civilian infrastructure, including hospitals and medical personnel, water systems, ports, airports and markets, amounts to a grave violation of international law;

2. Deeply regrets the loss of life caused by the conflict and the suffering of those caught up in the fighting, and expresses its condolences to the families of the victims; reaffirms its commitment to continuing to support Yemen and the Yemeni people;

3. Calls on all parties to the conflict to cease hostilities immediately; urges Saudi Arabia and other actors involved to further lift the ongoing blockade of Yemen: calls on all directly or indirectly involved states and relevant actors, including Iran, to apply maximum pressure on all parties to work towards de-escalation and to immediately cease providing political, military and financial support to military actors on the ground, either directly or by proxy;

4. Stresses that only a political, inclusive and negotiated solution to the conflict can restore peace and preserve the unity, sovereignty, independence and territorial integrity of Yemen; calls on all international and regional actors to engage constructively with the parties in Yemen to enable a de-escalation of the conflict and a negotiated settlement;

5. Supports the efforts of the Special Envoy of the UN Secretary-General for Yemen, Martin Griffiths, to restart the political process; takes note of his statement to the UN Security Council of 11 September 2018 'that despite the absence of one of the sides to the Consultations in Geneva last week, and even if it certainly did not go as planned, we still managed to relaunch the political process with solid support clearly from the Yemeni people and the international community'; welcomes Mr Griffiths' visit to Sana'a on 16 September 2018; calls for the Special Envoy to be given full and unhindered access to all parts of the territory of Yemen; calls on the VP/HR and all EU Member States to provide Mr Griffiths with political backing with a view to reaching a negotiated and inclusive settlement;

6. Condemns all terror attacks in the strongest terms; is deeply concerned about the increased presence in Yemen of criminal and terrorist groups, including AQAP and ISIS/Daesh; calls on all parties to the conflict to take resolute action against such groups; condemns the presence of foreign fighters and calls for the removal of all such fighters from Yemen;

7. Calls on all the parties to the conflict to allow for immediate and full humanitarian access to the conflict-affected areas in order to assist the population in need; calls on the Council and the UN Security Council, in implementing UN Security Council Resolution 2216 (2015), to identify the individuals obstructing the delivery of humanitarian assistance in Yemen and to impose targeted sanctions on them;

8. Stresses that the UN Security Council has underlined its support for the UN Verification and Inspection Mechanism (UNVIM), and that the EU fully supports the continuation of UNVIM and the full and unhindered implementation of its mandate;

9. Calls on all parties to immediately cease all attacks against freedom of expression, and to release all journalists and human rights defenders detained solely for having exercised their human rights; calls on all parties to cease obstructing the work of international media and humanitarian personnel in relation to the conflict;

10. Calls on all parties to the conflict to take the necessary measures to ensure effective, impartial and independent investigations into all alleged violations and abuses of human rights and alleged violations of international humanitarian law, in accordance with international standards; is deeply concerned about

reports of denial of freedom of religion or belief, which include discrimination, unlawful detention, the use of violence, and abuses of human rights, including sexual and other violence against women, men, girls and boys, in violation of international standards;

11. Calls on all parties to the conflict to end the recruitment or use of children as soldiers and to put a stop to other grave violations committed against them in violation of applicable international law and standards; calls on all parties to release any children who have already been recruited and to cooperate with the UN with a view to their rehabilitation and reintegration into their communities; supports the vital work of UNICEF in Yemen;

12. Calls on the Specialised Criminal Court in Houthi-controlled territory in Sana'a to acquit and release Asmaa al-Omeissy, Saeed al-Ruwaished and Ahmed Bawazeer, who were forcibly disappeared, tortured and sentenced to death after a grossly unfair trial for allegedly aiding an enemy country;

13. Calls on the Specialised Criminal Court in Sana'a to immediately release the 25 followers of the Baha'i faith who are currently detained for peacefully practising their religion and face charges punishable by death;

14. Reminds all parties to the conflict that they are accountable under international law for any crimes committed; urges the Member States to take all necessary measures to hold alleged perpetrators to account, notably through national or international prosecution of individuals, groups and organisations suspected of such violations or the application of the principle of universal jurisdiction, and by investigating and prosecuting the alleged perpetrators of atrocity crimes in Yemen;

15. Praises the work undertaken by the UN GEE on Yemen and expresses its full solidarity with its Chairman, Kamel Jendoubi; welcomes the annual report of the UN High Commissioner for Human Rights of 24 September 2018 on the situation in Yemen, in which the UN Human Rights Council decided to extend the mandate of the GEE for a further period of one year, renewable as authorised by the Human Rights Council, to include gathering evidence of war crimes and crimes against humanity committed in Yemen, in order to prosecute and punish those guilty of such violations; calls for a referral of the situation in Yemen to the International Criminal Court (ICC); urges Yemen to join the ICC, which would allow for the prosecution of all those responsible for the crimes committed during the conflict, in the absence of a UN Security Council referral;

16. Calls for the European Union and all Member States to provide cohesive, prompt and effective support to the GEE across all relevant UN bodies, and in the Human Rights Council in particular;

17. Urges the Council, the VP/HR and the Member States to oppose extrajudicial killings, including the use of drones, to reaffirm the EU's position under international law and to ensure that Member States do not perpetrate, facilitate or otherwise take part in unlawful lethal operations; urges the Council to adopt a Common Position on the use of armed drones;

18. Calls on the EU to take the initiative at the next Human Rights Council meeting to raise the issue of membership by states with deeply questionable human rights records;

19. Urges the VP/HR, the EEAS and the Member States to continue to conduct a dialogue with the countries of the region on human rights and fundamental freedoms; expresses its readiness to hold a constructive and open dialogue with authorities of the countries of the region on the fulfilment of their international human rights commitments; calls for an exchange of expertise on judicial and legal matters in order to strengthen the protection of individual rights in the countries of the region;

20. Calls on the Council to effectively promote compliance with international humanitarian law, as provided for in the relevant EU guidelines; reiterates, in particular, the need for the strict application by all EU Member States of the rules laid down in Common Position 2008/944/CFSP; recalls, in this regard,

Parliament's resolutions on the situation in Yemen of 25 February 2016 and 30 November 2017; urges all EU Member States in this context to refrain from selling arms and any military equipment to Saudi Arabia, the UAE and any member of the international coalition, as well as to the Yemeni Government and other parties to the conflict;

21. Denounces the destruction of Yemeni cultural heritage by the airstrikes of the Saudi-led coalition, including the Old City of Sana'a and the historic city of Zabid; regrets and recalls the responsibility of the coalition for this destruction and stresses that it will be held accountable also for such acts; calls on the UN Secretary-General to refer the issue of the protection of all cultural sites under threat from the conflict in Yemen to the Security Council, with a view to the adoption of a resolution on the matter;

22. Welcomes the UN 2018 Yemen Humanitarian Response Plan and the 2018 High-Level Pledging Event for the Humanitarian Crisis in Yemen, in which international donors pledged more than USD two billion; deplores, however, the fact that a funding gap still exists for Yemen; welcomes the fact that the EU is committed to assisting those affected by the conflict in Yemen and has pledged EUR 107,5 million; calls on all donors to swiftly disburse their pledges; welcomes the fact that the EU will continue to provide development assistance to Yemen, giving priority to interventions directed at stabilising the country, and will work in stable areas with local authorities to promote resilience, to help to maintain the provision of basic services and to foster sustainable livelihoods for communities;

23. Reserves the right to reconsider the matter until a negotiated solution is reached; recommends that its Subcommittee on Human Rights monitor human rights developments in Yemen and produce a report on the violations of human and civil rights perpetrated in the country;

24. Instructs its President to forward this resolution to the Council, the Commission, the Vice-President of the Commission / High Representative of the Union for Foreign Affairs and Security Policy, the governments and parliaments of the Member States, the Secretary-General of the United Nations, the Secretary-General of the Gulf Cooperation Council, the Secretary-General of the League of Arab States and the Government of Yemen.

INDEX

Printed in the United States
by Baker & Taylor Publisher Services